Erica Mindel

Erica Mindel

Yale Language Series

العربية للمبتدئين

كتاب الطالب

منذر يونس

ELEMENTARY ARABIC

An Integrated Approach

Student Workbook

Munther A. Younes
Illustrations by Micah Garen

Yale University Press   New Haven and London

To my fellow Arabs, whose language, rather than being their servant, has been transformed into yet another tyrant.

Cover photograph copyright © 1991 by George Baramki Azar. Illustrations by Micah Garen. Audio recordings by Ni'mat Barazangi, Abir Abdelnaby, Samer Alatout, Mohammed Mudarris, and Munther A. Younes.

Printed in the United States of America by BookCrafters, Inc., Chelsea, Michigan.

ISBN: 0-300-06085-8 (workbook)

A catalogue record for this book is available from the British Library.

The paper in this book meets the guidelines for permanence and durability of the Committee on Production Guidelines for Book Longevity of the Council on Library Resources.

10   9   8   7   6   5   4   3

Contents

Acknowledgments   xi

Introduction   xiii

Lesson 1: The Classroom   1
  Listen 1-6
  Read 1-2

Lesson 2: Arab Countries, Directions, Big/Small   3
  Listen 1-4
  Read 1
  Reading Arabic
  Read 2-5

Lesson 3: Telling Time   13
  Listen 1-5
  Read 1-6

Lesson 4: Days of the Week   17
  Listen 1-5
  Read 1-8
  Dictation

Lesson 5: Months of the Year   21
  Listen 1-4
  Read 1-7

Lesson 6: Seasons, Weather   26
  Listen 1-4
  Read 1-7
  Dictation
  Grammar: The definite article, the sun and moon letters

Lesson 7: Home, Transportation   32
  Listen 1-8
  Read 1-8
  Read and write
  Grammar: The construct الإضافة

Lesson 8: Family, Professions   40
  Listen 1-8
  Read 1-8
  Read and write
  Dictation
  Grammar: Number (dis)agreement

Lesson 9   50
  Listen: Sharif's family
  Dialogue: Dan and Ali on the plane
  Read: Sharif's family
  Grammar: Possession

Lesson 10   54
  Listen: Maryam
  Dialogue: Dan and Ali on the plane
  Read: Names, addresses, professions
  Grammar: Possession (continued)

Lesson 11   59
    Listen: Ayman
    Dialogue: At the airport
    Read: Entry visa
    Grammar: Subject/person markers on the perfect verb
Lesson 12   64
    Listen: Sharif comes to America
    Dialogue: In the taxi to the hotel
    Read: Taxi fares
    Grammar: Negation; sound and broken plurals
Lesson 13   69
    Listen: Sharif loses his suitcase at the Ithaca airport
    Dialogue: Dan at the hotel
    Read: Amman's hotels
    Grammar: Verb types
Lesson 14   74
    Listen: Sharif's room in the hotel
    Dialogue: Dan in the taxi to the airport
    Read: Match the word with the picture; application for a driver's licence
    Grammar: Sentence types
Lesson 15   81
    Listen: Sharif meets Muhammad
    Dialogue: At the airport with the policeman
    Read: The airport "Lost and Found"
    Grammar: Object pronouns
Lesson 16   86
    Listen: Sharif and Muhammad in the restaurant
    Dialogue: At the airport with the policeman
    Read: Match the word with the picture; Arab embassies in the U.S.
    Grammar: Subject/person markers on the perfect verb (the plural)
Lesson 17   91
    Listen: Muhammad talks to Sharif over the phone about an apartment
    Dialogue: Dan finds his passport
    Read: A Jordanian passport
    Grammar: Lame verbs
Lesson 18   96
    Listen: Sharif and Muhammad go to Walid's apartment
    Dialogue: The hotel receptionist tells Dan about a restaurant
    Read: For rent
    Grammar: The comparative and superlative
Lesson 19   102
    Listen: Sharif and his cousin
    Dialogue: Dan in the restaurant
    Read: As-Salam Restaurant menu
    Song: عمّي بو مسعود
    Grammar: Subject/person markers on the imperfect

Lesson 20   110
    Listen: Sharif and Walid on the way to Chicago
    Dialogue: Al-Quds Restaurant
    Read: Arab airline offices in the U.S.
    Grammar: Wanting with بدّ

Lesson 21   115
    Listen: Addresses in Irbid
    Dialogue: Dan talks to Abu Sharif over the phone
    Read: Hijazi buses
    Grammar: Ordinal numbers

Lesson 22   120
    Listen: Sharif's cousin's house
    Dialogue: Abu Sharif gives Dan directions to Irbid
    Read: The Arab countries
    Grammar: Plural possessive pronouns

Lesson 23   128
    Listen: Sharif comes back from Chicago
    Dialogue: Abu Sharif and Dan at the bus station
    Read: The Arab world
    Grammar: Prepositions followed by ما; the imperfect of hollow verbs; the
        imperative

Lesson 24   134
    Listen: Sharif trying to sleep on the plane
    Dialogue: Dan meets Abu Sharif's family
    Read: The weather in the Arab world
    Song: طيري يا طيّارة
    Grammar   Possession with عند; negation in MSA; قد + imperfect

Lesson 25   141
    Listen: Ayman comes back from Saudi Arabia
    Dialogue: Abu Sharif and Um Sharif ask Dan about Sharif
    Read: Rich and poor in the Arab world

Lesson 26   146
    Listen: Um Sharif and Suad making coffee for the guests
    Dialogue: Lunch at Abu Sharif's house
    Read: Jordan
    Grammar: Pronouns attached to prepositions; the imperfect of assimilated verbs
    in فصحى

Lesson 27   153
    Listen: Sharif's apartment in Ithaca
    Dialogue: American coffee
    Read: Jerash
    Grammar: Objects preceding their subjects; pronouns of separation

Lesson 28   158
    Listen: Sharif cooks in his apartment
    Dialogue: Abu Sharif insists that Dan spend the night at his house
    Read: Amman
    Grammar: Cases

Lesson 29   164

- Listen: Sharif's father
- Dialogue: Um-Khalid and Dan
- Read: Syria

Lesson 30   171

- Listen: Sharif's mother
- Dialogue: Dan and the neighbor Abul-Abid
- Read: Damascus
- Grammar: Subject/person markers in MSA

Lesson 31   178

- Listen: Abdalla
- Dialogue: Finding an apartment for Dan
- Read: Lebanon

Lesson 32   185

- Listen: Suad
- Dialogue: Dan is sick
- Read: Beirut

Song: بابوري رايح بابوري جاي

Lesson 33   193

- Listen: Working in Saudi Arabia and studying in America
- Dialogue: Dan renting an apartment
- Read: Iraq
- Grammar: Verb types (continued)

Lesson 34   200

- Listen: Sharif in the market
- Dialogue: Dan in the market
- Read: The Kurds
- Grammar: Negation with ليس and غير; pronouns attached to conjunctions

Lesson 35   208

- Listen: Muhammad el-Hassan
- Dialogue: On the bus to Irbid
- Read: Egypt (1)

Lesson 36   214

- Listen: Muhammad el-Hassan
- Dialogue: Study in America
- Read: Egypt (2)

Song: سافر مع السلامة

Lesson 37   221

- Listen: Cathy wants to study Arabic
- Dialogue: American universities
- Read: Egyptian universities, al-Azhar
- Grammar: Plural object pronouns suffixes

Lesson 38   230

- Listen: Cathy
- Dialogue: Places Dan visited in Jordan
- Read: Jamal Abdul-Nasser
- Grammar: Roots, patterns, and using the dictionary; relative adjectives النسبة

Lesson 39   237
    Listen: Hassan
    Dialogue: Dan wants to visit other Arab countries
    Read: Nawal el-Saadaawi
    Grammar: Forms of the verb: I, II, V
Lesson 40   248
    Listen: Hassan
    Dialogue: Um Sharif is worried that Sharif will marry an American
    Read: Sudan
    Grammar: Form VII
Lesson 41   256
    Listen: Hassan
    Dialogue: Dan talks to Abu Sharif on the phone
    Read: Tayyib Saleh, سوزان وعلي
    Grammar: Forms III and VI
Lesson 42   261
    Listen: Hassan
    Dialogue: Dan at the post office
    Read: Saudi Arabia
Lesson 43   267
    Listen: President Bush and Secretary of State Baker
    Dialogue: The weather in Ithaca
    Read: Makka
    Song: القلب يعشق كل جميل
Lesson 44   273
    Listen: Bush eats فول with an Egyptian family
    Dialogue: Suad and the Tawjihi exam
    Read: Oil in Saudi Arabia
Lesson 45   279
    Listen: Juha (I might have left through the other door)
    Dialogue: Suad and the Tawjihi exam
    Read: Yemen
    Grammar: Form VIII
Lesson 46   286
    Listen: Juha, the cat, and the meat
    Dialogue: Dan and Jalal want to go to the market
    Read: The Kingdom of Saba'
    Grammar: Form X
Lesson 47   296
    Listen: Juha and the soup of the rabbit soup
    Dialogue: Dan and Jalal in the market
    Read: Important events in Arab-Muslim history
Lesson 48   302
    Listen: Juha (Do you know what I am going to say?)
    Dialogue: Interview with Maryam el-Nabilsi
    Read: The Prophet Muhammad, Qur'an, and Hadith
    Grammar: Passive voice in فُصحى, قد + perfect

Lesson 49   311
   Listen: Juha and the neighbor's pot
   Dialogue: Interview with Yousif Salameh
   Read: Palestine (1)
   Grammar: More on using the dictionary
Lesson 50   318
   Listen: Juha loses his shoes
   Dialogue: Interview with Dan
   Read: Palestine (2)
   Grammar: Negation with لم in فُصحى
Lesson 51   325
   Listen: Juha's donkeys
   Dialogue: Interview with Ibrahim Abul-Laban
   Read: Jerusalem
   Grammar: كل, بعض, etc. with pronominal suffixes
Lesson 52   331
   Listen: Juha and his son carry the donkey
   Dialogue: Interview with Muhammad Salman
   Read: Mahmoud Darwish, سجّل أنا عربي
   Grammar: The resumptive pronoun; the future in فُصحى
Lesson 53   339
   Listen: Juha (ان شاء الله)
   Dialogue: Dan in the taxi to the airport
   Read: Water in the Middle East

Appendix   349
   Notes on Reading
   The Numerals
   Days of the Week
   Months of the Year
   Seasons of the Year
   Arab Countries and Their Capitals
   Forms of the Arabic Verb
   Additional Readings
Arabic-English Glossary   363
Photograph Credits   401

Acknowledgments

I would like to express my gratitude to Roger Allen and Dilworth Parkinson for reading a draft of this book and making valuable comments and suggestions. I am also indebted to my colleague Michel Nicola for discussing with me the content and approach of the book and for encouraging me to develop it into its present form. I am particularly indebted to him for sharing materials that he developed for use in his classes at the Defense Language Institute in Monterey, California. The content, format, and approach used in the first eight lessons of the present book were heavily influenced by these materials. My wife, Rebecca, spent many hours discussing with me the problems of teaching Arabic and the solutions implemented in this book. The book has greatly benefited from her insight and critical thinking.

I would also like to thank the embassies of Jordan, Lebanon, Saudi Arabia, Syria, and Yemen in Washingon, D.C., and the office of the Egyptian Tourist Authority in New York City for providing me with the photographs of Arab cities and monuments used in the Student Workbook. Special thanks are due to Mahmoud Zawawi, director of the Arabic section at the Voice of America in Washington, D.C., for providing me with a tape of one of the songs used in the Student Workbook, which I was not able to obtain even in the Arab world.

This project could not have been completed without the generous financial support of the Consortium for Language Teaching and Learning. I am grateful to the Consortium and particularly to its director, Peter Patrikis, for their continued interest and support.

Micah Garen gave his time and energy wholeheartedly to the task of bringing my imaginary characters to life with humor and cultural authenticity, thus making the book more useful and enjoyable.

I am also grateful to Ni'mat Barazangi, Abir Abdelnaby, Samer Alatout, and Mohammed Mudarris for generously giving time from their busy schedules to assist with the audio recordings.

I would like to thank Eliza Childs, Cynthia Wells, and Judith Calvert of Yale University Press for their invaluable assistance in the editing, design, and publication of the book.

Finally, my deepest gratitude goes to my students at Cornell University and the University of Wisconsin-Milwaukee, who over a number of years served as enthusiastic participants in my experiment with a new method of teaching Arabic.

Introduction

This book integrates an Arabic colloquial dialect with Modern Standard Arabic (MSA) in a way which reflects the use of Arabic by native speakers. Arabs communicate in the colloquial in everyday situations, and they use MSA for reading, writing, and formal speaking. For example, when an Arab talks to a waiter in a restaurant, he uses the dialect, but when he reads the menu he reads MSA.

Arabs from different parts of the Arab world speak different dialects, but MSA is the same everywhere. This is why the majority of Arabic programs prefer to teach MSA. However, students who learn to speak only MSA will not be able to use it in conversation; not only will they sound funny, but they will also find it very difficult, if not impossible, to understand what is being said to them.

I believe that teaching a spoken dialect for everyday conversation and MSA for reading, writing, and formal speaking is the most effective way to prepare students to function in Arabic. I also believe that if a student masters any Arabic dialect well enough, he/she will be able to function in other dialects, just as native speakers from different areas of the Arab world do.

The colloquial Arabic dialect used in this course is Levantine (Syrian) Arabic. It is one of the major Arabic dialects.

Suggestions for Using the Textbook

This book includes reading selections, vocabulary lists, and questions on the listening selections, the dialogues, and the reading selections. It also includes grammar notes, different types of exercises, and a comprehensive Arabic-English glossary. All listening selections and dialogues and most reading selections are recorded on tape and copies of the tapes accompany the book.

The book can be divided into two parts: lessons 1 through 8 and lessons 9 through 53. The goal of the first part is to introduce the Arabic writing system, the numbers, and about 150 high-frequency words related to personal identification, school, time, weather, home, family, and work, which are then used as a basis for further vocabulary (and other skill) building.

In the second part, the focus is shifted toward developing the skill to listen and read for comprehension without deliberately introducing the words at the beginning of each lesson and without expecting full mastery of new words. The lessons in this part generally have a similar format and consist of listening, speaking, reading, grammar, and exercises. Most of these activities can be worked on outside class with the help of the book and the cassette tapes--at home, in the library, or in a park, where you have more time and where you are more relaxed and rested. Each of these activities will be discussed briefly.

Listen اسمع

The purpose of the listening selections is to help you develop the ability to listen to Arabic and to understand the gist of what you listen to. All selections include language material that has not been fully covered in the class and you are not expected to understand the details of every selection, but you are encouraged to guess meaning from context. The focus is on developing the skill of listening for comprehension. Words are repeated in subsequent lessons and in varying contexts, and you will gradually start recognizing and then internalizing these words, to

varying degrees, of course, with more language input. The questions on each selection focus on the main points, and if you can answer these questions, then the goal is achieved. Listen to the selection as a whole as many times as needed with minimal help from the vocabulary lists, which should be used only to aid comprehension and not for memorization.

Dialogue حوار

The dialogues are intended for oral comprehension and production. Listen to a dialogue as many times as needed until you can answer the questions and are able to act out the dialogue. I am not suggesting memorization of the dialogue, but rather understanding it and using it as a basis for a dialogue dealing with a similar situation, using as many words from the dialogue as you wish as well as words and expressions you have acquired previously. Your teacher may choose to give you the texts of the dialogues as a reference, particularly if needed in acting out the dialogue, but these texts should not be used as reading exercises.

Read اقرأ

The reading selections have been prepared with the goal of developing the skill of silent reading comprehension. Thorough comprehension should not be the goal of such selections, nor should the skill to read aloud or the skill to translate Arabic into English. Questions that aid comprehension are provided, and they can be used as part of a homework assignment and/or as a basis for an informal discussion of the selection.

Write اكتب

Of the four language skills, writing receives the least emphasis at this stage, because it is my view that the time available to the college student in a first-year Arabic course is better utilized in developing the more useful skills of listening, speaking, and reading. However, writing can be helpful in reinforcing the other skills, and this is the main reason for including writing exercises in the book. This is an activity that you can do outside of class for the most part.

Grammar قواعد

Emphasis in the course is on intelligibility rather than on grammatical accuracy. As long as you understand what you hear or read and can make yourself understood when communicating a message, then discussion of grammatical structures should be avoided and class time used to work on the other language skills.

However, an explanation of grammatical structures may be necessary, especially when you need it to help your understanding of spoken or written materials. This is why brief grammatical notes are included at various points in the book. They are intended for you to read on your own, not as grammatical drills to be used during class. If you have trouble understanding a point or a concept, your teacher can help you in the class or during office hours.

الدرس رقم ١ (LESSON 1)

اسمع ١ (Listen 1)

(The numbers 1-10)

اسمع ٢

Match the picture with the sentence you hear.

 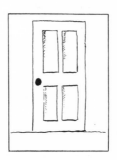 

How many doors does the room have?

_____

اسـمـع ٤

1. How many books does Abdalla have?

_____

2. Which page should he open the book to?

_____

اسـمـع ٥

1. Who are the people talking?

_____

2. Does Abdalla have a book?

_____

اسـمـع ٦

1. How many male students?

_____

2. How many female students?

_____

3. How many teachers?

_____

اقـرا ١ (Read 1)

١، ٢، ٣، ٤، ٥، ٦، ٧، ٨، ٩، ١٠

٢، ٤، ٦، ٨، ١٠، ٩، ٧، ٥، ٣، ١

٤، ٨، ٣، ٢، ٩، ٦، ٥، ٧، ١، ١٠

اقـرأ ٢

Match the two occurrences of each word in the following and identify the word occurring only once.

باب، كتاب، أنا، اسم، افتح، اسم، كتاب، افتح، باب، اكتب، أنا

٢

الدرس رقم ٢

اسمـع ١

(The numbers 11-20)

اسمـع ٢

Write in English the names of the Arab countries and cities you hear in each sentence.

1. _____   2. _____   3. _____
4. _____   5. _____   6. _____
7. _____   8. _____   9. _____
10. _____   11. _____
12. _____ _____

اسمـع ٣

Write the name, country, and profession of each of the three people interviewed.

<u>Name</u>   <u>Country</u>   <u>Profession</u>

اسمـع ٤

1. What are the names of the people talking?
_____

2. What do they do?
_____

3. Where is Halab (Aleppo)?
_____

١.   ١١، ١٢، ١٣، ١٤، ١٥، ١٦، ١٧، ١٨، ١٩، ٢٠

٢.   ١٢، ١٤، ١٦، ١٨، ٢٠، ١١، ١٣، ١٥، ١٧، ١٩

٣.   ٣، ٨، ١٤، ١٢، ١٦، ١٩، ١، ٦، ٥، ٢

Reading Arabic

A number of observations are of particular relevance before you start reading and writing Arabic.

1. Unlike English, Arabic is written and read from right to left.

2. Letters are always joined to one another.

3. A letter may have more than one shape according to its place in the word.

4. Short vowels are not represented regularly as part of the alphabet, but they are sometimes indicated as diacritical marks above or below the letters to assist beginning readers.

The Arabic letters are organized into groups according to their basic shape. Within the same group, letters are generally distinguised by the placement and number of their dots. Most letters represent sounds that are similar to English sounds; others are quite different. Do not let this intimidate you. First, these sounds are a minority. Second, and probably more important, language is not just sounds: context is often more important than individual sounds and words in getting the meaning of what is said or read. This means that even if you miss a certain sound in a word, you will be able to get the meaning from other available information: the topic, other words and sounds, etc.

In the following, the Arabic letters will be introduced in alphabetical order and next to each one the corresponding English letter. For letters representing sounds not found in English, a phonetic transliteration is given based on the International Phonetic Association (IPA) set of symbols. If you are not familiar with this alphabet, either your teacher or a native speaker of Arabic can show you what sounds these letters represent. But do not dwell too long on the pronunciation of individual sounds; the sentences and the message behind them are what matters the most. You will develop a feel for the Arabic letters and the sounds they stand for in time and without much extra effort.

Each letter will be listed in its different shapes if it has more than one. Initial position means at the beginning of the word, final means at the end of the word, and medial means inside the word. Five letters are described as nonjoining. This means that they are joined to a preceding letter, but not to a following one. Under "Name" is shown the Arabic name for the letter. (More on reading in the Appendix.)

The Arabic Alphabet

	Name	English	Final Separate	Final Joined	Medial	Initial	
nonjoining	الف	a (cat)	--	--	--	ا	اد/ ✓
	باء	b	ب	--	--	بـ	ﭐ ✓
	تاء	t	ت	--	--	تـ	✓ ﮞ ✓
	ثاء	th (thin)	ث	--	--	ثـ	ادﭐ ✓
	جيم	j	ج	--	--	جـ	ﭐﭐﻋ ✓
	حاء	ħ (IPA) h	ح	--	--	حـ	ﮞ ✓
	خاء	x (IPA)	خ	--	--	خـ	ﭐﭐ ✓
nonjoining	دال	d	--	--	--	د	ﭐ ✓
nonjoining	ذال	th (the)	--	--	--	ذ	ﭐﭐ ✓
nonjoining	راء	r	--	--	--	ر	ﭐ (below line) ✓
nonjoining	زاي	z	--	--	--	ز	ﭐ ✓
	سين	s	س	--	--	سـ	ﭐ ✓
	شين	sh	ش	--	--	شـ	ﭐ ✓
	صاد	ṣ (IPA)	ص	--	--	صـ	ﭐ ✓
	ضاد	ḍ (IPA)	ض	--	--	ضـ	
	طاء	ṭ (IPA)	--	--	--	ط	ﭐ ✓
	ظاء	ḏ̣ (IPA)	ʿ --	--	--	ظ	
	عين	ʕ (IPA)	ع	ع	عـ	عـ	ﭐ ✓
	غين	ɣ (IPA)	غ	غ	غـ	غـ	✓
	فاء	f	ف	--	--	فـ	ﭐ ✓
	قاف	ḳ (IPA)	ق	--	--	قـ	ﭐ ✓
	كاف	k	ك	--	--	كـ	ﭐ ✓
	لام	l	ل	--	--	لـ	ﭐ ✓
	ميم	m	م	--	--	مـ	ﭐ ✓
	نون	n	ن	--	--	نـ	ﭐ ✓
	هاء	h	ه	ـﻪ	ﻬ	هـ	ﭐ ✓
nonjoining	واو	oo (moon), w (we)	--	--	--	و	ﭐ ✓
	ياء	ee (seen), y (yes)	ي	--	--	يـ	✓

٥

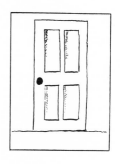

باب	كتاب	بيروت
بـ ا ب	كـ تـ ا ب	بـ يـ ر و ت

سوريا	تونس	كندا
سـ و ر يـ ا	تـ و نـ س	كـ نـ د ا

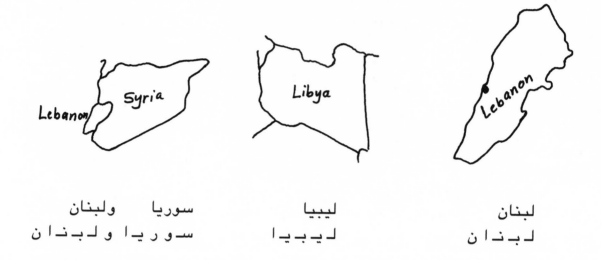

سوريا   ولبنان
سـوريـا ولـبـنـان

ليبيا
لـيـبـيـا

لبنان
لـبـنـان

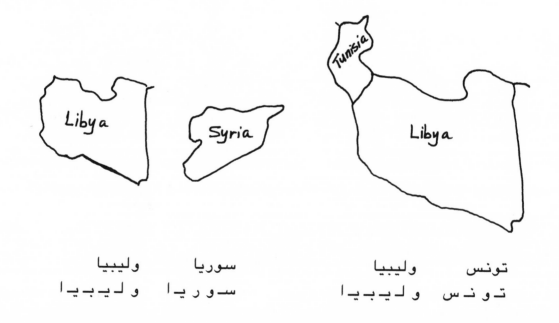

سوريا   وليبيا
سـوريـا ولـيـبـيـا

تونس   وليبيا
تـونـس ولـيـبـيـا

صغير	باب	كبير	باب
ص غ ي ر	ب ا ب	ك ب ي ر	ب ا ب

ليبيا	شرق	مصر
ل ي ب ي ا	ش ر ق	م ص ر

ليبيا	غرب	شمال	تونس
ل ي ب ي ا	غ ر ب	ش م ا ل	ت و ن س

أريزونا	غرب	كاليفورنيا
أ ر ي ز و ن ا	غ ر ب	ك ا ل ي ف و ر ن ي ا

سوريا	شمال	شرق	لبنان
س و ر ي ا	ش م ا ل	ش ر ق	ل ب ن ا ن

مصر	شمال	السودان
م ص ر	ش م ا ل	ا ل س و د ا ن

Match the names of the countries and states with the corresponding maps.

٤. اليمن   ٣. فلوريدا   ٢. مصر   ١. سوريا

٨. سوريا ولبنان   ٧. كاليفورنيا   ٦. تونس   ٥. تكساس

اقرأ ٥

Read the sentences and answer the questions.

١. مريم من لبنان.

Where is Maryam from?

_____

٢. سليم من مصر.

Where is Saleem from?

_____

٣. دمشق في جنوب سوريا.

Where is Damascus?

_____

٤. سوزان من سان فرانسسكو.

Where is Suzanne from?

_____

٥. علي طالب من اليمن. وسليم أستاذ من مصر.

What does Saleem do?

_____

اسـمـع ١

(The numbers 21-30)

اسـمـع ٢

Match the picture with the sentence you hear.

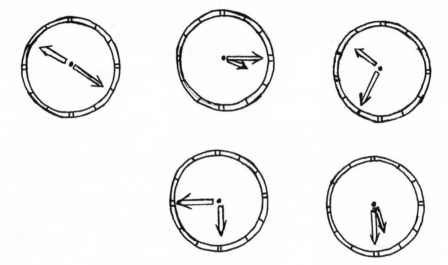

اسـمـع ٣

1. What name or names are mentioned?

_____

2. What time is it?

_____

اسـمـع ٤

1. What time did Waleed come?

_____

2. What time did Nadya come?

_____

اسمع ٥

1. Which city is Abdalla from?

_____

2. Is it big or small?

_____

3. Where is it located?

_____

اقرأ ١

١. ٢١، ٢٢، ٢٣، ٢٤، ٢٥، ٢٦، ٢٧، ٢٨، ٢٩، ٣٠

٢. ٢١، ٢٣، ٢٥، ٢٧، ٢٩، ٣٠، ٢٨، ٢٦، ٢٤، ٢٢، ٢٠

٣. ١، ٥، ١٠، ٢، ١٥، ٣٠، ١٤، ٢٤، ٤، ١٨

٤. ١١، ٣، ٨، ١٤، ٢٢، ١٦، ٢٦، ٦، ٧، ١٧

اقرأ ٢

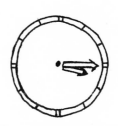

ثلاثة وربع

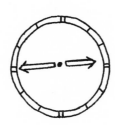

ثلاثة الا ربع

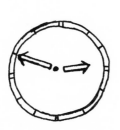

ثلاثة الا عشرة

سبعة وعشرة

ستة وعشرة

سبعة الا عشرة

١٤

اقرأ ٣

١. ليبيا شرق تونس.

Where is Libya?

_____

٢. لبنان غرب سوريا.

Where is Lebanon?

_____

٣. السودان جنوب مصر.

Where is Sudan?

_____

٤. الكويت شمال شرق السعودية.

Where is Kuwait?

_____

اقرأ ٤

Match the name of each city or country with the letters it is made up of.

ب ي ر و ت	بغداد
ت و ن س	مصر
ا ل ي م ن	بيروت
ب غ د ا د	تونس
م ص ر	لبنان
ا ل خ ر ط و م	اليمن
د م ش ق	عمّان
ج دّ ة	الخرطوم
ع مّ ا ن	جدّة
ل ب ن ان	دمشق

اقرأ ٥

اسمي سليم. أنا طالب. أنا من مدينة حلب. حلب مدينة كبيرة في شمال سوريا. هذا علي. علي أستاذ من طرابلس عاصمة ليبيا. وهذا محمود. محمود طالب من مدينة القدس في فلسطين.

1. What does Saleem do?

He is a student

2. What does Ali do?

_____

3. Where is Mahmoud from?

He is from Jerusalem in Palestine

اقرأ ٦

Circle the letter that you hear in the following pairs.

٤. ب، ت   ٣. ح، ﻟ   ٢. ا، ك   ١. ب، ش

٨. ك، عـ   ٧. ط، ح   ٦. مـ، ك   ٥. ت، ق

الدرس رقم ٤

اسـمـع ١

(The numbers 10-100)

اسـمـع ٢

1. How many days does he go to the university?

_____

2. Which days?

_____

اسـمـع ٣

What day is it?

_____

اسـمـع ٤

Days of the week: write in English the name of the day or days you hear in each sentence. Some sentences do not contain names of days.

1. _____   2. _____
3. _____   4. _____
5. _____   6. _____
7. _____   8. _____
9. _____

اسـمـع ٥

1. How many Yemens are there now?

_____

2. Where was South Yemen?

_____

اقرأ ١

١. ١، ٢، ٣، ٤، ٥، ٦، ٧، ٨، ٩، ١٠٠

٢. ٢، ٤، ٦، ٨، ١٠٠، ٩، ٧، ٥، ٣، ١

٣. ١، ٥، ١، ٢، ٢، ١١، ٣، ١٤، ١٦، ٤، ١٨

٤. ١١، ٣، ٨، ١٤، ٢١، ١٢، ١٦، ٢٦، ١٧، ١٠٠

٥. ٣، ٨، ٢٨، ٨٢، ٣٨، ٦٧، ١٤، ٤١، ٦٢، ٨٦

اقرأ ٢

Match the numbers in the two columns.

ثلاثة	١	אחת
ستة	٢	שבע
ثمانية	٣	אחד
اربعة	٤	ארבעה
واحد	٥	חמש
تسعة	٦	שישה
عشرة	٧	עשר
سبعة	٨	שמונה
اثنين	٩	שניים
خمسة	١٠	שלושה

اقرأ ٣

Circle the number you hear.

٣– ٤٥، ٤٠	٢– ١٥، ٥٠	١– ٢٣، ٣٠
٦– ٢، ١٢	٥– ٢٦، ٦٢	٤– ٦٢، ٧٢
٩– ٣٧، ٧٣	٨– ٦٨، ٧٨	٧– ٨٠، ٦٨
		١٠– ٢٣، ٣٢

less than

اقرأ ٤

أيام الأسبوع: السبت، الأحد، الإثنين، الثلاثاء، الأربعاء، الخميس، الجمعة

اقرأ ٥

Word search: find the following words. You can go down or right to left.

قطر، مِصر، اليَمَن، العِراق، بَيروت، الكويت، دِمشق

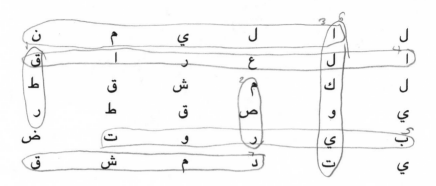

ل	ا	ل	ي	م	ن
ل	ل	ع	ر	ا	ق
ل	ك	ش	ق	ط
ي	و	ص	ق	ط	ر
ب	ي	ر	و	ت	ض
ي	ت	م	ش	د	ق

اقرأ ٦

Match the name of each country with its capital by drawing lines connecting the two.

الأردن	القاهرة
تونس	بيروت
سوريا	عمّان
مصر	بغداد
اليمن	تونس
لبنان	دمشق
السودان	صنعاء
السعودية	الخرطوم
العراق	الكويت
الكويت	الرياض

Circle the word you hear.

(٣) ثلاثة	(١٥٠) افتح ١.
(٨) ثمانية	سبعة ٢.
(٢) اثنين	(20) عشرين ٣.
(50) خمسين	(٩) تسعة ٤.
(٨) ثمانية	(٣) ثلاثة ٥.
(٤) أربعة	(40) أربعين ٦.
(٧) سبعة	(٥) خمسة ٧.
(20) عشرين	(10) عشرة ٨.
(٧) سبعة	(٦) ستة ٩.
(٩) تسعة	(٧) سبعة ١٠.

اقرأ ٨

Circle the letter you hear in each pair.

٤. ط، س	٣. ث، ت	٢. ج، ي	١. خ، ث
٨. ك، ق	٧. م، ن	٦. ر، د	٥. س، ش

إملاء (Dictation)

١، ٢، ٣، ٤، ٥، ٦، ٧، ٨، ٩، ١٠.

الدرس رقم ٥

اسمـع ١

Which month is it?

_____

اسمـع ٢

1. What does Nabeel Hassan do?

_____

2. Where is he from?

_____

3. When did he come to the U.S.?

_____

اسمـع ٣

1. How many pages are there?

_____

2. What is the total cost?

_____

اسمـع ٤

Translate each number and the noun it refers to (e.g., three books, two months, etc.).

1. _____ 2. _____
3. _____ 4. _____
5. _____ 6. _____
7. _____

اقرأ ١

١.   ١٠، ١٠٠، ٢٠٠، ٣٠٠، ٤٠٠، ١٠٠٠، ٢٠٠٠، ٣٠٠٠، ١٠٠٠٠٠٠

٢.   ١٢، ١٦، ٢٦، ٦١، ٩١، ٧٧، ٧٨، ٨٧، ١٩

٣.   ١.١، ١.٢، ١.٥، ٧٠٠، ٢.١، ٢.٢، ٣.١

٤.   ٣٠، ١٣، ٢٣، ٣٢، ٦، ٤٥، ١٧، ٢٧، ٧١

٥.   ١١٠٠، ١٢٠٠، ١٢.١، ١٩١٠، ١٩٢٣، ١٩٥٠، ١٩٦٧، ١٩٩٠

٦.   ٢٣، ٣٢، ١١٣٢، ٢١.٧، ١٩٨٠، ١٩٩١، ٢١٠، ١٩١، ٣١٤، ٦٦٠

٢١

اقرأ ٢

Circle the number you hear.

١. ١٥، ٢٥   ٢. ١١، ١٢   ٣. ١٧، ٢٧   ٤. ١٥، ٥١

٥. ١٤، ٤١   ٦. ٢٦، ٢٧   ٧. ٧٣، ٣٧   ٨. ٥٣، ٦٣

٩. ٨، ٣.   ١٠. ٦٦، ٧٧

اقرأ ٣

Circle the word or phrase you hear.

١. ثلاثة (3)   ثمانية (8)

٢. ثلاثة وأربعين (43)   ثلاثة وعشرين (23)

٣. سوريا   السعودية

٤. سبعة (7)   تسعة (9)

٥. دقيقة   دمشق

٦. سبعة (7)   أسبوع

٧. الثلاثاء   ثلاثة (3)

اقرأ ٤

شهور السنة: كانون الثاني، شباط، آذار، نيسان، أيّار، حزيران، تمّوز، آب،
أيلول، تشرين الأوّل، تشرين الثاني، كانون الأوّل

٢٢

answer

اقرأ ٥

١. الشهر الماضي كان شهر آب.

Past month was the month of aug.

What was last month? _____ اب

٢. هذا الشهر هو شهر أيلول.

this month is sept

What is this month? _____ أيلول

first day

٣. السبت أوّل يوم في الأسبوع في مصر.

saturday is the first day of the week in Egypt

What is the first day of the week in Egypt? _____ السبت

٤. الإثنين هو أوّل يوم في الأسبوع في لُبنان.

What is the first day of the week in Lebanon? _____ الاثنين

٥. يومُ الأحد هو أوّل يوم في الأسبوع في أمريكا.

What is the first day of the week in America? _____ يوم الاحد

٦. يوم الجمعة هو آخر يوم في الأسبوع في ليبيا.

What is the last day of the week in Libya? _____ يوم الجمعة

اقرأ ٦ (خريطة)

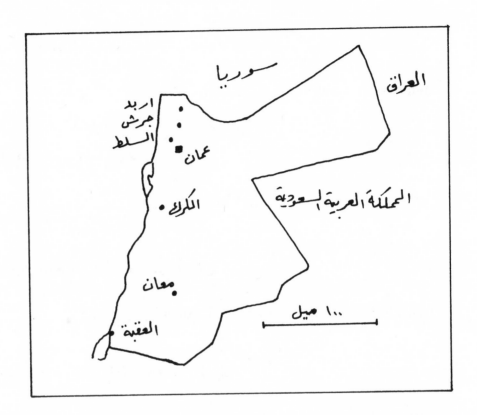

(جدول المسافات بالكيلومترات بين المدن الأردنية)

	الحدود السورية	السلط	معان	الكرك	جرش	إربد	الحدود العراقية	العقبة	عمان	
										عمان
								٣٢٨		العقبة
							٦٤٥	٣٣١		الحدود العراقية
						٣.٩	٤١٢	٨٩		إربد
					٣٨	٣١١	٣٧٤	٥١		جرش
				١٦.	١٩٨	٤٣٤	٢٣٧	١١٨		الكرك
			١٤٤	٢٥٧	٢٩٥	٥٢٨	١١٧	٢١٢		معان
		٢٣٦	١٣٩	٥.	٨٩	٣٥١	٣٠٣	٣.		السلط
	٩٣	٢٩٨	٢.٢	٤٣	٢٥	٣١٢	٤١٤	٩٤		الحدود السورية
٩.	٤٤	٢٣٣	١٣٩	٥٩	٩٢	٣.٨	٣٤٩	٢٣		الزرقاء

٢٤

What are the distances in kilometers between:
1. Amman and Irbid _____
2. Amman and Jerash _____
3. Ma'an and the Iraqi border _____
4. Aqaba and the Syrian border _____
5. Al-Karak and Al-Salt? _____

اقرأ ٧

You will hear four phrases. Reconstruct them by joining the appropriate words in the following.

| كتاب | سوريا | واحد | والأربعاء | عاصمة | ولبنان |
| الإثنين | مصر | القاهرة | | والجمعة |

الدرس رقم ٦

1. What is the population of Ithaca?

_____

2. How is the weather in the summer?

_____

3. How long is the winter?

_____

اسـمـع ٢

1. How is the weather in the winter in Florida?

_____

2. How is the weather in the winter in California?

_____

اسـمـع ٣

1. What month is it?

_____

2. What is he complaining about?

_____

اسـمـع ٤

1. What is the weather like in the summer in Syria?

_____

2. What is the weather like in the winter in California?

_____

3. Where does snow fall in California?

_____

Match the words with the pictures by copying each word under the corresponding picture.

١. صيف	٢. ربيع	٣. خريف
٤. شتاء	٥. مطر	٦. ثلج

اقرأ ٢

Read the sentences and answer the questions.

١. فصول السنة: الصيف، الخريف، الشتاء، الربيع.

What is the last season mentioned? _____

٢. الطقس في إثاكا بارد في الشتاء.

When is it cold in Ithaca? _____

٣. الطقس في الاسكا بارد في الشتاء والخريف والربيع.

How is the weather in Alaska in the fall? _____

اقرأ ٣

Match the singular with its plural.

ولايات	طالب
طلّاب	مدينة
ساعات	دولة
دقائق	ولاية
مُدُن	ساعة
دُوَل	دقيقة

اقرأ ٤

قنصليات السعودية ومصر في الولايات المتحدة

السعودية

رقم التلفون	المدينة	رقم التلفون	المدينة
(٢٠٢) ٣٤٢-٣٨٠٠	واشنطن دي سي	(٢١٣) ٢٠٨-٦٥٦٦	لوس انجلس
(٧١٣) ٧٨٥-٥٥٧٧	هيوستن-تكساس	(٢١٢) ٧٥٢-٢٧٤٠	نيويورك

مصر

رقم التلفون	المدينة	رقم التلفون	المدينة
(٢١٢) ٦٥٩-٧١٢٠	نيويورك	(٣١٢) ٦٧٠-٢٦٣٣	شيكاغو

What are the telephone numbers of the Saudi consulate in Houston and the Egyptian consulate in New York?

_____

_____

اقرأ ٥

Circle the word you hear.

١.	اثنين	الإثنين
٢.	ثمانية	ثمانين
٣.	الأحد	واحد
٤.	تسعة وأربعين	تسعة وربع
٥.	أربعة	ربع
٦.	ثلاثة وأربعين	ثلاثة وربع
٧.	ثلاثة وثلث	الثلاثاء
٨.	أسبوعين	سبعة وأربعين

اقرأ ٦

Circle the letter you hear in each pair.

١. ق، ك	٢. كـ، ف	٣. خ،ح	٤. س، ب
٥. ف، ق	٦. لا، ا	٧. خ، ط	٨. م، ل
٩. ع،ح	١٠. ن، ب		

٢٩

Reconstruct the four phrases you will hear by joining the appropriate words in the following.

الماضي	وشباط	الطقس	والصيف	الربيع
كانون الثاني	والخريف	اليوم	الشهر	بارد

املاء

١١، ١٢، ١٣، ١٤، ١٥، ١٦، ١٧، ١٨، ١٩، ٢٠.

باب كبير.

تونس وليبيا.

The Definite Article, the Sun and Moon Letters

Definiteness in Arabic is expressed by attaching the prefix الـ "the" to nouns and adjectives:

باب كبير	baab kabiir	"big door"
الباب الكبير	ilbaab ilkabiir	"the big (the) door"

(Note that الباب كبير is a full sentence that is translated as *The door is big*.)

If الـ is followed by a *sun letter* it is assimilated to (becomes the same as) that letter, which results in a doubled consonant in pronunciation but not in writing. The sun letters are the following: ت، ث، د، ذ، ر، ز، س، ش، ص، ض، ط، ظ، ن، ل. (The pronunciation of all these consonants involves the front part of the tongue (the tip and the blade):

الشمس	<u>ish</u>shams	"the sun"
الساعة	i<u>s</u>saaʕa	"the watch, the clock, the time"
الثلاثاء	i<u>thth</u>alaathaaʔ	"Tuesday" (*th* as in *thin*)

لـ remains unchanged before moon letters, which include all the consonants not listed above:

القمر	il<u>k</u>amar	"the moon"
الأربعاء	ilʔarbiʕaaʔ	"Wednesday"
الخميس	ilxamiis	"Thursday" (x = IPA)
الكويت	ilkuwait	"Kuwait"

الدرس رقم ٧

1. Does he live on campus?

_____

2. Is the house big?

_____

3. How many bedrooms does it have?

_____

4. Is the house far? How far?

_____

1. How many bedrooms are in Abdalla's apartment?

_____

2. Is the kitchen big or small?

_____

1. How many bathrooms does he want?

_____

2. Does he want a dining room?

_____

1. Where was he before coming to the U.S.?

_____

2. When did he come to the U.S.?

_____

3. How did he come to the U.S.?

_____

4. How long did the car take to get to the U.S.?

_____

1. How did he go to New York?

_____

2. How long did the plane take?

_____

3. How long does the bus take?

_____

1. Is the house close or far?

_____

2. What street name is mentioned?

_____

3. Is the house on the right or the left?

_____

1. What does Waleed want?

_____

2. How many cars does he have?

_____

According to the dialogue, is San Francisco far from Los Angeles?

_____

Match each word with the corresponding picture.

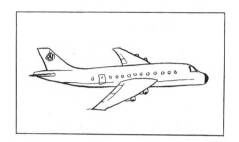

٤. غرفة جلوس	٣. غرفة نوم	٢. مَطبخ	١. شارع
٨. يمشي	٧. طيّارة	٦. سيّارة	٥. حمّام

اقرأ ٢

١. بيت كبير وبعيد عن الجامعة.

Is the house far from the university?

البيت وبعيد عن الجامعة

٢. عنوان البيت هو ٢١ شارع الجامعة.

What is the address of the house?

عنوان البيت هو ٢١ شارع الجامعة

٣. يوسف أستاذ في جامعة "كاليفورنيا" في "بيركلي". هو ساكن في بيت كبير قريب من الجامعة. في بيت يوسف أربع غرف نوم، وغرفة جلوس، وحمّام واحد ومطبخ كبير. بيت يوسف على شارع صغير. عنوان البيت هو: ٢١٣ شارع "واشنطن".

1. What does Yousif do?

يوسف أستاذ

2. Where does he live?

يوسف تمكن في كاليفورنيا

3. How many bedrooms does Yousif's house have?

أربع غرف

4. Is the street where Yousif's house is big or small?

بيت يوسف على شارع صغير

5. What is the address of Yousif's house?

٢١٣ شارع واشنطن

اقرأ ٣

Match each of the words in the first column with its opposite in the second. There is one extra word in the first column.

أَخِر	كبير
صغير	الماضي
يمين	شمال
غرب	أول
بعيد	قبل
جنوب	قريب
بعد	شرق
	يسار

اقرأ ٤

Match the singular with its plural. One word in the singular column does not have a matching plural.

أسابيع	يوم
عناوين	أسبوع
شوارع	شهر
شهور	سنة
سنوات	حمام
أيام	شارع
	عنوان

اقرأ ٥

مِصْر دَوْلَة عَرَبِيَة كَبيرة في شَمال شَرْق إفْريقيا. هي شَرْق ليبيا وشَمال السودان. هي قَريبَة مِن السَعودِية وبَعيدَة عَن العِراق. عاصِمَة مِصْر مَدينَة القاهرة. القاهرة مَدينَة كَبيرة.

close to = قريبة من

According to the paragraph:
1. Where is Egypt? _____ شرق ليبيا وشمال السودان
2. Is Egypt far from Iraq? _____ بعيدة عن العراق
3. Is Cairo a big city? _____ نعم القاهرة مدينة كبيرة

اقرأ ٦

Circle the letter you hear.

٤. و، د	٣. ك، ل	٢. ج، ح	١. ن، ي
٨. ع، ح	٧. خ، ج	٦. ف، ق	٥. لا، ر
		١٠. ث، ت	٩. س، ش

Read aloud.

٢. سوريا ولبنان.   ١. ثلاث طالبات.

٤. غرفة نوم وغرفة جلوس.   ٣. العراق والكويت.

٨. مطبخ كبير وحمّام صغير.   ٧. سيّارة أمريكية كبيرة.

١٠. سيّارتي في البيت.   ٩. هذا بيت كبير.

١٢. جامعة "عين شمس" جامعة مصرية كبيرة.   ١١. عنوان الجامعة.

(handwritten annotations: "female students (3)"; "sleepingroom & living room"; "big kitchen small broom"; "my car is in the house"; "university" "is a big egyptian university")

Reconstruct the five phrases you will hear by joining the appropriate words in the following.

عاصمة	والسودان	جلوس	بعيدة	غرفة	دمشق
مصر	الشمالي	سوريا	نوم	الجامعة	الجنوبي
	وغرفة	بعيدة	واليمن	وحمّام	اليمن

(handwritten annotations: (egypt) (sudan) (sitting) (for feminine) (san) (Damascus); "egypt"; "northern"; "syria"; "sleeps"; "university"; "& the room"; "& yemen"; "bathroom"; "southern"; "yeah")

اقرأ واكتب

Join the letters to form words, phrases, and sentences.

١. ك م   ش ق ة   ف ي   ا ل ب ي ت؟

٢. ث ل ا ث   ش ق ق.

٣. ل ي ب ي ا   و م ص ر   و ا ل س و د ا ن.

٤. ا ل ص ي ف   و ا ل خ ر ي ف   و ا ل ش ت ا ء   و ا ل ر ب ي ع.

قواعد

The Construct (الإضافة)

When two or more nouns are closely associated, as in the case of possession or something being part of something else, they form a special grammatical construction called *the construct* (إضافة):

اسم المعلم	ism ilmuʕallim	"the teacher's name"
عاصمة سوريا	ʕaaṣimit suurya	"the capital of Syria"
باب الغرفة	baab ilɣurfi	"the door of the room"
شارع الجامعة	shaariʕ iljaamʕa	"university street"

The following two points about the إضافة are important to remember at this stage: first, the ـة of التاء المربوطة is pronounced like any other ت in the first part of the إضافة:

غرفة نوم	ɣurfit noom	"bedroom"
عاصمة سوريا	ʕaaṣimit suurya	"the capital of Syria"
ولاية كاليفورنيا	wilaayit California	"the state of California"
مية طالب	miit ṭaalib	"a hundred students"
جامعة كورنيل	jaamiʕit Cornell	"Cornell University"

Second, the first part of the إضافة never takes the definite article; it is made definite by association with the second part.

غرفة نوم	"a bedroom"
غرفة النوم	"the bedroom"

The following three phrases are ungrammatical:

الغرفة النوم

الغرفة نوم

الجامعة جورجتاون

٣٨

Note that if three or more nouns are found in an إضافة relation, each two of them form an إضافة construction to which the above two points apply:

عنوان بيت الطلاب   "The address of the students' house (dormitory)"

طالبة جامعة الكويت "The University of Kuwait (female) student"

In the two phrases, none of the words عنوان، بيت، طالبة، جامعة can have the definite article. In the second phrase the تاء مربوطة of both طالبة and جامعة is pronounced as ت.

الدرس رقم ٨

اسـمـع ١

1. How many houses do they own?

_____

2. Where are his parents now?

_____

3. When did they go to Florida?

_____

4. When do they return to New York?

_____

اسـمـع ٢

1. How many brothers does Yousif have?

_____

2. How many brothers and sisters does the other speaker have?

_____

اسـمـع ٣

1.Where is Said from?

_____

2. Does he have a house in Amman?

_____

3. How many people are in the whole family?

_____

4. What is Said's mother's name?

_____

5. Where does his father work?

_____

6. What does his mother do?

_____

1. How many children does my sister have?
_____
2. How old are they?
_____
3. Who lives close to my sister's house?
_____

What does his father do?
_____

1. What do Yousif's parents do?
_____
2. What does the other person's father do?
_____

1. Does Yousif like the dorm?
_____
2. Why?
_____
3. Is the other person's apartment big?
_____
4. Where does he eat?
_____

1. Where does Waleed eat?

_____

2. Why?

_____

3. Where does the other person eat?

_____

Match each word with the corresponding picture.

اقرأ ٢

Circle the phrase you hear.

سوريا وليبيا	١. سوريا ولبنان
بيروت قريبة	٢. باب كبير
هو من سوريا؟	٣. هو من مصر؟
ليبيا أكبر من تونس	٤. ليبيا قريبة من تونس
العراق شرق سوريا	٥. الأردن جنوب سوريا
ثلاثة وخمسين	٦. الثلاثاء والخميس
اثنين وأربعين	٧. الإثنين والأربعاء

اقرأ ٣

مصر للطيران

٩٩ رحلة أسبوعياً الى ١٨ مدينة في الشرق الأوسط والشرق الأقصى
وبلدان الخليج العربي ومنها الى جميع أنحاء آسيا

الثلاثاء	مانيلا	الثلاثاء	طوكيو
السبت	بومباي	الثلاثاء	بانكوك
كل يوم	جدة	الإثنين/الجمعة	كراتشي
كل يوم	عمّان	كلّ يوم	الظهران
كل يوم	الكويت	كل يوم	بغداد
الاثنين/الخميس/الجمعة/الأحد	دُبيّ	كل يوم	ابو ظبي
الاثنين/الثلاثاء/الخميس	مسقط	كل يوم	الدوحة
الأحد/الخميس	البحرين	الثلاثاء/الخميس	الشارقة
الثلاثاء/الجمعة	صنعاء	الخميس	رأس الخيمة

للاستعلام: مكتب مصر للطيران، تلفون ٢٤٥.٢٦٠/ ٢٤٥.٢٧٠/ ٢٤٥٤٤..

every ١

1. How many flights does Egypt Air have to the Far East and the Middle East each week?

_____

2. How many flights per week does Egypt Air have to Bangkok, Muscat, San'a?

_____

3. On what days does Egypt Air fly to Dubai?

_____

4. If you miss the Sunday flight to Bahrain, when is the next flight that you can catch?

_____

5. To which cities does Egypt Air have daily flights?

_____

اقرأ ٤

Match the singular with its plural. One word in the singular column does not have a matching plural.

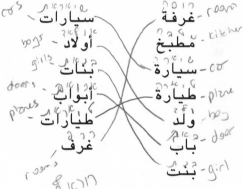

اقرأ ٥

Rewrite the following words grouping them into related families. A family is a group of words that derive from the same root, which generally consists of three letters.

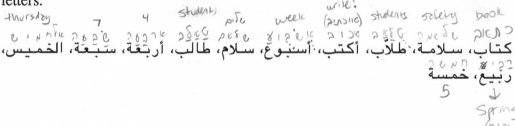

كتاب، سلامة، طلّاب، أكتب، أسبوع، سلام، طالب، أربعة، سبعة، الخميس، ربيع، خمسة

٤٥

اقرأ ٦

Listen to the sentences and phrases and reconstruct them by joining the appropriate words.

سكرتير *seeratery*	أولاد *boys*	ويسار *Sicne ופsar*	خمسة *5*	وطَبيب *חומר*
ومهنّدس *engineer*	يمين *right*	وبنت *2 girl*	الجامعة *university*	الأمريكية
مُستشفى *hospital*		وطَبيبة *girl doctor*	عنْدي *w/me*	أستاذ *teacher*

اقرأ ٧

Read aloud.

انتِ	انتَ	أنا	أختْ	أخ	أمّ	أب	١.
	انتِ	هي	هو	في	مِن	كَم	لا	٢.
صغير	كبير	كتاب	شهر	بيت	يوم	باب	٣.
سوريا	لُبنان	طالِب	بارِد	بنات	بِنت	وَلَد	٤.

اقرأ ٨ (Greetings)

(أ is the greeting and ب is its response.) *translate to hebrew*

when answering these questions, you add Jc before

שלום עליכם	peace be on you	السلام عليكم	أ-
עליכם השלום	on you peace	وعليكم السلام	ب-
בוקר טוב	good morning	صباح الخير	أ-
בוקר אור	good morning	صباح النّور	ب-
ערב טוב	good evening	مساء الخير	أ-
ערב טוב	good evening	مساء النّور	ب-
שלום	hello, hi	مرحبا	أ-
ברוכים הבאים	hello, welcome	أهلاً وسهلاً	ب-
שלום שלום			

أ- كيف حالَك، حالِك؟ how are you? مה שלומך

ب- الحمدلله thank God ברוך ה

كويّس good, fine } כל טוב/בסדר

بخير well, fine

أ- مع السلامة good-bye } להתראות

ب- مع السلامة good-bye } להתראות

أ- شُكراً thank you תודה

ب- عَفواً you are welcome בבקשה

اقرأ واكتب

Join the letters to make up words and sentences, then read what you have written.

١. ا ف ت ح   ك ت ا ب ك.

٢. س ت ة   كُ ت ب.

٣. ا ن ت   اوّ ل   ط ا ل ب.

٤. ا ق ر أ   ص ف ح ة   ب ه ذا   ا ل ك ت ا ب.

٥. ا ق ر أ   رُ ب ع   ا ل ك ت ا ب.

٦. ه و   أ س ت ا ذ   و أ ن ا   ط ا ل ب.

٧. م ص ر   أ ك ب ر   م ن   ا ل أ ر د ن.

املاء

١٠، ٢٠، ٣٠، ٤٠، ٥٠، ٦٠، ٧٠، ٨٠، ٩٠، ١٠٠.

سوريا ولبنان.

مصر والسودان.

قواعد

Number and (Dis)Agreement

A noun in Levantine Arabic can be singular, dual, or plural, and an adjective can be singular or plural.

The singular

A *book* or *one book* is expressed as كتاب واحد or simply كتاب, with the number following the noun it refers to or no number at all. (Note that واحد كتاب is ungrammatical.)

The dual

The dual is expressed by attaching the suffix ين (een) to the noun. If the noun ends in التاء المربوطة, then *t* of التاء المربوطة is pronounced when the dual suffix is added. (Note that اثنين كتاب is ungrammatical.)

كتاب كتابين	kitaabeen	"two books"
صفحة صفحتين	ṣaffiiteen	"two pages"

The plural

Nouns and adjectives are pluralized in a variety of ways, but for the most part they follow general patterns. One easy plural category to remember is plurals of words ending in a تاء مربوطة. Many such words are pluralized by deleting the تاء مربوطة and adding the suffix ات in its place. At this stage I suggest that you try to remember the plurals of the individual nouns and adjectives as they are introduced; you will develop a feel for the plural patterns later.

You will find the following observations concerning number particularly useful in improving your overall Arabic language skills because they involve frequently used constructions:

1. For the numbers 3-10, the plural form of the noun is used and the noun follows the number. (Note that the تاء مربوطة of the number is dropped before the noun.)

ثلاث كتب	thalath kutub	"three books"
أربع كتب	arbaʕ kutub	"four books"
عشر كتب	ʕashar kutub	"ten books"
ثلاث صفحات	thalath ṣaffiaat	"three pages"
سبع صفحات	sabʕ ṣaffiaat	"seven pages"
عشر صفحات	ʕashar ṣaffiaat	"ten pages"

2. For the number 11 and above, the singular form of the nouns is used. (Note the addition of the suffix *ar* to the numbers 11-19 when a noun follows them.)

احداشر كتاب	ifidashar kitaab	"eleven books"
عشرين كتاب	ʿishriin kitaab	"twenty books"
الف كتاب	alf kitaab	"a thousand books"
خمسطاشر صفحة	xamistashar ṣaffia	"fifteen pages"
مليون صفحة	malyoon ṣaffia	"a million pages"

3. After كم "how many" only the singular form of the noun is used:

كم ولد عندك؟	"how many boys, children do you have?"
كم غرفة في بيتكم؟	"how many rooms are in your house?"
كم أخ وأخت عندك؟	"how many brothers and sisters do you have?"

اسـمـع

أسئلة

1. How old is Sharif?
_____

2. Where does his family live?
_____

3. How many sisters does he have? What are their names?
_____

4. How old is Sharif's father?
_____

5. What does Sharif's mother do?
_____

كلمات جديدة

engineering	هَنـدسـة	to study	درَس (يدرُس)
		housewife	رَبَّة بيت

أسئلة

1. Where is he going?

_____

2. Where is he from in America?

_____

3. How far is Ithaca from New York City by car?

_____

4. What is the population of Ithaca?

_____

كلمات جديدة

about, approximately	حَوالي	of course	طَبعاً
		only	بَسّ

family

عائلة أبو شريف

علي سمارة   +   حليمة أبو اللبن
(الأب، ٥٦ سنة)   (الأم، ٥١ سنة)

مريم	شريف	أيمن	عبدالله	سعاد
بنت	ولد	ولد	ولد	بنت
٣١ سنة	٢٨ سنة	٢٥ سنة	٢١ سنة	١٨ سنة

أسئلة

1. What is Sharif's mother's name?

_____

2. How old is she?

_____

3. How old is Sharif's father?

_____

4. How many brothers does Sharif have?

_____

5. What are the names of Sharif's sisters?

_____

قواعد

Possession

Possession in nouns is expressed by attaching a pronoun suffix to the noun.

كتاب +ـُـه	كتابه	kitaab-u	"his book"
كتاب +ها	كتابها	kitaab-ha	"her book"
كتاب +َك	كتابك	kitaab-ak	"your, m.s. book"
كتاب +ك	كتابك	kitaab-ik	"your, f.s. book"
كتاب+ ي	كتابي	kitaab-i	"my book"

تمارين (Exercises)

١. اكتب

Attach the singular possessive pronoun suffixes corresponding to هو، هي، انتَ،
انتِ، أنا to the following nouns:

اسـم، عُمر، بيـت

٢. اكتب

Make your own family tree: write your name, the names of your parents, brothers,
and sisters.

٣. اقرأ

Match the singular with its plural. One word in the singular column does not have
a matching plural.

أطبّاء	عائلة
مدارس	أخ
عائلات	أخت
أخوات	رَقم
إخوان	مهندس
أرقام	طبيب
	مدرسة

اسمع

أسئلة

1. How old is Maryam?
_____
2. How long does it take to get from her apartment to her parents' house?
_____
3. How long did she study in school?
_____
4. How many children does she have? How old are they?
_____
5. What does Maryam's husband do?
_____

كلمات جديدة

to get married	تزوّج	husband	زوج
teacher	معلّم	when	لمّا
		language	لُغة

حوار

أسئلة

1. What are the names of the two people speaking?

_____

2. What does Dan do?

_____

3. How many students attend Cornell University?

_____

4. Where does Dan's sister live?

_____

5. How many brothers and sisters does Ali have?

_____

كلمات جديدة

	polite way of asking the name		الإسم الكريم
honored, pleased to meet you	تشرّفنا	welcome, hello	أهلاً
people, family	أهل	to do	عمل (يعمل)
		but	لكِن

اقرأ

الإسم	سليمان علي عبد القادر
العُمر	٣٥ سنة
العنوان	جَبَل الحسين–عمان، قُرب سينما الحسين
رقم التلفون	٦٩١٢٤٣
المهنة	معلّم

الإسم	ليلى أبو زيد
العمر	٢٠ سنة
العنوان	البنك العربي–عمان
رقم التلفون	٦١٧٦٥٦
المهنة	محاسبة

الإسم	عبدالله علي سمارة
العمر	٢١ سنة
العنوان	إربد–الحارة الغربية–قرب بقالة فلسطين
رقم التلفون	———
المهنة	طالب؛ يعمل في مطعم ايام الخميس والجمعة

الإسم	جميلة أحمد قاسم
العمر	٢١ سنة
العنوان	كلّية الطب–الجامعة الأردنية
رقم التلفون	٦٦١٢٥١
المهنة	طالبة

أسئلة

1. How old is Suleiman Abdelqader?

_____

2. What is Layla Abu-Zayd's address?

_____

3. What does Abdalla Samara do?

_____

4. What is Layla Abu-Zayd's telephone number?

_____

5. How old is Jamila Qasim?

_____

number	رَقم	close to	قُرب
accountant	مُحاسب	profession	مِهنة
college of medicine	كُلّيّة اَلطِبّ	neighborhood, quarter of a city	حارَة

قواعد

Possession (continued)

If the noun to which the pronoun suffix is attached ends in التاء المربوطة

(ـة), then a ت appears in the place of التاء المربوطة:

غرفة+ ه	غرفته	ɣurfi-t-u	"his room"
غرفة +ها	غرفتها	ɣurfi-t-ha	"her room"
غرفة +ك	غرفتك	ɣurfi-t-ak	"your, m.s. room"
غرفة +ك	غرفتك	ɣurfi-t-ik	"your, f.s. room"
غرفة +ي	غرفتي	ɣurfi-t-i	"my room"

تمارين

١. اكتب

Attach the singular possessive pronoun suffixes corresponding to هو، هي، انتَ،

انتِ، أنا to the following nouns:

عنوان، مدينة، سيارة

٢. املاء

١. ٢١، ٢٢، ٢٣، ٢٤، ٢٥، ٢٦، ٢٧، ٢٨، ٢٩، ٣٠.

٢. أنا طالب.

٣. أنا من لبنان.

٤. دمشق عاصمة سوريا.

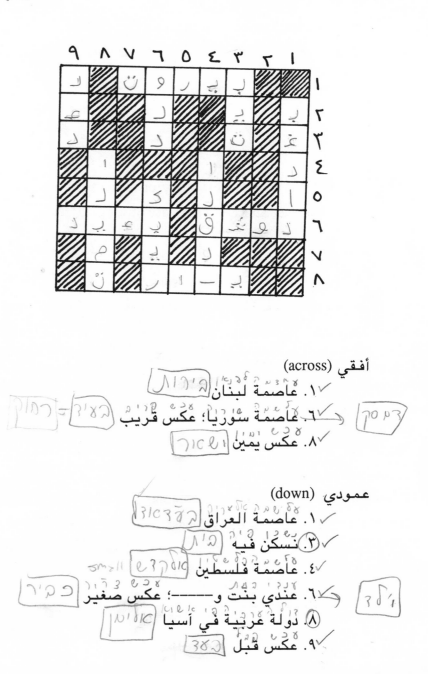

أفقي (across)

١. عاصمة لبنان בֵּירוּת

٦. عاصمة سوريا؛ عكس قريب قْסَم = رَחوק

٨. عكس يمين يَسار

عمودي (down)

١. عاصمة العراق بَغْداد

٣. نسكن فيه بَيت

٤. عاصمة فلسطين אַלקُدس small الْقدس

٦. عندي بنت و ـــــــ؛ عكس صغير كبير

٨. دولة عربية في آسيا الأردن

٩. عكس قبل بعد

اسمـع

أسئلة

1. What does Ayman do?

_____

2. Where did he go to school?

_____

3. How long did he work in Irbid?

_____

4. Where does he work now?

_____

5. Where is Jedda?

_____

6. What does his wife do?

_____

كلمات جديدة

to take	أخَذ	married	مُتزوّج
to travel	سافَر	then	بَعدين
history	تاريخ	the Red Sea	البحر الأحمر

لا، لا، مش عنوانك في أمريكا. عنوانك هون في الأردن.

أسئلة

1. What is Daniel's father's name?

الاسم ان دنيال هو هنري

2. How old is Daniel?

دنيال هو ٤٩

3. What is his address in Jordan?

العنوان في الأردن هو فندق ادنس جين

4. What does he do?

دنيال هو طالب

كلمات جديدة

pilot	طَيّار	to mean, in other words	يَعني
		hotel	فُندُق

اقرأ

وزارة الداخلية *interior ministry*

تأشيرة دخول - *Permision of entry*

اسم الأب ____ هنري	اسم الأب	الإسم ____ دانيل	رقم
اسم العائلة ____ وليمز		اسم الأم ____ اليزابث	
مكان الولادة ____ نيويورك - أمريكا		تاريخ الولادة ____ ١٩٦٢\١٢\٢٧	

الجنسية ____ أمريكي

رقم جواز السفر ____ أ ٧٦٢٥٣ تاريخ ومكان الصدور ____ واشنطن دي سي

المهنة ____ طالب

العنوان في الأردن ____ فندق الأندلس - عمان

مدّة الزيارة ____ ٣ شهور

أسئلة

1. When was Dan born?

_____

2. Where was he born?

_____

3. What is his passport number?

_____

4. What is his address in Jordan?

_____

5. How long is he staying in Jordan?

_____

كلمات جديدة

Ministry of the Interior	وزارَة الداخليّة
date	تاريخ
birth	ولادة
place	مَكان
nationality	جِنسيّة
passport	جَواز سَفَر
period, duration, length	مُدّة
visit	زِيارَة

قواعد

Subject/Person Markers on the Perfect Verb

Arabic verbs have two aspects or tenses: the perfect and the imperfect. The perfect corresponds roughly to the past tense in English and generally indicates completed action, and the imperfect corresponds to the present tense and indicates actions that have not been completed.

Different persons are expressed on the perfect verb by attaching different suffixes to it, except in the case of the third person masculine singular (the one corresponding to *he wrote*, *he was*, etc.).

The singular

كتب	katab	"to write"
(هو) كتب	katab	"he wrote"
(هي) كتبَتْ	katab-at	"she wrote"
(انتَ) كتبتْ	katab-t	"you, m.s. wrote"
(انتِ) كتبتِ	katab-ti	"you, f.s. wrote"
(أنا) كتبتُ	katab-t	"I wrote"

تمارين

١. اكتب

Conjugate the following perfect verbs in the singular (هو، هي، انتَ، انتِ، أنا):

أخذ، سافر، كتب، درس

٢. تكلّم

Create a dialogue with another student in the class in which you ask and answer questions relating to name, family, place of residence, what family members do, etc.

Pretend that you are traveling to Jordan to take an Arabic summer course that will
last two months. Fill out the following form accordingly.

وزارة الداخليـة
تأشيرة دخول

اسم الأب بابا   الإسم اريقة

اسم العائلة ميندل   اسم الأم شبيلة

مكان الولادة نويورك   تاريخ الولادة ١٩٩٢/٢/٢٠

الجنسية اوريكلي - nationality

date & place issued (passport)   ١٠/١٠   تاريخ ومكان الصدور   رقم جواز السفر - passport #

المهنة طالبين - profession

العنوان في الأردن - where are you staying

مدة الزيارة - length of the visit

الدرس رقم ١٢

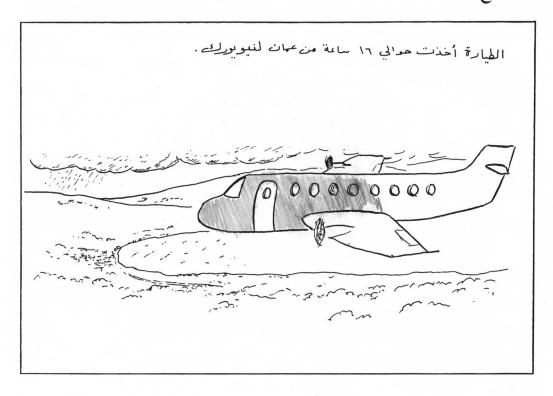

الطيارة أخذت حوالي ١٦ ساعة من عمان لنيويورك .

1. When did he come to America?
_____

2. How did he go from Irbid to Amman?
_____

3. Where did the plane stop on the way from Amman to New York?_____

4. How long did the plane take from Amman to New York?
_____

كلمات جديدة

I want	بدّي	now	هَلّأ
how	كيف	to talk, tell	حَكى (يحكي)
to fly, take off	طار	airport	مَطار

٦٤

أسئلة

1. Where is he going?
_____

2. Where is he from?
_____

3. Where did he learn Arabic?
_____

4. Is Cornell a big university?
_____

كلمات جديدة

to learn	تعلّم	please, go ahead	تفضّل

إقرأ

أجرة سيارات التاكسي من مطار علياء الدولي

إلى	دينار	فلس
عمان-البلد	----	٢
عمان-موقف باصات العبدلي	٢٥٠	٢
السلط	٥٠٠	٥
جرش	٥٠٠	٦
إربد	----	٩
الزرقاء	٢٥٠	٤
مأدبا	٢٥٠	٢
الكرك	٥٠٠	٨
معان	----	١٤
العقبة	----	١٩

أسئلة

What is the taxi fare from Alia' International Airport to: downtown Amman, Jerash, Ma'an, Aqaba?

كلمات جديدة

downtown	البلَد	fare (rent)	أجرَة
fils (monetary unit)	فِلس	stop (bus stop)	مَوقِف
dinar (monetary unit, 1,000 fils)	دينار		

قواعد

Negation

Verbs are generally negated by inserting the particle ـما before the verb to be negated:

أنا ما فتحت الباب.

"I did not open the door."

Verbless (or equational) sentences (see Sentence Types in Lesson 14) are negated by inserting مش before the adjective, noun, or prepositional phrase:

الطقس في الكويت مش كويس.	"The weather in Kuwait is not good."
أبوه مش طبيب.	"His father is not a doctor."
أمه مش في المكتب.	"His mother is not in the office."

Sound and Broken Plurals

Plurals are of two main types in Arabic: sound and broken. Only a minority of nouns take sound plurals; the majority take broken plurals.

Sound plurals

Sound plurals are of two types, too: masculine and feminine. *Masculine sound plurals* are formed by adding the suffix ين (iin) to the noun.

معلّم-معلّمين	"teacher-teachers"
مُهندس-مهندسين	"engineer-engineers"
طيّار-طيّارين	"pilot-pilots"

Feminine sound plurals are formed by adding the suffix ات (aat) to the noun. If the noun ends in التاء المربوطة, then التاء المربوطة is dropped:

معلمة-معلّمات	"teacher-teachers"
طالبة-طالبات	"student-students"
تلفون-تلفونات	"telephone-telephones"
صفحة-صفحات	"page-pages"

٦٧

Broken plurals

These plurals are formed mainly by changing the vowels of the word; the consonants are usually not affected. Think of the English *goose-geese, foot-feet*. Broken plurals follow certain patterns, but as was suggested earlier, it is advisable at this point to try to remember the plurals of nouns individually as you hear or read them.

باب–أبواب	"door-doors"
ألف–آلاف	"a thousand-thousands"
يوم–أيام	"day-days"
طالب–طُلّاب	"student-students"
أسبوع–أسابيع	"week-weeks"
شَهر–شُهور	"month-months"
بيت–بُيوت	"house-houses"
كتاب–كُتُب	"book-books"
مدينة–مُدن	"city-cities"
غرفة–غُرف	"room-rooms"

تمارين

١. املاء

١. ١، ٢، ٣، ٥، ١١، ١٩، ٢٠، ١، ٩، ٦، ١٥
٢. بيروت مدينة كبيرة.
٣. قطر دولة عربية.
٤. الخميس والسبت.

٢. تكلّم

Create a dialogue with another student in which one of you is a taxi driver and the other a passenger.

الدرس رقم ١٣

اسمع

أسئلة

1. How long was he on the plane?

_____

2. What happened to his suitcase?

_____

3. What did he leave at the airport?

_____

4. How far was the hotel from the university?

_____

كلمات جديدة

noon	ظُهر	to arrive	وَصَل
tired	تَعبان	to be (see grammar section)	كان، كُنت
suitcase	شَنطة	to look for	فتّش على
I left	خلّيت	to say (see grammar section)	قال–قُلت

٦٩

أسئلة

1. When did Dan reserve a room in the hotel?

_____

2. Did he want a room with a bathroom?

_____

3. What happened to Dan's passport?

_____

4. What is the number of the room where Dan will be staying?

_____

كلمات جديدة

to reserve	حَجَز	service	خدمة
possible	مُمكن	if you please	لوَ سَمحت، من فَضلك
		Mr.	سَيّد

اقرأ

فنادق عمّان

العنوان	التلفون	عدد الغرف	الدرجة	اسم الفندق
الشميساني	٦٦٢٦٤٠	٢٩٦	xxxxx	عمان-ماريوت
شارع الحسين بن علي	٦٦٥١٦٧	٢٢١	xxxxx	هوليدي إن
شارع الجامعة	٦٦٥١٢١	١٧٥	xxxxx	القدس- جيروسلم فرانتل
جبل عمان-الدوار الثالث	٦٤١٣٦١	٣٧٨	xxxxx	الأردن انتركونتننتال
الشميساني	٦٦٧١٥٠	٩٩	xxxxx	الشرق الأوسط
المدينة الرياضية	٦٦٠٠٠٠	٣٠٠	xxxxx	قصر ريجنسي-ريجنسي بالاس
مطار علياء الدولي	٨٥١٠٠٠	٣٠٠	xxxx	بوابة علياء
الشميساني	٦٦٥١٦١	١٠٠	xxxx	السفير -امباسادور
جبل عمان-الدوار السابع	٨١٥٠٧١	٣٠٠	xxxx	فندق عمرة

أسئلة

1. How many rooms does the Holiday Inn have?

_____

2. What is the address of the Holiday Inn?

_____

3. Where is Bawwabat Alia' located?

_____

4. What is the telephone number of Ash-Sharq Al-Awsat Hotel?

_____

5. How many rooms does the Ambassador Hotel have?

_____

كلمات جديدة

mountain	جَبَل	number	عَدَد

قواعد

Verb Types

Arabic verbs are divided into categories according to their consonant structure. Most verbs derive from a three-consonant root. A verb is called *sound* if it has three consonants in its three consonant positions, no doubling of any two consonants, and no و, ي, or أ in any of the three positions. Verbs like كتب, عرف, سمع, etc. are sound verbs. The three consonants of a sound verb are generally maintained in the same order regardless of the suffixes attached to them. *Hollow* verbs have و or ي in place of the second consonant of the root. The و and ي of hollow verbs generally appear as ا in the perfect: كان، راح، نام، جاب. The ا of hollow verbs is replaced by a short vowel when certain subject/person markers are suffixed to the verb:

هو كان	huwwa kaan	"he was"
هي كانت	hiyya kaan-at	"she was"
انتَ كنت	inta kun-t	"you, m.s were"
انت كنت	inti kun-ti	"you, f.s. were"
أنا كنت	ana kun-t	"I was"

تمارين

١. اكتب

Conjugate the following perfect verbs in the singular (هو، هي، انتَ، انتِ، أنا):
Sound verbs:

وصل، فتّش، تعلم

Hollow verbs:

نام، قال، طار

Match the singular with its plural. One word in the singular column does not have a matching plural.

٣. تكلّم

Create a dialogue with another student in which one of you is a tourist and the other a hotel receptionist.

الدرس رقم ١٤

اسمـع

أسئلة

1. How much was the room in the hotel?

2. Why couldn't he sleep well?

3. Did he tell his family that he had lost his suitcase?

4. Who did he talk to after talking to his family?

5. Was the airport far?

6. How much did he pay for the taxi?

كلمات جديدة

to be happy	انبَسط	I slept	نِمت (نام)
early	بَدري	to wake up	صِحِي
to lose	ضيَّع	to be happy	انبِسط ٦
		to ask	سأَل

من مدينة اثاكا في ولاية نيويورك، مدينة
اثاكا صغيرة. كان أنا باحكي عربي كويس،
وتعلمت عربي في ...

أسئلة

1. Where is Dan going?

_____

2. How do you know that Dan was upset?

_____

3. Why was he upset?

_____

كلمات جديدة

why	ليش	to do	عمل
sorry	أَسِف	upset	زَعلان
lost and found box	صَندوق المَوجودات	God willing	إن شاء الله

Match the word or phrase with the picture in the following:

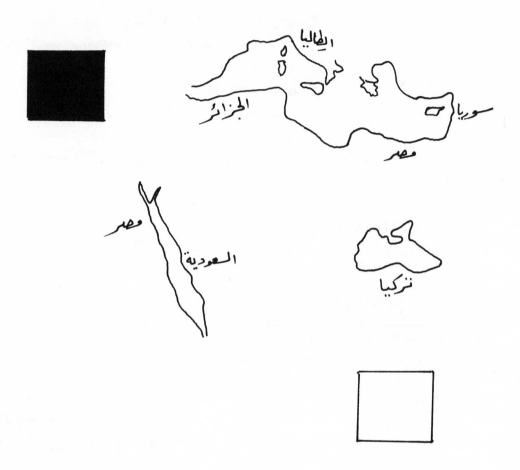

أبيض	أسود
البحر الأحمر	البحر الأسود
	البحر الأبيض المتوسط

وزارة الداخلية–دائرة السير
طلب للحصول على رخصة قيادة سيارة

الإسم:	عبدالله علي سمارة
العنوان:	اربد–الحارة الغربية–قرب بقالة فلسطين
تاريخ الولادة:	١٩٧٢ /٦/١٥ مكان الولادة: إربد
الجنس:	ذكر لون الشعر: أسود لون العينين: بنّي
الطول:	١٧٦ سم الوزن: ٧٥ كغم

تاريخ تقديم الطلب: ١٩٩٣ /٢/٧   التوقيع: عبدالله علي سمارة

أسئلة

1. When was Abdalla born?

_____

2. What color eyes does he have?

_____

3. How much does he weigh?

_____

4. When was the application submitted?

_____

كلمات جديدة

male	ذَكَر	grocery store	بقّالة
eyes	عينين	hair	شَعَر
kilogram	كغم (كيلوغرام)	height, (length)	طول

Sentence Types

Arabic sentences are of two general types: those with verbs and those without verbs. Sentences that have verbs are called *verbal sentences*, and sentences without verbs are called *equational sentences*.

Equational sentences:

أنا معلم	"I am a teacher."
البيت كبير	"The house is big."

Verbal sentences:

الطيّارة أخذت ساعتين.	"The plane took two hours."
هو أجا مبارح.	"He came yesterday."

Whereas English sentences generally do not start with a verb, Arabic sentences starting with a verb are quite common.

أخذت الطيّارة ساعتين.	"The plane took two hours."
وصل أحمد اليوم.	"Ahmad arrived today."

The order of these sentences is not strictly verb-subject; the other order is also common:

الطيّارة أخذت ساعتين.

أحمد وصل اليوم.

If the subject of the equational sentence is indefinite, it is placed after the predicate:

عنده ثلاث سيارات.	"He has three cars."
في إثاكا جامعة كبيرة.	"There is a big university in Ithaca."

تمارين

١. اكتب

Pretend that you are applying for a driver's licence in an Arab country and you are given the following form to fill out.

وزارة الداخلية-دائرة السير
طلب للحصول على رخصة قيادة سيارة

	الإسم:
	العنوان:
مكان الولادة:	تاريخ الولادة:
لون الشعر:	الجنس:
الوزن:	الطول:

لون العينين:

تاريخ تقديم الطلب: التوقيع: _____

٢. إملاء

١. ١٢، ٢، ٢٠، ٨، ١٠، ١٥، ١٣، ٣٠، ٨٠، ١٠٠.

٢. شباط وآذار.

٣. مصر دولة كبيرة.

٤. مدينة الكويت عاصمة دولة الكويت.

الدرس رقم ١٥

اسمع

- اسمي محمد. الاسم الكريم؟
- شريف.

أسئلة

1. Where is Muhammad from?

_____

2. When did he come to the U.S.?

_____

3. What does he study?

_____

4. Was Sharif (the speaker) hungry?

_____

كلمات جديدة

to meet	التقى (يلتقي)	one day	في يوم من الأيام
hungry	جوعان	when	إمتى
		let's go	يالله

٨١

أسئلة

1. When did Dan lose his passport?

_____

2. What is Dan's father's name?

_____

3. Does Dan remember his passport number?

_____

4. Where was Dan's passport issued? When?

_____

كلمات جديدة

		yes, can I help you	نعم
unknown	غير معروف	to remember	ذَكَر (يذكُر)
to sit down	قَعَد (يقعُد)	issue	صُدور
to see	شاف (يشوف)	to let	خلّى (يخلّي)

اقرأ

مطار علياء الدولي
صندوق الموجودات

١. شنطة كبيرة لونها أسود، باسم السيد أحمد سَلمان.
العنوان: السالمية، الكويت. مكتوب عليها "ملابس للأولاد".
٢. شنطة يد صغيرة لونها بنّي.
٣. جواز سفر أمريكي باسم دانيل جوزف وليمز.
٤. جاكيت رجالي لونه بنّي.
٥. قلم "باركر" لونه أسود.
٦. كتاب بعنوان "جمهورية أفلاطون" باسم سليم عبدالله الشافعي.

أسئلة

1. Who does the big black suitcase belong to?

_____

2. What is written on it?

_____

3. What color is the handbag?

_____

4. What is the title of the book that was found?

_____

كلمات جديدة

| written | مَكتوب | Mr. | سيِّد |
| hand | يَد | clothes | ملابِس |

قواعد

Object Pronouns

Pronoun suffixes attached to verbs function as objects in a way similar to English pronouns in object position, as in *I saw them*, *He visited her*. They follow subject/person markers.

كتبت	katab-t	"I wrote"
كتبته	katab-t-u	"I wrote it, m.s."
كتبتها	katab-t-ha	"I wrote it, f.s."

سأله	saʔal-u	"he asked him"
سألها	saʔal-ha	"he asked her"
سألك	saʔal-ak	"he asked you, m."
سألك	saʔal-ik	"he asked you, f."
سألني	saʔal-ni	"he asked me"

سألته	saʔal-t-u	"I asked him"
سألتها	saʔal-t-ha	"I asked her"
سألتَك	saʔal-t-ak	"I asked you, m.s."
سألتِك	saʔal-t-ik	"I asked you, f.s."

Note that for the pronoun corresponding to *me*, a ن is added between the subject marker and the object pronoun: سألني.

تمارين

١. اقرأ

Rewrite the following words grouping them into related families. For each family identify the root and give its general meaning in English.

هندسة، يعرف، قريب، درس، مهندس، أولاد، مدرسة، طيارة، ولد، سافر، طيار، ولادة، تقريباً، معروف، مطار، سفر.

٢. اكتب

For each of the following verbs, attach the object pronoun given next to it:
Example:

سأل+انتَ= سألكَ

١. أخذّتْ+هو
٢. كتبَتْ+هي
٣. تعلّمْتْ+هي
٤. وصلتَ+أنا
٥. فتّشتَ على (فتّشْتْ عليـ)+انتِ

Translate the following into Arabic:
     1. He lost you, f.s.
     2. You, m.s. wrote it, f.
     3. I asked him.
     4. She reached me.

٣. تكلّم

Create a dialogue with another student in which one of you is a traveler who reports the loss of a passport or a suitcase and the other is a policeman or an airport employee who writes down the information.

الدرس رقم ١٦

اسمــع

أسئلة

1. How far was the restaurant?

2. Were there a lot of people?

3. What did he (the speaker) eat and drink?

4. What did they exchange?

كلمات جديدة

people	ناس	to enter	دَخَل
to return	رَجَع	water	ميّة

أسئلة

1. What is Dan's full name?

_____

2. What is Dan's father's name?

_____

3. What is the problem?

_____

4. Why did the policeman want to talk to the American embassy?

_____

5. What did Dan tell him to do instead?

_____

6. Did the policeman agree to do that?

_____

كلمات جديدة

middle	وَسَط	full	كامِل
to wait	استنّى	OK	طَيّب
picture	صورَة	embassy	سَفارَة

Write under the picture the word that refers to it from the list below.

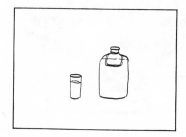  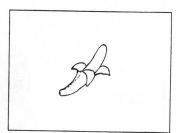

  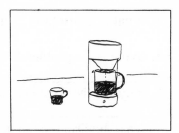

بطاطا	عصير برتقال	شاي	قهوة	دجاج
	موز	سمك	حليب	تفاح

اقرأ ٢

السفارات العربية في الولايات المتحدة

السفارة	رقم التلفون	السفارة	رقم التلفون
المملكة العربية السعودية	(٢٠٢) ٣٤٢-٣٨٠٠	مصر	(٢٠٢) ٢٣٢-٥٤٠٠
لبنان	(٢٠٢) ٩٣٩-٦٣٠٠	المغرب	(٢٠٢) ٤٦٢-٧٩٧٩
قطر	(٢٠٢) ٣٣٨-٠١١١	الجزائر	(٢٠٢) ٣٢٨-٠٥٣٠
الإمارات العربية المتحدة	(٢٠٢) ٣٣٨-٦٥٠٠	اليمن	(٢٠٢) ٩٦٥-٤٧٦٠
البحرين	(٢٠٢) ٣٤٢-٠٧٤١	السودان	(٢٠٢) ٣٣٨-٨٥٦٥
سوريا	(٢٠٢) ٢٣٢-٦٣١٣	تونس	(٢٠٢) ٨٦٢-١٨٥٠
عُمان	(٢٠٢) ٣٨٧-٢٠١٤	الأردن	(٢٠٢) ٩٦٦-٢٦٦٤
مكتب الإعلام الفلسطيني	(٢٠٢) ٤٦٦-٣٣٤٨		

What are the telephone numbers of the following embassies:

Saudi Arabia_____   United Arab Emirates _____

Syria _____   Yemen _____

Algeria _____

كلمات جديدة
الولايات المتحدة   the United States

قواعد

Subject/Person Markers on the Perfect

The plural

كتب	katab	"to write"

(هم) كتبوا	katab-u	"they wrote"
(انتو) كتبتوا	katab-tu	"you, pl. wrote"
(احنا) كتبنا	katab-na	"we wrote"

راح	raafi	"to go"

(هم) راحوا	raafi-u	"they went"
(انتو) رُحتوا	rufi-tu	"you, pl. went"
(احنا) رُحنا	rufi-na	"we went"

تمارين

١. اكتب

Conjugate the following perfect verbs in the plural (هم، انتو، احنا):

عرف، سافر، كان، نام، رجع

٢. املاء

١. ٢٣، ٣٢، ٨، ٣٠، ٢٧، ٧٢، ٧٦، ١٧، ٧، ٤٤

٢. مدينة تونس عاصمة تونس.

٣. الشهر الماضي كان شهر ايلول.

٤. الطقس في بيروت بارد في الشتاء.

الدرس رقم ١٧

أسئلة

1. What time did Muhammad call?

_____

2. What did he ask Sharif?

_____

3. Who is Walid?

_____

4. Did Sharif know what "roommate" meant?

_____

كلمات جديدة

to find	وَجَد	night, evening	ليل
to like	حَبّ (يحبّ)	friend	صاحِب
		have to, must	لازِم

أسئلة

1. Where was the passport?

_____

2. What was the problem?

_____

3. What names are written in Jordanian passports?

_____

4. Is there an elevator in the hotel?

_____

كلمات جديدة

policeman	شُرطي	problem	مُشكِلة
grandfather	جَدّ	to think	فَكَّر
key	مفتاح	to understand	فِهِم
straight	دُغري	elevator	مِصعَد

اقرأ

المملكة الأردنية الهاشمية
جواز سفر
صدر في   عمان
بتاريخ   ٧/٧/ ١٩٩١
وزير الداخلية/الجوازات
مدير الجوازات العام

رقم الجواز   ج٢٤١٩٢٧

صورة حامل الجواز

اسم حامله   ايمن علي سمارة
مكان الولادة   إربد
تاريخ الولادة   ٢/٣/ ١٩٦٨
اسم الوالدة   حليمة

المهنة   معلم
مكان الإقامة   إربد-الحارة الغربية-قرب بقالة فلسطين
الطول   ١٧٦ سم
لون العينين   بني
لون الشعر   اسود
فوارق خاصّة   ــــــــــــــ

صورة الزوجة

اسم الزوجة   ليلى عبدالله أبو زيد
مكان الولادة   نابلس
تاريخ الولادة   ٦/٨/ ١٩٧٢
لون العينين   بنّي
الطول   ١٧٤ سم
فوارق خاصّة   _____

الأولاد

الجنس	مكان الولادة	تاريخ الولادة	الاسم
أنثى	جدة-السعودية	٢٣/١١/ ١٩٩٢	ريما

أسئلة

1. When was the passport issued?

_____

2. When was Mr. Samara born? Where?

_____

3. What does Mr. Samara do?

_____

4. What is the color of his eyes?

_____

5. When was Layla Abu-Zayd born? Where?

_____

6. Who is taller Mr. Samara or his wife?

_____

7. How many children do Mr. Samara and his wife have?

_____

8. Where was Rima born?

_____

كلمات جديدة

mother	والدة=أمّ	carrier, holder	حامِل
centimeter	سم=سنتمتر	residence	إقامة
female	أنثى	sex	جِنس

قواعد

Lame Verbs

In lame verbs the last position in the three-consonant root skeleton has و or ي, which is generally realized as ا or ى, both pronounced *aa*. Some of the verbs that belong in this category are: حكى, مشى, التقى, and. When person markers are sufixed to these verbs, the long vowel occupying the third consonantal position is either deleted or is changed to ي, depending on the individual person marker. This is shown in the conjugation of the verb حكى.

حكى	fiaka	"he spoke"
حكت	fiakat	"she spoke"
حكوا	fiaku	"they spoke"
حكيت	fiakeet	"you, m.s. spoke"
حكيتِ	fiakeeti	"you, f.s. spoke"
حكيتوا	fiakeetu	"you, pl. spoke"
حكيت	fiakeet	"I spoke"
حكينا	fiakeena	"we spoke"

تمرين

اكتب

Conjugate the following perfect verbs in all persons, i.e., singular and plural

(هو، هي، هم، انتَ، انتِ، انتو، أنا، احنا):

مشى، التقى

الدرس رقم ١٨

اسمع

1. What time did he walk to the university?

_____

2. Where did he meet Muhammad and Walid?

_____

3. What did they drink?

_____

4. How did they go to Walid's apartment?

_____

5. How many bedrooms did Walid's apartment have?

_____

6. How many bathrooms?

_____

7. Was the apartment far or close to the university?

_____

8. What was the monthly rent?

_____

9. Did Sharif decide to live with Walid?

_____

كلمات جديدة

bus stop	مَوقف باص	to ride	رِكِب
cheap, inexpensive	رَخيص	clean	نَظيف
plus, in addition to	زائد	rent	أجرة
to decide	قرّر	electricity	كَهرَباء

حوار

أسئلة

1. Which restaurant is closer?

_____

2. How is the food at As-Salam Restaurant?

_____

3. How far is As-Salam Restaurant?

_____

4. Is As-Salam Restaurant on the right or on the left?

_____

كلمات جديدة

closer	أقْرب	which?	أيّ؟
to reach	وصِل (يوصَل)	cleaner	أنظف
		excellent	مُمتاز

٩٨

اقرأ

للايجار

عمان-

شقة سوبر ديلوكس، غرفتين نوم، غرفة طعام، صالون معيشة، برندة زائد حمامين. مطبخ أمريكي، وديزاين أمريكي كامل. انتين مركزي وكراج وهاتف في بناية حديثة ديلوكس.
الموقع: جبل عمان-الدوار السابع، هاتف ٨٢٤٦٤٥.

القاهرة-

شقة مفروشة خلف نادي السيارات، لمدة طويلة. ت ٨٤٢٢٦٣
٤ غرف، ٢ نوم، بالتلفون لمدة طويلة. ت ٨٤٤٦٨٦
مكتب مفروش بالتلفون، وصالة، ٣٥ ش شامبليون، شقة ١٢، ت ٧٦٩٨٧٨، ٩١٣٧٩٣
شقة مفروشة سوبرلوكس وصالة وجراج، بالتلفون، لمدة طويلة. مكتب أو عيادة، مدينة نصر، ت، ٢٦٩٤٣١.

أسئلة

1. How many bedrooms does the apartment in Amman have?

_____

2. How many bathrooms?

_____

3. Where is it located?

_____

4. How many apartments are advertised for long-term rent in Cairo?

_____

5. What is the address of the office that is adveritsed for rent in Cairo?

_____

كلمات جديدة

telephone	هاتف= تلفون	living room	صالون مَعيشة
location	مَوقِع	building	بناية
long	طَويل	furnished	مَفروش

قواعد

The Comparative and Superlative

The comparative and superlative are formed in the same way: they have the structure أفعَل (ʔafʕal) of the corresponding adjective:

كبير–أكبَر   "big-bigger, biggest"

بارد–أبرَد   "cold-colder, coldest"

The comparative is generally followed by the preposition مِن, and the superlative directly by the noun compared:

السودان أكبر من مصر بالمساحة.   "Sudan is bigger than Egypt in area."

مصر أكبر دولة عربية بعدد السكان.   "Egypt is the largest Arab country in population."

أكثر الدول العربية في آسيا.   "Most Arab countries are in Asia."

تمارين

١. اكتب

Conjugate the following perfect verbs in all persons, i.e., singular and plural (هو، هي، هم، انتَ، انتِ، انتو، أنا، احنا). Note that although the verbs التقى and تعلّم are not simple verbs consisting of the three basic root consonants and accompanying vowels, they are conjugated the same way as simple verbs.

سمع، تعلّم، وصل، قال، دخل، التقى

٢. اكتب

Write the comparative and superlative form for each of the following:

صغير، كثير، قريب، بعيد، نظيف، رخيص

٣. املاء

١. ٣٣، ٨٥، ٩١، ٢٣، ٢٨، ١٠٢، ١١٠، ١٢١، ١٣٢، ٢٠١

٢. بيت كبير وبعيد عن الجامعة.

٣. يمين ويسار.

٤. غرفة نوم وغرفة جلوس وحمام.

٤. تكلّم

Create a dialogue with another student in which one of you gives the other
directions to a restaurant in town.

الدرس رقم ١٩

أسئلة

1. What does Sharif's cousin do?
_____

2. How long has it been since Sharif saw his cousin?
_____

3. How long does it take to drive by car from Ithaca to Chicago?
_____

4. How long does the bus take?
_____

5. When is Sharif thinking of going to Chicago?
_____

كلمات جديدة

there	هُناك	cousin (father's side)	ابن عَمّ
another time	مَرّة ثانية	expensive	غالي

أسئلة

1. What did he drink first?

_____

2. Are there vegetable dishes that have chicken in them?

_____

3. What dish did he order?

_____

4. What did he have for dessert?

_____

كلمات جديدة

rice	رزّ	thing, something	شيء
fava beans	فول	baked, grilled	مشوي
other than	غير	to give	أعطى (يعطي)
		something sweet	شيء حلو

اقرأ

مطعم السلام
مأكولات عربية وغربية
مفتوح كل يوم من الساعة الثامنة صباحاً الى العاشرة مساء

الفطور

حمص	٤٠٠ فلس
فول	٤٠٠ فلس
سندويشة فلافل	٣٥٠ فلس
بيض مقلي أو مسلوق (عدد ٢)	٤٠٠ فلس

الغداء

خضار باللحمة (فاصوليا، بامية، ملوخية، بطاطا)	٩٠٠ فلس
دجاج مشوي (ربع دجاجة)	دينار و ١٠٠ فلس
شيش كباب (خروف)	دينار و٤٠٠ فلس
سمك	دينار واحد
رز	٢٠٠ فلس
سلطة خضار	٢٥٠ فلس

المشروبات

شاي	٢٥٠ فلس
قهوة	٢٥٠ فلس
عصير فواكه (برتقال، تفاح، جزر)	٤٥٠ فلس
حليب	٢٥٠ فلس
بيبسي، ميراندا، سفن أب	٤٠٠ فلس

الحلويات

بقلاوة	٣٠٠ فلس
كنافة	٣٥٠ فلس

1. What is the price of a hummus plate at Al-Salam Restaurant?

_____

2. How much is grilled (baked) chicken?

_____

3. What kind of drinks are available at Al-Salam Restaurant?

_____

كلمات جديدة

food, dishes	مأكولات
in the morning	صَباحاً=في الصباح
in the evening	مساءً=في المساء
breakfast	فطور
lunch	غداء
lamb	خَروف
salad	سَلَطَة
sweets	حِلويّات

أغنية

عمّي بو مسعود (كلمات وألحان الياس رحباني)

عمّي بو مسعود

عيونه كبار وسود

بياكل ما بيشبع

عمي بو مسعود

شو تروّقت اليوم

يا عمي بو مسعود؟

ها، ها، ها...

تروقت خمسين بيضة

وشربت برميل حليب

و١٦ صحن مربّى

وبعدني جوعان.

عمي بو مسعود...

شو راح تتغدى

يا عمي بو مسعود؟

ها، ها، ها...

راح آكل عشر خواريف

وبدي اشرب نهر ميّ

وآكل مية ليمونة

وراح أبقى جوعان.

قواعد

Subject/Person Markers on the Imperfect
Different persons are expressed in the imperfect verb by attaching a prefix or, in some cases, both a prefix and a suffix to the verb:

هو يكتب   huwwa yi-ktub   "he writes, is writing"

هي تكتب   hiyya ti-ktub   "she writes, is writing"

انتَ تكتب   inta ti-ktub   "you, m.s. write, are writing"

انتِ تكتبي   inti ti-ktub-i   "you, f.s. write, are writing"

أنا أكتب   ana a-ktub   "I write, am writing"

The prefix *b-* is attached to imperfect verbs in Levantine Arabic when these verbs are used to express habitual or progressive actions.

هو بيكتب   huwwa byiktub   "he writes, is writing"

Note also that in place of the English infinitive Arabic uses fully conjugated verb forms, but without the ب:

بيحب يسافر   He likes to travel. ("he likes he travels")

بتحب تسافر   She likes to travel. ("she likes she travels")

تمارين

١. اقرأ

Match the singular with its plural. One word in the singular column does not have
a matching plural.

مكان	صور
سفارة	أصحاب
صورة	مشاكل
صاحب	أشياء
مشكلة	سفارات
موقف	أماكن
شيء	مواقف
بناية	

٢. اكتب

Conjugate the following verbs in the imperfect singular:

عرف، شرب، كتب، سمع

٣. تكلّم

Create a dialogue with another student in which one of you is a customer in a
restaurant and the other is a waiter.

اسمع

وصلنا شيكاغو في نفس اليوم، الساعة تسعة في الليل.

أسئلة

1. Where did Walid's friend live?

_____

2. How will Sharif come back from Chicago?

_____

3. When did they start the trip to Chicago?

_____

4. When did they arrive in Chicago?

_____

5. Why was Sharif able to find his cousin's house quickly?

_____

كلمات جديدة

same	نفس	to visit	زار (يزور)
to buy	اشترى	trip	رِحلة
quickly	بسُرعة	map	خَريطة

أسئلة

1. Where is Al-Quds Restaurant located?

2. How much does it cost to take a taxicab to the restaurant?

3. How is the food at Al-Quds Restaurant in terms of quality and price?

4. How is the *knafi*?

5. Why did he decide to eat at As-Salam Restaurant?

كلمات جديدة

better, the best	أحسن	if	إذا
tastier	أطيب	especially	خصوصاً
as you wish	على كيفك	like	مثل

اقـرأ

دليل أمريكا
شركات الطيران العربية في الولايات المتحدة

هيوستن

رقم التلفون	شركة الطيران	رقم التلفون	شركة الطيران
٦٢٦-١٥٩. (٧١٣)	الخطوط الجوية الكويتية	٨٥.-٧٢٢٧ (٧١٣)	الخطوط الجوية السعودية
٩٧٧-٧٤٤٣ (٧١٣)	طيران الشرق الأوسط	٧٨٣-٩٦.. (٧١٣)	طيران الخليج

واشنطن دي سي

رقم التلفون	شركة الطيران	رقم التلفون	شركة الطيران
٣٩٣-١٥١٥ (٢.٢)	الخطوط الجوية المغربية	٣٣٣-٣٨.. (٢.٢)	الخطوط الجوية السعودية
٢٩٣-.٤٤٤ (٢.٢)	طيران الخليج	٨٥٧-.٤.١ (٢.٢)	الخطوط الجوية الأردنية
٨٨٧-٥٣.٣ (٢.٢)	طيران الشرق الأوسط	٤٢٤-١١٢٨ (٨..)	الخطوط الجوية الكويتية

نيويورك

رقم التلفون	شركة الطيران	رقم التلفون	شركة الطيران
٢٢٣-١٧٧٥ (٨..)	الخطوط الجوية المغربية	٧٥٨-٤٧٢٧ (٢١٢)	الخطوط الجوية السعودية
٥٨١-٥٦.. (٢١٢)	مصر للطيران	٩٤٩-..٦. (٢١٢)	الخطوط الجوية الأردنية
٢٢٣-.٨.٤ (٨..)	طيران الشرق الأوسط	٣١٩-١٢٢٢ (٢١٢)	الخطوط الجوية الكويتية

شيكاغو

رقم التلفون	شركة الطيران	رقم التلفون	شركة الطيران
٢٢٣-.٤٧. (٨..)	الخطوط الجوية الأردنية	٧٨٢-٧٩٥٦ (٣١٢)	الخطوط الجوية المغربية
		٢٦٣-٣٨٥٨ (٣١٢)	الخطوط الجوية الكويتية

What are the telephone numbers of the following airline offices:
the Saudi airlines in New York _____
the Moroccan airlines in Chicago _____
the Kuwaiti airlines in Washington, D.C. _____
the Middle East airlines in Houston _____

كلمات جديدة

Gulf Air	طيران الخليج	airline	شركة طيران=خطوط جوية

Wanting with بدّ

The word بدّ is used in combination with a pronoun suffix (the same set of suffixes that are used to indicate possession) to express the equivalent of the English verb *to want* in Levantine Arabic:

بدّه	bidd-u	"he wants"
بدها	bid-ha	"she wants"
بدّك	bidd-ak	"you, m.s want"
بدّك	bidd-ik	"you, f.s. want"
بدّي	bidd-i	"I want"

تمارين

١. املاء

١. ١٨٣، ٢٢، ٣٨٤، ٥.٦، ٦٢٠، ٩١٩، ١٩١٩، ١٩٩١، ١١٨٨، ١٩٦٧

٢. أنا طالب من البحرين.

٣. أنا طالب وأبي معلّم.

٤. القاهرة عاصمة مصر.

٥. بيت سليم كبير وبيت علي صغير.

٢. اقرأ (كلمات متقاطعة)

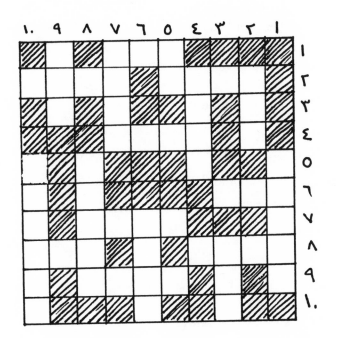

عمودي	أفقي
١. أمّ	١. ——— وأنت
٢. دولة عربية صغيرة في آسيا	٢. عكس بعيد؛ عكس يسار
٣. عكس غرب	٤. أستاذ
٤. يشتغل	٦. عكس آخِر
٥. زوج الأم	٧. خامس شهر في سوريا ولبنان
٦. من اليمن	والأردن ولبنان وفلسطين
٧. جمع يوم	٨. عاصمة سوريا؛ جذر (root) سافر
٨. يدرس فيها الطلاب	٩. فيها ملابس
٩. اليوم فيه نهار (day) و———	
١٠. دولة عربية كبيرة في آسيا	

اسـمـع

أسـئـلة

1. Why did Sharif know Irbid well?

_____

2. Did he know the names of the streets there?

_____

3. Where is Sharif's house in Irbid?

_____

4. What is the name of the shop on the right?

_____

5. What do you need in America to find your way around?

_____

كلمات جديدة

قبل ما=قبل	before
أسامي (م. إسم)[1]	names
عناوين (م. عنوان)	addresses
دكاكين (م. دكّان)	shops
حارة	neighborhood, quarter (of a city)
رئيسي	main
حتّى	until
مَخبز	bakery
حدّ	one, anyone, someone

---

١ م.-= مـفرد singular

حوار

أسئلة

1. Who is talking to whom?

_____

2. Where is Dan now?

_____

3. Why can't Dan go today?

_____

4. When is he going?

_____

كلمات جديدة

letter	رِسالة
thank God for your safe arrival	الحمد لله على السلامة
may God keep you safe (answer to الحمدلله على السلامة)	الله يسلمك
busy	مشغول
therefore	إذن

١١٧

باصات حجازي

خدمة سريعة، نظيفة، مريحة

أجرة الباصات ومواعيد مغادرتها من عمان الى المدن الأخرى

الأجرة	اليوم وموعد المغادرة	المدينة
دينار واحد	كل يوم/كل ساعة ابتداء بالسادسة صباحاً	جرش
دينارين	كل يوم/كل ساعة ابتداء بالسادسة والنصف	إربد
٥ دنانير	كل يوم/الثامنة صباحاً	معان
٨ دنانير	كل يوم/الثامنة صباحاً	العقبة
١٢ دينار	السبت والثلاثاء/التاسعة صباحاً	جدّة
١٢ دينار	السبت والاثنين والأربعاء/التاسعة صباحاً	بغداد
٧ دنانير	الأحد والثلاثاء والخميس/التاسعة والنصف صباحاً	دمشق
١٧ دينار	الثلاثاء/التاسعة والنصف صباحاً	استانبول

أسئلة

1. When does the first bus leave for Irbid?

_____

2. What is the fare from Amman to: Ma'an, Baghdad, Istanbul?

_____

3. How often does the bus go from Amman to: Jerash, Jedda, Damascus, Baghdad?

_____

4. What time does the bus leave for Irbid, Aqaba, Damascus, Ma'an?

_____

كلمات جديدة

sixth	سادس	beginning (at)	ابتداء بـ
		half	نِصف=نص

قواعد

Ordinal Numbers

Ordinal numbers from 2 to 10 are formed following the pattern فاعِل
(faaʕil):

اثنين-ثاني

ثلاثة-ثالث

أربعة-رابع

خمسة-خامس

ستة-سادس

سبعة-سابع

ثمانية-ثامن

تسعة-تاسع

عشرة-عاشر

Note that ثاني does not have a final consonant and that سادس is not
regularly derived from ستة.

اسمـع

أسئلة

1. How many bedrooms does Sharif's cousin's house have?

_____

2. Does it have a large front yard?

_____

3. How many children does his cousin have?

_____

4. How old is Nadya?

_____

5. What grade is Tariq in?

_____

6. Where does his cousin's wife work?

_____

guests	ضيوف (ضيف)	residential	سَكَني
behind	وراء	yard	حَديقة
that, which	اللي	in front of	قُدّام
class, grade	صَفّ	trees	شَجَر
wife	زوجة	private	خاصّة

حوار

روح لمحطة الباصات في العبدلي
واسأل عن باصات حجازي.

أسئلة

1. Does Dan know Abu Sharif's address in Irbid?
_____

2. Why is America mentioned?
_____

3. How is Abu Sharif going to help Dan to get to his (Abu Sharif's) house?
_____

4. How are Hijazi buses?
_____

5. How often is there a bus to Irbid?
_____

6. How long does the bus take from Amman to Irbid?
_____

كلمات جديدة

station	مَحطّة	coming	جاي
		fast	سريع

اقرأ

الدول العربية

العاصمة	المساحة (كيلومتر مربّع)	عدد السكّان (بالمليون)	اسم الدولة
القاهرة	١.٠٠٢.٠٠٠	٥٤.٧	جمهورية مصر العربية
الجزائر	٢.٣٨١.٧٥١	٢٥.٦	جمهورية الجزائر الشعبية الديمقراطية
الرباط	٤٤٦.٥٥٠	٢٥.٦	المملكة المغربية
الخرطوم	٢.٥٠٥.٨١٢	٢٥.٢	الجمهورية السودانية
بغداد	٤٣٤.٩١٣	١٨.٨	الجمهورية العراقية
الرياض	٢.٢٥٠.٠٧٠	١٥	المملكة العربية السعودية
دمشق	١٨٥.١٨٠	١٢.٦	الجمهورية العربية السورية
صنعاء	٥٢٧.٩٧٠	٩.٨	جمهورية اليمن
مغاديشو	٦٣٧.٦٥٥	٨.٤	جمهورية الصومال الديمقراطية
تونس	١٦٤.١٥٢	٨.١	الجمهورية التونسية
طرابلس	١.٧٥٩.٩٩٨	٤.٢	الجماهيرية العربية الليبية الشعبية الاشتراكية
عمّان	٩٦.٥٩٩	٤.١	المملكة الأردنية الهاشمية
بيروت	١٠.٤٠٠	٣.٣	الجمهورية اللبنانية
الكويت	١٧.٨٢٠	٢.١	دولة الكويت
نواكشوط	١.٠٣٠.٧٠٠	٢	جمهورية موريتانيا الإسلامية
أبو ظبي	٨٢.٨٨٠	١.٦	الإمارات العربية المتحدة
مسقط	٢١٢.٤٥٨	١.٥	سلطنة عمان
المنامة	٦٢٠	٠.٥	دولة البحرين
الدوحة	١١.٤٣٧	٠.٥	دولة قطر
جيبوتي	٢٢.٠٠٠	٠.٤	جمهورية جيبوتي
	١٣.٧٧٠.٠٠٠	٢٢٤	المجموع

أسئلة

1. What is the smallest Arab country in area?

_____

2. Which Arab countries have the same number of inhabitants?

_____

3. What are the capitals of the following countries: Yemen, Bahrain, Mauritania, Libya, and Oman?

_____

area	مَساحة	population	عَدد السُكّان
popular	شَعبيّة	republic	جُمهوريّة
socialist	اشتراكية	kingdom	مملكة
sultanate	سَلطنة	united	مُتّحدة

قواعد

Plural Possessive Pronouns

The suffixed pronouns هُم، كُم، نا are used to indicate possession by plural referents:

كتابهُم	"their book"
كتابكُم	"your, pl. book"
كتابنا	"our book"

You may recall that when a noun ends in تاء مربوطة the تاء مربوطة is replaced by a regular ت when a possessive suffix is added.

مدينة	"city"
مدينتهم	"their city"
مدينتكم	"your city"
مدينتنا	"our city"

تمارين

١. اقرأ

Match the singular with its plural. One word in the singular column does not have a matching plural.

رَسائل	خَريطة
شركات	شركة
ضيوف	دُكّان
خرائط	مخبز
محطات	جُمهورية
دكاكين	رسالة
مخابز	ضيف
	مَحطّة

٢. اقرأ واكتب

Rewrite the following words, grouping them into related families. For each family identify the root and give its general meaning in English.

زار، سَريع، مَخبِز، مَشغول، سكَني، ثالث، شركة، افتح، بسُرعة، اشتراكيّة، مفتاح، زيارة، خَبز، اشتغل، ثلاثة، ساكِن، الثلاثاء، سُكّان.

٣. تكلّم

Create a dialogue with another student in which one invites the other to his/her house and gives directions on how to get there.

٤. اكتب

Fill in the names of the Arab countries on the following map.

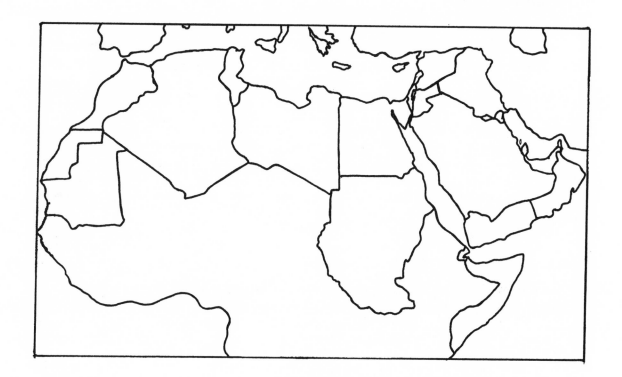

٤. الجزائر	٣. موريتانيا	٢. اليمن	١. مصر
٨. عُمان	٧. تونس	٦. المغرب	٥. الصومال
١٢. العراق	١١. البحرين	١٠. ليبيا	٩. السودان
١٦. لُبنان	١٥. السعودية	١٤. قَطر	١٣. الأردن
٢٠. الإمارات العربية	١٩. الكويت	١٨. سوريا	١٧. جيبوتي

٥. اكتب

Attach the plural possessive pronoun suffixes corresponding to هم، انتو، احنا to the following nouns:

استاذ، شقة، عنوان، سيارة، مكتب، مشكلة، صورة

٦. املاء
١. سليم مهندس. هو من مصر.
٢. مريم من بيروت عاصمة لبنان.
٣. أنا من دمشق عاصمة سوريا.
٤. لبنان دولة عربية صغيرة والعراق دولة عربية كبيرة.

الدرس رقم ٢٣

اسمع

أسئلة

1. How long did the trip from Chicago take?
_____

2. Why didn't he eat at his cousin's house?
_____

3. When did the plane leave O'Hare Airport?
_____

4. What did the hostess say first?
_____

5. When will the plane land at the Pittsburgh airport?
_____

كلمات جديدة

hostess	مُضيفة	trip	رحلة
going to	رايح	to hear	سمِع
		to land	نزِل (يِنزِل)

حوار

أسئلة

1. How long did the trip from America take?

_____

2. How many hours was Dan in the plane?

_____

3. At which airports did the plane stop?

_____

4. Did Dan have to change planes on his trip from Ithaca to Amman?

_____

كلمات جديدة

to stop   وَقَّف   not bad   مش بطّال

اقرأ

العالم العربي

في العالم العربي ٢٠ دولة: ١١ في آسيا و٩ في إفريقيا. الدول العربية التي في آسيا هي: العراق، الكويت، البحرين، قطر، الإمارات العربية المتحدة، عُمان، اليمن، السعودية، الأردن، سوريا ولبنان. والدول العربية التي في إفريقيا هي: مصر، السودان، جيبوتي، الصومال، ليبيا، تونس، الجزائر، المغرب، وموريتانيا.

العالم العربي كبير: سكانه أكثر من ٢٢٠ مليون نسمة. أكثر سكان العالم العربي مسلمون، ولكن هناك كثير من المسيحيين، وخصوصاً في لبنان ومصر. كان هناك كثير من اليهود في العراق والمغرب واليمن ومصر ولكن أكثرهم هاجروا الى إسرائيل بعد سنة ١٩٤٨.

أكثر سكان العالم العربي عرب يتكلمون اللغة العربية، ولكن هناك أقليات كثيرة مثل الأكراد في العراق، البربر في شمال إفريقيا، الأرمن في لبنان وسوريا، والشركس والشيشان في الأردن وسوريا.

أسئلة

1. How many Arab countries are in Asia? How many are in Africa?

_____

2. What is the population of the Arab world?

_____

3. Which Arab countries have large Christian minorities?

_____

4. Which Arab countries had Jewish minorities?

_____

5. Which non-Arab minorities are mentioned? Where do they live?

_____

كلمات جديدة

that, which (f.)	التي=اللي	world	عالَم
person (people)	نَسَمة	more than	أكثر
there is, there are	هُناك=فيه	Muslim	مسلم
Jews	يهود (م. يهودي)	Christian	مسيحي
to speak	تكلّم (يتكلّم)=حَكى	to emigrate	هاجر
		minority	أقلّيّة

Prepositions Followed by ما

Prepositions are generally followed by nouns. In cases where a verb follows instead of the noun, the particle ما is inserted between the preposition and the verb:

قبل الظهر	"before noon" but,
قبل ما أجا	"before he came"

In such cases ما does not add to the meaning of the preposition, so قبل and قبل ما mean exactly the same thing. Other words (prepositions and nouns functioning like prepositions) that behave in a similar way and that you will encounter in this book are: بعد "after," أوّل "first, at the beginning," بدل "instead," بدون "without," and مثل "like, as."

The Imperfect of Hollow Verbs

Whereas the vowel of the perfect form of hollow verbs is always ا, it is realized in one of three ways in the corresponding imperfect form: ا, ي, or و, depending on the individual verb. There is no general rule determining what vowel a certain hollow verb takes in the imperfect, but it may be helpful to mention that in terms of frequency و verbs are the most common, followed by ي and ا verbs, in that order.

The subject markers attached to hollow verbs in the imperfect are the same as those attached to sound verbs (and all other verbs in the imperfect for that matter).

(هو) يروح	y-ruufi	"he goes"
(هي) تروح	t-ruufi	"she goes"
(انتَ) تروح	t-ruufi	"you, m.s. go"
(انتِ) تروحي	t-ruufii	"you, f.s. go"
(أنا) أروح	a-ruufi	"I go"

So far, you have seen only the imperfect verb conjugation with singular persons. The following are the plural person conjugations:

(هم) يروحوا	y-ruufi-u	"they go"
(انتو) تروحوا	t-ruufi-u	"you, pl. go"
(احنا) نروح	n-ruufi	"we go"

The Imperative

The imperative form of the verb can be derived from the imperfect form following two steps:

1. drop the imperfect prefix
2. insert a(n) epenthetic vowel if the resulting form begins with a two-consonant cluster.

يشوف-شوف	"See, look!"
يكتب-كتب-اكتب	"Write!"

The pronunciation of the inserted vowel depends on the *stem* vowel of the verb. The stem vowel is the vowel between the second and third consonants of the root. If the stem vowel is ُ (u), the inserted vowel is pronounced as ُ (u), and if it is ِ (i) or َ (a), then the inserted vowel is ِ (i).

اكتب	uktub	"Write!"
إعرف	iʕrif	"Know!"
اسمع	ismaʕ	"Listen, hear!"

تمارين

١. اكتب

Fill in the blank spaces in the following.

العالم العربي ـــــــ: يزيد سكانه على ٢٢٠ ـــــــ نسمة. أكثر سكان العالم ـــــــ مسلمون، ولكن هناك كثير من المسيحيين، وخاصة في ـــــــ ومصر. كان هناك كثير من اليهود في العراق والمغرب واليمن ومصر ولكن أكثرهم ـــــــ لإسرائيل بعد سنة ١٩٤٨.

أكثر سكان ـــــــ العربي عرب يتكلمون اللغة ـــــــ، ولكن هناك أقليات كثيرة مثل الأكراد في ـــــــ، البربر في ـــــــ إفريقيا، الأرمن في لبنان و ـــــــ، والشركس والشيشان في ـــــــ وسوريا.

١٣٢

٢. اكتب

Conjugate the following verbs in the imperfect with all (singular and plural) subject/person markers (هو، هي، هم، انتَ، انتِ، انتو، أنا، احنا)

كان، قال، نام، طار، زار

٣. اكتب

Form the imperative (in the second person, singular and plural) of the following verbs:

كتب، دخَل، درَس، فتَح، قال

٤. تكلّم

Create a dialogue with another student in which one of you asks the other about a trip he/she has recently made.

الدرس رقم ٢٤

اسمع

أسئلة

1. How long did they wait at the Pittsburgh airport?

_____

2. What time did the plane leave for Ithaca?

_____

3. Did he order anything to drink?

_____

4. Why couldn't he sleep the third time he tried?

_____

1. Name the people to whom Dan was introduced.

_____

2. Where is Abdalla?

_____

3. What does Suad do?

_____

كلمة جديدة

| the Tawjihi exam | توجيهي | market | سوق |

اقرأ

الطقس في العالم العربي

العالم العربي كبير: مساحته أكثر من ١٣ مليون كيلومتر مربع، ولكنّ أكثره صحراء. مثلاً ٩٧٪ من مساحة مصر و٩٩.٩ من مساحة السعودية صحراء أو مناطق صخرية.

أكبر الصحاري في العالم العربي هي الصحراء العربية الكبرى في شمال إفريقيا وصحراء الربع الخالي في المملكة العربية السعودية.

يختلف الطقس من بلد الى بلد ومن منطقة الى منطقة في نفس البلد في العالم العربي. في المناطق الصحراوية الطقس حار جداً في الصيف، وبارد في الشتاء: قد تصل درجة الحرارة في الصيف الى أكثر من ١٢٠ درجة فهرنهايت في شهور حزيران وتمّوز وآب (يونيو ويوليو وأغسطس). ولا ينزل في الصحاري مطر كثير أو ثلج.

وفي المناطق الجبلية مثل شمال العراق وجبال لبنان وجبال أطلس في شمال إفريقيا الطقس بارد في الشتاء ومعتدل في الصيف، وينزل في هذه المناطق ثلج ومطر كثير.

أسئلة

1. What is the total area of the Arab world?

_____

2. What percentage of Egypt is desert or rocky areas?

_____

3. What are the two largest deserts in the Arab world?

_____

4. What is the weather like in desert areas?

_____

5. On which areas does snow fall?

_____

كلمات جديدة

square	مُربَّع
desert	صَحراء
for example	مَثلاً
areas, regions	مَناطق (م. منطقة)
rocky	صَخري
the Empty Quarter	الرُبع الخالي
to differ	اختلَف (يختلِف)
country	بَلَد
hot	حارّ=حامي
very	جدّاً
may	قَد
to reach	وَصل (يَصِل)
temperature ("degree of heat")	دَرَجة الحرارة
to fall	نَزَل (يَنزِل)
mountainous	جَبلي
moderate	مُعتدِل

أغنية

طيري يا طيّارة (فيروز)

يا ورق وخيطان	طيري يا طيّارة طيري
على سطح الجيران	بدّي أرجع بنت صغيرة
على سطح الجيران	وينساني الزمان
	(طيري يا طيارة...)

عالنسمة الخجولة	علّي فوق سطوح بعاد
وردّوا لي الطفولة	أخذوني معهن الاولاد
وغناني زمان	ضحكات الصبيان
والعمر اللي كان	ردّت لي كتبي ومدرستي
على سطح الجيران	وينساني الزمان
	(طيري يا طيارة...)

مع هالورق الطاير	لو فينا نهرب ونطير
شو صاير شو صاير	تا نكبر بعد بكير
ميل بهالبستان	ويا زهر الرمّان
ويحلوّ الزمان	تا يتسلّوا صغار الأرض
على سطح الجيران	وينساني الزمان
	(طيري يا طيارة...)

Possession with عند

The preposition عند is used in combination with a pronoun suffix to express the idea of possession in a way that parallels the use of the English verb *to have* to indicate possession in sentences like:

I have a Japanese car.
He has two brothers.

عنده	ʕind-u	"he has"
عندها	ʕind-ha	"she has"
عندَك	ʕind-ak	"you, m.s have"
عندِك	ʕind-ik	"you, f.s. have"
عندِي	ʕind-i	"I have"

Negation (in MSA)

Unlike Levantine Arabic, verbs in MSA are negated in different ways according to their tense. Verbs in the perfect are negated by using مـا in the same way it is used in Levantine:

ما عرف عنهم شيئاً.   "He did not know anything about them,"

or by using لم and the imperfect form of the verb (more on this in Lesson 50):

لم يعرف عنهم شيئاً.   "He did not know anything about them."

Verbs in the imperfect are negated by using لا:

لا يعرف عنهم شيئاً.   "He does not know anything about them."

قد + Imperfect

When the word قـد precedes a verb in the imperfect, it gives the meaning of possibility:

قد تصل درجة الحرارة الى أكثر من ١٢٠ درجة.

"The temperature may reach more than 120 degrees."

١. اقرأ

Match each of the words in the first column with their opposites in the second.
There is one extra word in the first column.

أخذ	وجد
قُدّام	يمين
ضيّع	كثير
غالي	وراء
ذَكَر	أعطى
يسار	رخيص
بارِد	أنثى
	حارّ

٢. املاء

١. تونس بعيدة عن العراق.
٢. سيارتي في البيت.
٣. شارع الجامعة قريب.
٤. السبت والإثنين والأربعاء.

٣. تكلّم

Create a dialogue with another student in which each of you introduces his/her
family members to the other.

الدرس رقم ٢٥

1. Who went to the airport to welcome Ayman?

_____

2. Why did his mother and Suad stay at home?

_____

3. What time did they reach the house?

_____

4. How long has it been since his mother saw Ayman?

_____

5. Where did they sit?

_____

to welcome, meet	استقبل (يستقبِل)	in order to	حتّى
to cook	طبخ (يطبُخ)	to remain	ظلّ
happy	مَبسوط	to clean	نظّف (ينظِّف)
condition, how one is	حال	to greet	سلّم
		health	صِحّة

حوار

أسئلة

1. When was the last time Dan saw Sharif?

_____

2. Who is Sharif living with?

_____

3. How many times did Dan see Sharif's apartment?

_____

4. How many bedrooms does Sharif's apartment have?

_____

5. How does Sharif go to school?

_____

كلمة جديدة

last time	آخِر مَرّة	study	دِراسة

١٤٣

اقرأ

الدول الغنية والدول الفقيرة في العالم العربي

الدول الغنية

اسم الدولة	الدخل السنوي للدولة (بالمليون دولار)	السكان (بالمليون)	متوسط دخل الفرد (بالدولار)
قطر	٥٤٠٠	٠.٥	١٧.٧٠
الإمارات العربية	٢٢٠٠٠	١.٦	١١٩٠٠
الكويت	١٩١٠٠	٢.١	١٠٤١٠
البحرين	٣٥٠٠	٠.٥	٧٥٠٠
عُمان	٧٥٠٠	١.٥	٦١١٠
السعودية	٧٤٠٠٠	١٥	٥٤٨٠
ليبيا	٢٠٠٠٠	٤.٢	٥٤١٠

الدول المتوسطة

الجزائر	٥٩٠٠٠	٢٥.٦	٢٦٤٥
سوريا	٢.٣٠٠	١٢.٦	١٩٦٢
العراق	٣٤٠٠٠	١٨.٨	١٩٥٠
الأردن	٤٩٠٠	٤.١	١٧٨٠
تونس	٩٦٠٠	٨.١	١٢٧٠

الدول الفقيرة

جيبوتي	٣٣٣	٠.٤	١.٦٧
المغرب	١٨٠٠٠	٢٥.٦	٧٤٠
اليمن	٥٥١٠	٩.٨	٥٦٢
لبنان	١٨٠٠	٣.٣	٥٤٥
مصر	٢٥٦٠٠	٥٤.٧	٤٩٠
موريتانيا	٨٤٣	٢	٤٤٠
السودان	٨٥٠٠	٢٥.٢	٣٤٠
الصومال	١٥٠٠	٨.٤	١٩٠
الولايات المتحدة	٤٨٦٢٠٠٠	٢٥١.٤	١٩٨٠٠

1. Which Arab country has the highest gross national product (GNP)?

_____

2. Which has the lowest GNP?

_____

3. Which Arab country has the highest per capita income?

_____

4. Which has the lowest?

_____

4. What is the per capita income in the following countries:
   Kuwait _____
   Syria _____
   Egypt _____
   Yemen _____

كلمات جديدة

poor	فَقير	rich	غَني
average, middle	مُتوسّط	annual income	دخل سنَوي
		individual	فَرد

تمارين

١. اكتب

Conjugate the following verbs in the perfect with all persons:

فتح، عرف، طار، سأل، مشى

٢. اكتب

Conjugate the following verbs in the imperfect with all persons:

عرف، درس، قال، كان

٣. تكلّم

Create a dialogue with another student in which you ask and answer questions about your place of residence.

الدرس رقم ٢٦

اسمع

أسئلة

1. When did the neighbors start coming?

_____

2. Why did his mother have to go to the kitchen?

_____

3. Why did his mother become upset?

_____

4. What were the neighbors talking about?

_____

كلمات جديدة

to be upset	زِعِل	neighbors	جيران (م. جار)
		prices	أسعار (م. سِعر)

أسئلة

1. What did Dan want to drink?

_____

2. Has Dan eaten *mansaf* before?

_____

3. What kind of meat is in the *mansaf*?

_____

كلمات جديدة

rice	رُزّ	truly, in fact	فعلاً
lamb meat	لحمة خَروف	yogurt	لَبَن
		pork	لحم خنزير

١٤٧

الأردن

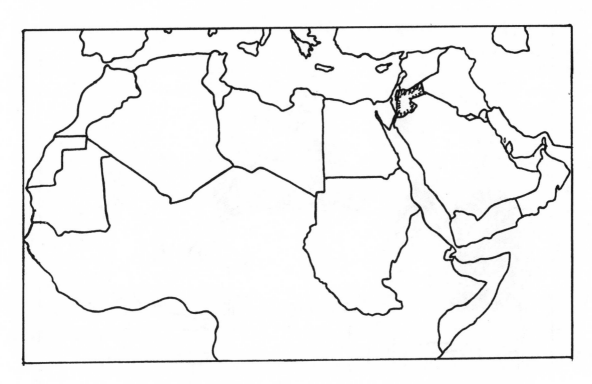

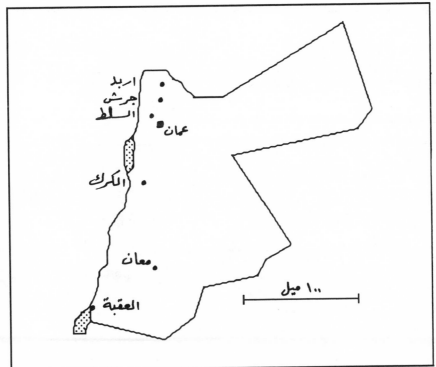

الإسم الكامل	المملكة الأردنية الهاشمية
المساحة	٣٧.٢٩٧ ميل مربع (٩٦.٥٩٩ كم مربع)
عدد السكان	٤.١ مليون نسمة
المدن الرئيسية	عمان (العاصمة ٩٧٢.٠٠٠)، الزرقاء (٢٢٠.٣٩٢)، اربد (٢٧١.٠٠٠)، السلط (١٣٤.١٠٠)
اللغة	العربية
الدين	الإسلام (٩٥٪)، المسيحية (٥٪)
اسم الحاكم	الملك حسين ابن طلال
سنة الاستقلال	١٩٤٦
العملة	الدينار
الدخل السنوي للفرد	١٧٨٠ دولار أمريكي

الأردن دولة عربية صغيرة تقع بين العراق والسعودية في الشرق وسوريا في الشمال واسرائيل في الغرب والسعودية والبحر الأحمر في الجنوب. عدد سكان الأردن أكثر من أربعة ملايين نسمة ومساحته حوالي ٣٨ الف ميل مربّع. من المدن الأردنية الكبيرة: عمان (العاصمة)، الزرقاء، إربد، السلط، جرش، والعقبة.

أكثر الأردن صحراء (حوالي ٨٠٪ من مساحته)، لكن هناك مناطق كثيرة فيها جبال وشجر وينزل عليها مطر وثلج مثل مناطق عمان وجرش وإربد.

الطقس في أكثر مناطق الأردن بارد في الشتاء، معتدل في الربيع والخريف، وحارّ في الصيف. ينزل أكثر الثلج والمطر في الشتاء في شهور كانون الأوّل وكانون الثاني وشباط (ديسمبر ويناير وفبراير).

أحسن مناطق الأردن للزراعة هي منطقة الغور. الطقس في الغور حار أكثر ايام السنة. أرض الغور خصبة وفيها ماء كثير لأن نهر الأردن يمر منها. أكثر خضار وفواكه الأردن تجيء من الغور.

أسئلة

1. What borders Jordan from the north and the south?

_____

2. What percentage of Jordan is desert?

_____

3. How is the weather in Jordan?

_____

4. How is the weather in the Ghor area?

_____

			كلمات جديدة
main	رَئيسي	cities	مُدُن (م. مدينة)
ruler	حاكم	religion	دين
currency	عُملَة	independence	استقلال
mountains	جبال (م. جبل)	to be located	وَقَع (يقع)
fertile	خَصب	agriculture	زراعة
to pass through	مَرّ (يمرّ)	river	نَهر
		to come	جاء (يجيء)

قواعد

Pronouns Attached to Prepositions

The pronoun suffixes that are used to indicate possession on nouns can also be attached to prepositions to express the equivalent of English constructions consisting of a preposition and an object pronoun, such as *on it, in them, to you,* etc.

مع	"with"	معه، معها، معهم، معَك، معك، معكم، معي، معنا
في	"in"	فيه، فيها، فيهم، فيك، فيك، فيكم، فيَّ، فينا
على	"on"	عليه، عليها، عليهم، عليك، عليكم، عليّ، علينا
من	"from"	منّه، منها، منهم، منّك، منّك، منكم، منّي، منّا
لـ (لـ)	"to, for"	اله، الها، الهم، الَك، الك، الكم، الي، النا
عن	"about"	عنّه، عنها، عنهم، عنّك، عنّك، عنكم، عنّي، عنّا

Note that when the preposition ends in a vowel, the second person feminine singular suffix is pronounced *ki* rather than *ik*. Compare معك maʕik "with you, f.s." with فيك fiiki "in you, f.s.".

As noted earlier, the same set of pronominal suffixes is attached to عند to indicate possession in the sense of the English *to have* and to بدّ to indicate wanting. You have seen these two particles only in their singular forms. Their full paradigms are shown here.

عنده	ʕind-u	"he has"
عندها	ʕind-ha	"she has"
عندهم	ʕind-hum	"they have"
عندَك	ʕind-ak	"you, m.s have"
عندك	ʕind-ik	"you, f.s. have"
عندكم	ʕind-kum	"you, pl."
عندي	ʕind-i	"I have"
عندنا	ʕind-na	"we"

بدّه	bidd-u	"he wants"
بدها	bid-ha	"she wants"
بدهم	bid-hum	"they want"
بدّك	bidd-ak	"you, m.s want"
بدّك	bidd-ik	"you, f.s. want"
بدكم	bid-kum	"you, pl. want"
بدّي	bidd-i	"I want"
بدنا	bid-na	"we want"

The Imperfect of Assimilated Verbs in فصحى

Verbs like وقع and وصل that have و as their first consonant are called *assimilated* verbs. In Modern Standard Arabic (Fuṣḥa فصحى) the و of these verbs is deleted when the verb is in the imperfect:

وقع	"was located"	يقَع	"is located"
وصل	"arrived, reached"	يصِل	"reaches"

تمارين

١. اقرأ

Match the singular with its plural. One word in the plural column does not have a matching singular.

مَناطق	مَسيحي
بِلاد	يَهودي
أغنياء	مِنطَقة
جيران	سِعر
يَهود	بَلَد
فُقراء	غني
مَسيحيّين	فقير
مُدُن	جار
أسعار	

٢. املاء

١. ساعة وربع.

٢. كم دقيقة في الساعة؟

٣. مصر شمال السودان وشرق ليبيا.

٤. فصول السنة هي الصيف والخريف والشتاء والربيع.

اسـمع

وليـش نفتـش على شـقةَ ثانيةً؟ هذه شـقةٌ نظيفة ورخيصة.

أسئلة

1. Why is he happy in the apartment?

2. How far is the bus stop?

3. How long does the bus take to the university?

4. When did Walid come to America?

5. Where did he study before coming to America?

6. Why isn't Muhammad living with them?

كلمات جديدة

young man	شـابّ	until now, still	لِسّه
		sociology	عِلم الاجتِماع

أسئلة

1. What did Dan want to drink?

_____

2. What did he want in it?

_____

3. What did Abu Sharif want to drink?

_____

كلمات جديدة

sugar	سُكَّر
without	بِدون
not possible, hard to believe	مِش مَعقول
to try	جرّب (يـجرّب)
God bless your hands	يـسلموا ايديك
bon appetit!	صِحّة وهناء

اقرأ

جرش

جرش مدينة أردنية تقع في منطقة جبلية على بعد حوالي ٣٥ كيلومتر شمال عمان على الطريق الرئيسي بين عمان وإربد. جرش مدينة صغيرة؛ عدد سكانها حوالي ٤٠ الف نسمة. يمر من جرش نهر صغير اسمه "وادي الدير". جرش مدينة قديمة فيها آثار يونانية ورومانية كثيرة. بناها اليونان، وبعد اليونان حكمها الرومان ثم العرب المسلمون.

دخل العرب المسلمون جرش سنة ٦٣٤ ميلادية، وفي القرن التاسع كان نصف سكان جرش مسلمين والنصف الثاني يونانيين.

في سنة ١٨٧٨ جاء الشركس الى جرش وبنوا بيوتاً فيها. والشركس هم مسلمون جاءوا من روسيا.

أسئلة

1. Where is Jerash located?
_____

2. What is the population of Jerash?
_____

3. When did the Muslim Arabs enter Jerash?
_____

4. What was the population of Jerash like in the ninth century?
_____

between	بـين	at a distance of	على بُعد
antiquities	آثار	ancient	قَديم
to build	بَنى	Greek	يوناني
and then	ثـُمّ=بعدين	to rule	حَكم
A.D.	ميلادية (م.)	to enter	دخل
Russia	روسيا	century	قَرن

قواعد

Objects Preceding Their Subjects

If the object of the verb is a pronoun, then it is attached to the verb, resulting in a verb-object-subject sequence:

حكم الرومان جرش.

Jerash the Romans ruled. = The Romans ruled Jerash.

The Romans ruled it is rendered as:

حكمها اليونان.   (literally: ruled it the Romans)

Pronouns of Separation

In equational sentences in which the subject and predicate are nouns, a pronoun that agrees in number and gender with the subject noun may be inserted between the subject and predicate. In such a position, the pronoun has a meaning similar to the English verb *to be*.

جرش (هي) مدينة أردنية.   "Jerash is a Jordanian city."

الشركس (هم) مسلمون.   "The Circassians are Muslims."

تمارين

١. اكتب

Fill in the blank spaces in the following.

جرش ـــــ أردنيـة تقـع في ـــــ جبليـة على بعد حوالي ٣٥ كيلومتـر ـــــ عمـان على الطريق الرئيسي بين عمـان وإربد. جرش مـدينة ـــــ ؛ عدد سكانها حوالي ٤٠ ألف ـــــ . يمر من جرش ـــــ صغيـر اسمـه "وادي الدير". جرش مدينة ـــــ فيها آثار يونانية ورومانية ـــــ . بناها اليونان، وبعد اليونان حكمها الرومان ثم ـــــ المسلمون.

دخل العـرب المسلمـون جرش سنة ٦٣٤ ميـلاديـة، وفي ـــــ التاسع كان نصف ـــــ جرش مسلمين والنصف الثاني يونانيين.

٢. اكتب

Replace the object noun in the following sentences with an object pronoun.

ضيّع أحمد الشنطة.
أخذت ليلى الكتاب.
فتح الأستاذ الباب.

٣. تكلّم

Create a dialogue with another student in which one of you is a host offering his guest something to drink.

الدرس رقم ٢٨

اسمـع

أسئلة

1. Where does he eat when he is busy?

_____

2. What kind of food does he (the speaker) cook at home?

_____

3. Why does Walid cook excellent Lebanese food?

_____

4. Does Walid like Chinese food?

_____

كلمات جديدة

Chinese صيني also كَمان

فيه حمامين، حمام عربي وحمام غربي.

أسئلة

1. Why did Dan want to go back to Amman?

_____

2. Did Abu Sharif let him go back?

_____

3. Where is Dan going to sleep?

_____

4. Is Dan tired?

_____

كلمات جديدة

morning	صُبح	tonight	الليلة
reserved	مَحجوز	nonsense	بَلا ... بلا بطّيخ
certainly	أكيد	don't worry	ولا يهمّك
idea	فِكرة	to rest	استراح (يـستريح)

اقرأ

عمّان

عمّان عاصمة الأردن وأكبر مدينة فيه. عدد سكانها حوالي مليون نسمة. تقع على سبعة جبال شمال شرق البحر الميّت، وتبعد عنه حوالي ٤٠ كم (٢٥ ميل). في عمان مركز الحكومة الأردنية وفيها مساجد وكنائس ومكتبات كثيرة. كانت عمان مركزاً مهماً للتجارة في الماضي والآن هي مركز للتجارة في الأردن وفي الشرق الأوسط.

عمان مدينة قديمة يزيد عمرها على ٣ آلاف سنة. كان اسمها ربة عمون وبعد ذلك صار فيلادلفيا ثم عمان. حكمها اليونان والرومان والعرب والأتراك. وفي سنة ١٩٢١ صارت عاصمة الأردن. كانت قرية صغيرة، ولكن بعد حرب ١٩٤٨ وحرب ١٩٦٧ بين العرب وإسرائيل صارت عمان مدينة كبيرة لأن كثيراً من الفلسطينيين جاءوا وسكنوا فيها.

1. What is the population of Amman?

_____

2. Where is it located?

_____

3. How old is Amman?

_____

4. Who ruled Amman through the ages?

_____

5. When did it become the capital of Jordan?

_____

6. What made it grow into a big city?

_____

كلمات جديدة

to be far from	يبعُد عن	the Dead Sea	البَحر الميّت
mosques	مَساجد (م. مسجد)	center	مَركَز
library	مكتبة	churches	كنائس (م. كنيسة)
trade, commerce	تجارة	important	مُهِمّ
now	الآن = هلًّا	past	ماضي
to exceed	زاد (يزيد) على	the Middle East	الشرق الأوسط
to become	صار	after that	بعد ذلك = بعدين
war	حَرب	village	قَرية
		because	لأنّ

قواعد

Cases

Only فـصــحـى has a case system; the spoken Arabic dialects do not have one. So knowledge of this system is useful in dealing with فـصــحـى, which is introduced in this course mainly for reading and writing purposes. Nouns and adjectives in فُصــحـى may have one of three cases, depending on their function in the sentence: nominative, accusative, or genitive. There are many rules and many exceptions to these rules, which can be quite intimidating even to native speakers of Arabic and can easily discourage the beginning nonnative learner of the language. A detailed account of the case system can be found in any standard grammar of فصحى Arabic, but for now only those parts of it that will help develop your reading skills will be introduced.

The three cases are indicated by certain endings. These endings vary

according to a number of factors, such as whether the noun or adjective is definite or indefinite, whether it has a sound plural ending, or whether it ends in التـــاء المربوطة. These endings are shown in the following table:

Case Endings in فصحى

	Singular and Broken Plural			Sound Plural	
	nominative	accusative	genitive	nom.	accus./gen.
definite masc.	الطالبُ	الطالبَ	الطالبِ	المعلمونَ	المعلمينَ
definite fem.	الطالبةُ	الطالبةَ	الطالبةِ	المعلّماتُ	المعلّماتِ
indefinite masc.	طالبٌ	طالباً	طالبٍ	معلمونَ	معلمينَ
indefinite fem.	طالبةٌ	طالبةً	طالبةٍ	معلّماتٌ	معلماتٍ

One point that you should keep in mind is that changes in case do not result in changes in meaning: they are only changes in form. So معلمٌ، معلماً، معلمٍ all mean the same thing: teacher. For purposes of this introductory course, only recognition of the cases is important. In dealing with reading materials, all you need to know about cases is that معلمٌ، معلماً، معلمٍ is one word with one meaning, as are such pairs as معلماتٌ/معلماتٍ and معلمونَ/معلمينَ. In dealing with listening materials in فصحى, such as listening to your teacher read a passage or listening to a tape, you will notice that case endings are also heard at the end of a noun to which a pronoun has been attached and at the end of the first term of إضافة constructions:

ومساحتُه حوالي ٣٨ الف ميل مربّع.
   "And its area is about 38,000 square miles."

عددُ سكّانها حوالي ٤٠ ألف نسمة.
   "Its population is about 40,000 people."

في عمّان مركزُ الحكومة الأردنية.
   "In Amman [there is, is found] the center of the Jordanian government."

تمارين

١. اقرأ واكتب

Rewrite the following words grouping them into related families. For each family identify the root and give its general meaning in English. One word does not belong to a family.

طيَران، رُبع، قَبل، وسَط، طيّار، مَربّع، أكثر، الأربعاء، يطبُخ، بعيد، كثير، موقِف، حَكم، حَجـز، استـقـبل، مَطبخ، بُعـد، وقّف، حـاكِم، تَعِب، أوسَط، محجوز، تَعبان، مكتبة، مُتوسّط، طار

٢. املاء

١. السودان أكبر من مصر وليبيا.

٢. مطار القاهرة كبير.

٣. هو ساكن في شقة صغيرة. في الشقة غرفة نوم واحدة.

٤. عندي بنت واحدة وولد واحد.

١٦٣

الدرس رقم ٢٩

أسئلة

1. How old is Abu Sharif?

_____

2. Where was he born?

_____

3. What does he own?

_____

4. When did he leave school? Why?

_____

5. When did he go to Irbid?

_____

كلمات جديدة

first thing	اوّل شيء
to be born	انولَد
the West Bank	الضفّة الغربيّة
to leave	ترَك
to help	ساعَد (يساعِد)
farm	مَزرَعة
farmer	مُزارِع
war	حَرْب

ـ أنا قلتِ لك بدي حمام، مش جورة في الأرض .

ـ هذا حمام عربي. اذا بدلك حمام غربي السفارة الأمريكيّة قريبة .

أسئلة

1. Who is Um-Khalid?

_____

2. How old is Dan?

_____

3. Why was Um-Khalid surprised?

_____

4. What did Um-Khalid offer to do?

_____

كلمات جديدة

pilgrim, someone who has performed the Hajj to the Muslim holy places   حَجّ

wife   مَرة = زوجة

ملاحظة (Note): متجوز/متزوج

The two sounds ز and ج of the Arabic root زوج and its derivatives are metathesized (they switch places) in informal spoken Arabic. They are never metathesized in written Arabic, and they generally maintain that order (زوج) in formal spoken Arabic.

Informal Spoken	Written/Formal Spoken	
جوز	زوج	"husband, couple, pair"
تجوّز	تزوّج	"to get married"
متجوّز	متزوّج	"married"

سوريا

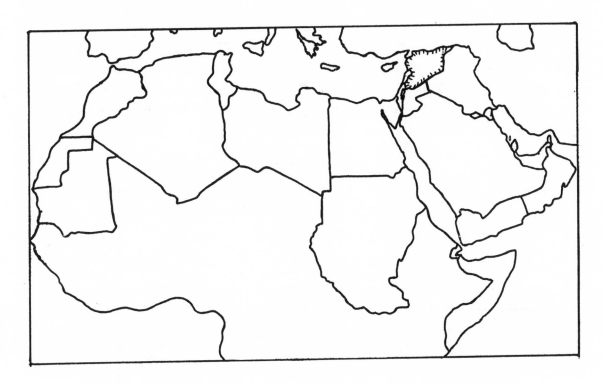

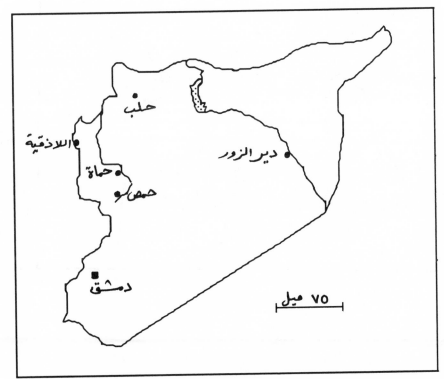

الإسم الكامل	الجمهورية العربية السورية
المساحة	٧١٫٥ الف ميل مربع
عدد السكان	١٢ مليون نسمة
المدن الرئيسية	دمشق (١٫٢٩٢٫٠٠٠)، حلب (١٫٢١٦٫٠٠٠)، حمص (٤٣١٫٠٠٠)،
	اللاذقية (٢٤١٫٠٠٠)، حماة (٢١٤٫٠٠٠)
اللغات	العربية، التركية، الكردية، الأرمنية
الدين	الإسلام (٩٠٪)، المسيحية (١٠٪)
اسم الحاكم	الرئيس حافظ الأسد
سنة الاستقلال	١٩٤٤
العملة	الليرة السورية
الدخل السنوي للفرد	١٢٦٠ دولار

سوريا دولة عربية في غرب آسيا. يحدّها من الشرق العراق ومن الشمال تركيا ومن الجنوب الأردن ومن الغرب اسرائيل ولبنان والبحر الأبيض المتوسط.

مساحة سوريا ٧١، ٤٩٨ ميل مربّع، وعدد سكّانها أكثر من ١٢ مليون نسمة. عاصمة سوريا مدينة دمشق، ومن المدن الرئيسية: حَلَب في الشمال، وحمص وحماة في الوسط، واللاذقيّة على شاطئ البحر الأبيض المتوسط.

اللغة الرسمية في سوريا هي اللغة العربية وهناك أقليات تتكلم اللغات التركية والكردية والأرمنية. أكثر سكان سوريا مسلمون، وفيها أقلّية مسيحية.

تاريخ سوريا طويل: دخلها المصريون سنة ١٥٠٠ قبل الميلاد (ق.م.)، ثم دخلها العبرانيون والآشوريون والكلدانيون والفرس واليونان. ومن سنة ٦٤ ق.م. الى سنة ٦٣٦ ميلادية (م.) كانت سوريا جزءاً من الامبراطورية الرومانية. دخل العرب سوريا سنة ٦٣٦ م.، وصارت دمشق عاصمة الدولة الإسلامية وصارت سوريا مركزاً تجارياً مهماً. ومن سنة ١٥١٦ الى الحرب العالمية الأولى كانت سوريا جزءاً من الإمبراطورية العثمانية. بعد الأتراك العثمانيين جاء الفرنسيون وحكموا سوريا من الحرب العالمية الأولى الى الحرب العالمية الثانية. استقلّت سوريا سنة ١٩٤٤.

Indicate whether each of the following statements is true or false.
1. Syria is located to the east of the Mediterranean. _____
2. Syria's full name is "the Syrian Arab Republic." _____
3. One of Syria's major cities is situated on the Mediterranean coast. _____
4. The majority of Syrians are Christians. _____
5. The names of only four Syrian cities are mentioned in the passage. _____
6. The Greeks ruled Syria after the Arabs. _____
7. Syria was an important trade center in the Muslim Empire. _____
8. Syria became independent right after the defeat of Turkey in World War I. _____
9. Syria was part of the Roman Empire for 700 years. _____

كلمات جديدة

to border	حدّ (يحدّ)	president	رئيس
official	رَسمي	shore	شاطِئ
the Hebrews	العبرانيون	B.C.	قبل الميلاد (ق.م.)
the Chaldeans	الكلدانيّون	the Assyrians	الآشوريّون
part	جُزْء	the Persians	الفُرس
		empire	امبراطوريّة
to become independent	استقلّ	World War I	الحرب العالميّة الأولى

تمرين

اقرأ

Match the singular with its plural. One word in the singular column does not have a matching plural.

مساجد	نَهر
قرى	مركز
مَكاتب	مسجد
أجزاء	كنيسة
أنهار	مَكتبة
مكتبات	مرّة
مَزارع	مَكتب
مراكز	مزرعة
كنائس	جُزْء
	قَرية

الدرس رقم ٣٠

اسمع

الله يرحم ايام زمان !
كنا نطبخ ونخبز ونغسل
وعمر الواحدة منا
٨ سنوات . بنات اليوم
عمر الواحدة ١٨ سنة
وما بتقدر تعلي بيضة .

أسئلة

1. What does Sharif's mother do?
_____

2. When does she help her husband?
_____

3. How long did she go to school?
_____

4. Why did she leave school?
_____

5. How many children did they have when they went to Irbid?
_____

كلمات جديدة

grandmother   جَدّة   sometimes   أَحْياناً

١٧١

أسئلة

1. Who came to see Dan?

_____

2. What did Dan say in answer to the question, "In your opinion, which is better Jordan or America?"

_____

3. When did Dan arrive in Jordan?

_____

4. How many siblings does Dan have?

_____

5. Is Dan's sister younger or older than he is?

_____

6. Where does an unmarried woman live in Jordan?

_____

كلمات جديدة

guest	ضيف	neighbor	جار
opinion	رأي	correct	مَزبوط
		by herself	لوحدها

اقرأ

دمـشق

دمشق عاصمة سوريا وأكبر مدينة فيها، تقع في جنوب غرب الدولة
قرب الحدود اللبنانية ويمر منها نهر بردى. عدد سكان دمشق حوالي مليون
وثلاثمئة الف نسمة. دمشق من أقدم المدن في العالم؛ يزيد عمرها على
٥٠٠٠ سنة.

في دمشق مركز الحكومة السورية وجامعة دمشق والمكتبة الوطنية
والجامع الأموي وجامع السلطان سليمان وقبر صلاح الدين، القائد المسلم
المعروف. ودمشق مركز الصناعة والتجارة والسياحة والبنوك، وفيها مطار
دولي كبير. وهي مشهورة بأسواقها القديمة مثل سوق الحميدية.

أكثر الناس في دمشق يسكنون في شقق، ولكن كثير منهم يسكنون
في بيوت قديمة جميلة.

كانت دمشق مدينة مهمة في زمن الآشوريين واليونان والرومان
البيزنطيين. دخل العرب المسلمون دمشق سنة ٦٣٥ م. وصارت عاصمة الدولة
الإسلامية في زمن الأمويين. وبعد العرب جاء الأتراك المسلمون وحكموا
دمشق من سنة ١٥١٦ م. الى الحرب العالمية الأولى. وبعد الأتراك جاء
الفرنسيون، الذين حكموا سوريا من سنة ١٩٢٠ الى سنة ١٩٤٤، سنة
استقلال سوريا.

1. What is the population of Damascus?

_____

2. How old is Damascus?

_____

3. Name two important landmarks found in Damascus?

_____

4. Where do most people live in Damascus?

_____

5. When did the Muslim Arabs enter Damascus?

_____

6. When did the Turks rule Damascus?

_____

7. Who ruled Damascus from 1920 until Syria's independence?

_____

كلمات جديدة

national	وَطنيّ	borders	حُدود
grave, tomb	قَبر	mosque	جامِع=مسجد
(well)-known	معروف	leader	قائد
tourism	سياحة	industry	صناعة
international	دَوْلي	bank	بنك (بنوك)
market	سوق (أسواق)	famous	مَشهور
beautiful	جَميل	people	ناس
the Umayyads	الأمويّين	time, era	زَمَن
		who (m. pl.)	الّذين=اللي

١٧٤

قواعد

Subject/Person Markers in MSA

The following table shows the person/subject markers of فـصـحـى. The Levantine Arabic verb paradigm is similar to that of فـصـحـى , with a few differences. (Dual forms in فـصـحـى as well as second and third person feminine plural forms are not included in the table since I do not believe that they are essential in an elementary Arabic course.)

كتب   "to write"

		Perfect		Imperfect	
هو	"he"	كتب	katab	يَكتُب	yaktub
هـي	"she"	كتبت	katabat	تَكتُب	taktub
هـم	"they"	كتبـوا	katabu	يَكتبون	yaktubuun
انتَ	"you, m.s."	كتبتَ	katabta	تكتُب	taktub
أنت	"you, f.s."	كتبت	katabti	تَكتُبـين	taktubiin
أنتـم	"you, pl.m."	كتبـتُمَ	katabtum	تكتبون	taktubuun
أنـا	"I"	كتبتُ	katabt	أكتُب	aktub
نـحن	"we"	كتبنا	katabna	نَكتُب	naktub

Note that ا is added after و of the plural (واو الجـمـاعـة) at the end of the verb to indicate plural person. This ا is written but is never pronounced.

تمارين

١. اقرأ (كلمات متقاطعة)

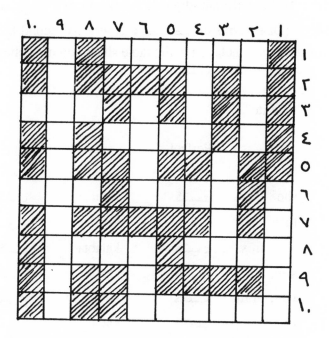

أفقي

١. شرق السعودية وغرب ايران

٣. نعمله من الحليب

٤. عكس غالي

٦. تلفون؛ نسافر فيه

٨. عكس حارّ؛ عكس وراء

١٠. جمع دكّان

عمودي

١. وسط المدينة

٢. عكس أقرب

٣. جمع شهر

٤. بندورة وبطاطا وخيار

٦. جمع ضيف؛ ١٠٠ سنة

٩. بحر صغير غرب الأردن ليس فيه سمك

١٧٦

٢. إملاء

١. الفندق قريب.

٢. أختي ربّة بيت.

٣. هو طبيب في مستشفى الجامعة.

٤. هي مهندسة وتعمل في مكتب.

٣. تكلّم

Create a dialogue with another student in which you compare the towns, cities, or countries you come from.

الدرس رقم ٣١

اسمـع

أسئلة

1. How old is Abdalla?

_____

2. Where did he attend high school?

_____

3. What does he do now?

_____

4. Why didn't his parents want him to go to America?

_____

5. How much does it cost to live and study in America for a year?

_____

6. Why does Abdalla's mother think that Yarmouk University is suitable for her son?

_____

كلمات جديدة

secondary	ثانَوي
College of Commerce, Business	كُلِّيّة التجارة
study	دراسة
travel	سَفَر
ticket	تَذكَرة
to cost	كلّف (يكلّف)
to bring, get	جاب (يجيب)
enough	كافي

حوار

طيب يوم الجمعة انا باجي للفندق وبنفتش على شقة مع بعض.

أسئلة

1. What is Dan going to study?

_____

2. Where is Dan going to live?

_____

3. Has Dan found an apartment?

_____

4. When is Abu Sharif going to meet Dan in Amman?

_____

5. Does Abu Sharif know Amman well?

_____

كلمات جديدة

subject, course	مادّة	literature	أدب
together	مع بعض	until now, so far	لحدّ هلأ
	all of it ("from its beginning to its end")	من أوّلها لآخرها	
don't mention it	لا شكراً على واجب	thanks a lot	شكراً جزيلاً

١٨.

لبنان

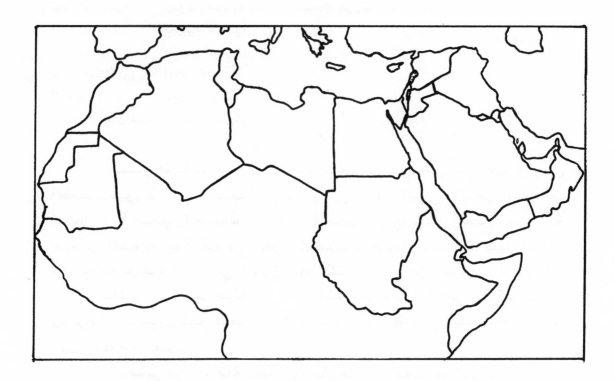

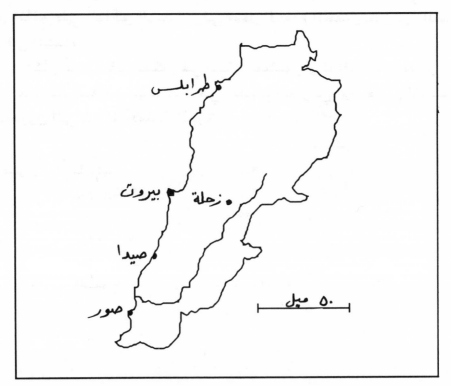

الإسم الكامل	الجمهورية اللبنانية
المساحة	١٥،٤٠٠ ميل مربع (١٠،٤٠٠ كم مربع)
عدد السكان	٣،٥٧٥ مليون نسمة
المدن الرئيسية	بيروت (العاصمة ٥٠٠،٠٠٠ نسمة)، طرابلس، صيدا، صور
اللغات	العربية، الأرمنية
اسم الحاكم	الرئيس الياس الهراوي
سنة الاستقلال	١٩٤١-١٩٤٦
العملة	الليرة اللبنانية
الدخل السنوي للفرد	٧٠٠ دولار أمريكي

لبنان دولة عربية في غرب آسيا. يحدّ لبنان من الشرق ومن الشمال سوريا ومن الجنوب اسرائيل ومن الغرب البحر الأبيض المتوسط. لبنان دولة صغيرة مساحتها ١٥،٤٠٠ ميل مربع. يتكون لبنان من أربع مناطق: المنطقة الساحلية في الغرب ثم منطقة جبلية ثم منطقة سهل البقاع ثم منطقة جبلية ثانية في الشرق. تقع أكثر الأرض الزراعية في لبنان في سهل البقاع الذي يزيد طوله على ١١٥ كيلومتر وعرضه على ١٥ كيلومتر. ويزرع اللبنانيون فيه الخضار مثل البندورة والبطاطا والبصل، والفواكه مثل التفاح والعنب.

الطقس في المنطقة الساحلية حار في الصيف ومعتدل في الشتاء، وينزل الثلج على المناطق الجبلية. وفي سهل البقاع الطقس حار في الصيف وبارد في الشتاء.

أكثر من نصف السكان في لبنان مسلمون والباقي مسيحيون، وفي لبنان أعلى نسبة مسيحيين في العالم العربي، وينقسم المسلمون والمسيحيون الى طوائف دينية كثيرة.

المسيحيون		
مارونيون	٩٠٠،٠٠٠	٢٥،١٪
روم اورثودكس	٢٥٠،٠٠٠	٧٪
أرمن	١٧٥،٠٠٠	٤،٩٪
روم كاثوليك	١٥٠،٠٠٠	٤،٢٪
طوائف أخرى	٥٠،٠٠٠	١،٤٪
المجموع	١،٥٢٥،٠٠٠	٤٢،٦٪

المسلمون	شيعة	۱٬۱۰۰٬۰۰۰	۳۰٫۸٪
	سنة	۷۵۰٬۰۰۰	۲۱٪
	دروز	۲۰۰٬۰۰۰	٥٫٦٪
	المجموع	۲٬۰٥۰٬۰۰۰	٥۷٫٤٪

أسئلة

1. What borders Lebanon on the west?

2. How many areas does Lebanon consist of? What are they?

3. Where is most of Lebanon's agricultural land located?

4. How is the weather in the coastal area?

5. What percentage of the total population of Lebanon is Christian?

6. What are the names of the Muslim sects in Lebanon?

كلمات جديدة

coastal	ساحلي	to consist of	تكوّن (يتكوّن)
width	عَرض	plain	سَهل
grapes	عنَب	onions	بَصَل
high	عالي	remaining	باقي
to be divided	انقَسم (ينقسم)	percentage, ratio	نسبة
Maronites	مارونيون	sects	طَوائف
total	مَجموع	other	أخرى

۱۸۳

اكتب

Fill in the blank spaces in the following.

لبنان ــــــ عربيـة في ــــــ ــــــ آسيـا. يحدّ لبنان من الشرق
ومن ــــــ سـوريا ومن الجنوب اسرائيل ومن الغرب ــــــ ــــــ ــــــ
المتوسط. ــــــ دولة صغيرة مسـاحتها ١٥،٤ ميل ــــــ ــــــ يتكون
لبنان من أربع ــــــ: المنطقة السـاحليـة في ــــــ ثم منطقة جبلية ثم
منطقـة سهل البقـاع ثم ــــــ جبليـة ثانيـة في الشرق. تقع أكثر الأرض
الزراعيـة في لبنان في ــــــ البقـاع الذي يزيد طولـه على ١١٥ كيلومتر
وعرضـه على ١٥ ــــــ ويزرع اللبنانيـون فيـه ــــــ مثل البندورة
والبطاطا والبصل ــــــ و ــــــ مثل التفاح والعنب.

الدرس رقم ٣٢

اسمع

أسئلة

1. What does Suad do?

_____

2. What does Suad have at the end of the year?

_____

3. What can Suad do if she passes the Tawjihi exam with high grades?

_____

4. Why is she thinking of studying in America?

_____

5. What subjects is Suad worried about?

_____

كلمات جديدة

end	نِهاية	class, grade	صَفّ
grade	علامة	the Tawjihi exam	امتحان التوجيهي
except	الا	high	عالي
afraid	خايف	math	رياضيّات

١٨٦

أسئلة

1. What did Dan want Abu Sharif to do?

_____

2. Where is the pain?

_____

3. Did Abu Sharif think it is a good idea to go to the hospital?

_____

4. Had Dan eaten *mansaf* before?

_____

5. What does Abu Sharif believe is the cause of Dan's sickness?

_____

6. What does Um Sharif think is the cause?

_____

كلمات جديدة

I hope you're OK	سلامتك	ask for, request, call	طلَب (يطلُب)
pain	وَجع	sick	مَريض
stomach	بَطن	head	راس
luck, lot	نصيب	poor, unfortunate	مَسكين
fatigue	تَعَب	to be sick	مرِض
everything	كُل شيء	to come out	طلِع (يطلَع)

١٨٨

اقرأ

بيروت

بيروت عاصمة لبنان وأكبر مدينة فيه. عدد سكانها أكثر من نصف
مليون نسمة. بيروت مدينة قديمة، يزيد عمرها على ٣٠٠٠ سنة.

تقع بيروت على الساحل الشرقي للبحر الأبيض المتوسط، وهي
المركز الثقافي والتجاري في لبنان، ومركز الحكومة ايضاً. فيها جامعات
وكليات كثيرة منها الجامعة الأمريكية، الجامعة العربية، الجامعة اللبنانية،
كلية بيروت الجامعية وجامعة سينت جوزف.

كانت بيروت قبل الحرب الأهلية مركزاً مهماً للتجارة والسياحة
والثقافة في الشرق الأوسط، ولكن الحرب الأهلية دمّرت التجارة والسياحة
والاقتصاد.

تاريخ بيروت طويل. اسّسها الفينيقيّون، وبعد الفينيقيّين حكمها
الآشوريون، وبعد الاشوريين حكمها اليونان والرومان. وصارت بيروت جزءاً
من الدولة العربية الإسلامية سنة ٦٣٥ ميلادية. ومن سنة ١٥١٦ الى الحرب
العالمية الأولى كانت بيروت جزءاً من الإمبراطورية العثمانية، ومن الحرب
العالمية الأولى وحتى استقلال لبنان سنة ١٩٤٦ كانت تحت الحكم الفرنسي.

أسئلة

1. What is the population of Beirut?

_____

2. How old is Beirut?

_____

3. Name two universities located in Beirut.

_____

4. What destroyed the commercial quarter of Beirut?

_____

5. Who founded Beirut?

_____

كلمات جديدة

also	أيضاً=كمان	cultural	ثقافي
to destroy	دَمَّر	civil war	حَرب أَهليّة
to found	أسّس	economy	اقتصاد
under	تَحت	the Phoenicians	الفَينيقيون

أغنية

بابوري رايح (موفق بهجت)

بابوري شق البحر وامواجه عليت فوق
ما ادري يا خلّي ميّ ما ادري غلبني الشوق

بابوري رايح رايح بابوري جاي
بابوري محمّل سكّر وشاي

بابوري رايح على بيروت
رايح يجيب مرجان وياقوت
عالبعد يا حبيبي راح اموت
بالله الحقوني بشربة ميّة

دخل الله عجّل يا بابور
وعلى دقّة قلبي لفّ ودور
بيني وبينهم سبع بحور
عجّل لا تمشي شويّة شويّة

حمّي بخارك عاالألفين
واسرع وسابق نظر العين
يا بابور لو تعرف رايح فين
لتطير طيران من فوق الميّة.

تمارين

١. اكتب

Fill in the blank spaces in the following.

بيروت ———— لبنان وأكبر ———— ———— فيه. عدد سكانها أكثر
من نصف ———— ———— نسمة. بيروت مدينة ———— ———— يزيد عمرها على
———— ٣...

تقع بيروت على الساحل ———— للبحر الأبيض ————،
وهي المركز الثقافي ———— في لبنان، و———— الحكومة ايضاً. فيها
جامعات وكليات كثيرة منها ———— الأمريكية، الجامعة العربية،
———— اللبنانية، كلية بيروت الجامعية و———— سينت جوزف.

كانت بيروت قبل ———— الأهلية مركزاً مهماً للتجارة والسياحة
والثقافة في ———— الأوسط، ولكن الحرب ———— ———— دمّرت التجارة
والسياحة و————.

٢. املاء

اسمي جمال. أنا طالب في الجامعة الأمريكية في بيروت. أنا ساكن
مع أبي وأمي وأخي وأختي في شقّة في مدينة بيروت.

٣. تكلّم

Create a dialogue with another student similar to the one between Abu Sharif and
Dan.

الدرس رقم ٣٣

اسمع

أسئلة

1. How long is he thinking of working in Saudi Arabia?

_____

2. Why does he want to save money?

_____

3. Can Suad go and work in Saudi Arabia?

_____

4. Would Suad's parents let her travel to America if she had money?

_____

كلمات جديدة

to think	فكّر (يفكّر)
to collect, save (money)	جَمَع (يجمَع)
in any case	على كل حال
to allow	سَمَح (يسمَح)

١٩٣

أسئلة

1. Did Abu Sharif want a furnished apartment?

_____

2. How many bedrooms does he want?

_____

3. What kind of bathroom did he want?

_____

4. How much is the rent going to be?

_____

كلمات جديدة

furnished	مفروش
how many?	كم واحد؟
for the sake of	على شان

العراق

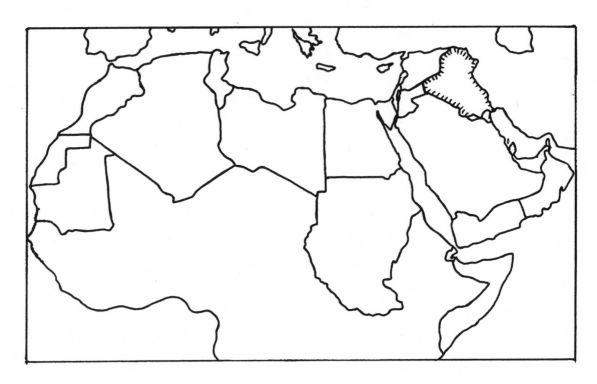

الإسم الكامل	الجمهورية العراقية
المساحة	١٢٠.١٦٧ ميل مربع (٤٣٤.٩١٣ كم مربع)
عدد السكان	١٨.٨٠٠.٠٠٠ نسمة
المدن الرئيسية	بغداد (العاصمة ٤.٦٤٨.٠٠٠ نسمة)، البصرة (٦١٦.٧٠٠)، الموصل (٥٧٠.٩٣٠)
اللغات	العربية، الكردية، الكلدانية، الآشورية، التركية
الدين	الإسلام (٩٧٪)، المسيحية (٣٪)
اسم الحاكم	الرئيس صدّام حُسين
سنة الاستقلال	١٩٣٢
العملة	الدينار
الدخل السنوي للفرد	١٩٥٠ دولار أمريكي

يقع العراق بين ايران في الشرق، تركيا في الشمال، سوريا والأردن في الغرب، والسعودية والكويت والخليج العربي في الجنوب. يمر من العراق نهران كبيران هما دجلة والفرات. يتكون العراق من مناطق صحراوية ومناطق زراعية خصبة ومناطق جبلية. تقع المناطق الصحراوية غرب نهر الفرات، والأراضي الزراعية الخصبة بين دجلة والفرات، والمناطق الجبلية في الشمال الشرقي.

يختلف الطقس في العراق من منطقة الى منطقة، ومن فصل الى آخر. ففي المناطق الجبلية في الشمال الطقس بارد في الشتاء ومعتدل في الصيف. وقد تصل درجة الحرارة الصفر المئوي (٣٢ درجة فهرنهايت) في شهر كانون الثاني (يناير) في تلك المناطق. أما في المناطق الأخرى (الوسط والجنوب والغرب) فالطقس معتدل في الشتاء وحار في الصيف. مثلاً في العاصمة بغداد، التي تقع في وسط العراق، متوسط درجة الحرارة ١٠ درجات مئوية (٥٠ درجة فهرنهايت) في شهر كانون الثاني و٣٣ درجة مئوية (٩٠ درجة فهرنهايت) في شهر تمّوز (يوليو). وقد تزيد درجة الحرارة في المناطق الجنوبية مثل مدينة البصرة على ٤٥ درجة مئوية (١١٣ درجة فهرنهايت) في شهور الصيف.

كذلك تختلف كمية المطر من منطقة الى منطقة في العراق. ففي المناطق الشمالية الشرقية قد تزيد كمية المطر على ١٠٠٠ مليمتر (٤٠ انش) في السنة، وفي الوسط والغرب والجنوب قد لا تصل ٢٥٠ ملمتر في السنة.

أكثر سكان العراق عرب مسلمون، ولكن هناك مسلمون غير عرب ومسيحيون. نسبة العرب حوالي ٧٥٪، ونسبة المسلمين حوالي ٩٧٪ من السكان. ينقسم المسلمون الى الشيعة وهم أكثر السكان، والسنّة، واليزيديون. واليزيديون أقلّيّة صغيرة تسكن في شمال العراق.

أهم الأقلّيات غير العربية في العراق: الأكراد والكلدانيون والآشوريون والأرمن واليهود. الأكراد مسلمون وهم أكبر أقلية غير عربية (حوالي ٢٠٪ من السكان)، والكلدانيون والآشوريون والأرمن أقليات مسيحية صغيرة، ويتكلمون لغات غير اللغة العربية، ويسكنون في شمال العراق.

أسئلة

1. What percentage of the Iraqis are Muslim?

_____

2. What is the average annual income of an Iraqi?

_____

3. What borders Iraq to the south?

_____

4. Where is the rich agricultural land located?

_____

5. How is the weather in the northern areas?

_____

6. How much rain falls on the northeastern areas of Iraq annually?

_____

7. What is the biggest non-Arab minority in Iraq?

_____

8. What is the religion of the Chaldeans?

_____

9. Do the Assyrians speak a language other than Arabic?

_____

كلمات جديدة

the Tigris River	دجلة	gulf	خليج
another, other	آخَر (أخرى .f)	the Euphrates River	الفُرات
centigrade	مئوي	zero	صفر
that (f.)	تلك	as for	أمّا . . . فـ
also	كذلك	average	مُتوسّط
millimeter	ملمتر	quantity	كمّيّة
		most important	أهمّ

Note

The phrase نهران كبيران in the passage translates as "two big rivers." It is the dual form of نهر كبير in the nominative case.

قواعد

Verb Types (continued)

It was mentioned earlier that Arabic verbs are divided into categories on the basis of their root elements. A verb is *sound* if it has three consonants in the three consonantal positions of the root, *hollow* if it has و or ي in the second consonant position, *lame* if it has و or ي in the third consonant position, and *assimilated* if it has و or ي in the first consonant postition. The و and ي of hollow and lame verbs are generally realized as ١ or ى in the perfect form of the verb. Another verb type is called the *doubled* verb. It is a verb in which the second and third consonants of the root are identical, as in حبّ (ḥabb) "to like, love."

تمارين

١. اكتب

Classify the following verbs into different types: sound, hollow, lame, assimilated, or doubled.

كتب، وجد، كان، مشى، ظلّ، فتح، سكن، عرف، عمل، حدّ، سمع، وصل، قال، حجز، نام

٢. اكتب

Fill in the blank spaces in the following:

أكثر ــــــــ العراق عرب مسلمون، ولكن هناك مسلمون غير عرب ومسيحيون. نسبة ــــــــ ــــــــ حوالي ٧٥٪، ونسبة المسلمين ــــــــ ٩٧٪ من السكان. ينقسم المسلمون الى الشيعة وهم أكثر السكان، والسنّة، واليزيديون. واليزيديون أقلية ــــــــ ويسكنون في ــــــــ العراق.

أهم الأقليات غير العربية في العراق ــــــــ والكلدانيون والآشوريون والأرمن واليهود. الأكراد مسلمون وهم أكبر أقلية غير عربية (حوالي ٢٠٪ من ــــــــ)، والكلدانيون والآشوريون والأرمن أقليات ــــــــ صغيرة، ويتكلمون لغات ــــــــ اللغة العربية، ويسكنون في شمال العراق.

٣. املاء

اسمي فريد. أنا طالب في جامعة جورجتاون. أنا أسكن في شقة صغيرة. هي قريبة من الجامعة. في شقتي غرفة نوم واحدة.

٤. تكلّم

Create a dialogue with another student in which one is a prospective tenant and the other a rental agent.

اسمــع

أسئلة

1. Why did he go to the vegetable market?
_____

2. Where did he go first?
_____

3. How much were the tomatoes that the first vendor had?
_____

4. How much were the tomatoes that the second vendor had?
_____

5. From whom did he buy fruits and vegetables?
_____

6. Where did he go after buying the fruits and vegetables?
_____

7. How much meat did he buy?
_____

8. What did he say to himself?
_____

كلمات جديدة

as you (pl.) know	مثل ما بتعرفوا
seller, vendor	بيّاع
piastre	قرش
be reasonable	حرام عليك
less than	أقلّ
how much, what is the price of	كم سعر
God	رَبّ
high prices, inflation	غلاء

- بكم كيلو البندورة من فضلك؟ كل شيء حسب التسعيرة الحكومية.

أسئلة

1. How many kinds of tomatoes are there?
_____
2. How much is a kilogram of local tomatoes?
_____
3. When did the cucumbers reach the store?
_____
4. What happens to local bananas?
_____
5. What vegetables and fruits did Dan buy?
_____
6. How much did he pay?
_____
7. How far is Ash-Sha'b grocery?
_____
8. Where is the butcher shop?
_____

كلمات جديدة

pricing	تَسعيرة	according to	حَسب
fresh	طازة	local, domestic	بلدي
watermelon	بطّيخ	to sell	باع (يبيع)
honey	عسل	like	زَيّ = مثل
enough	كافي	for sure	أكيد
butcher	لحّام	my dear sir	يا سيدي
hand	ايد	butcher shop	مَلحمة

تكلّم

Create a dialogue with another student in which one of you is a customer buying fruits and vegetables from a fruit vender or grocery keeper.

اقرأ

الأكراد

عائلة كردية في خيمة للاجئين في شمال العراق

يعيش الأكراد في بلاد كردستان وهي مناطق جبلية في ايران والعراق
وتركيا وسوريا وأرمينيا وأزربيجان. يزيد عدد الأكراد على ١٠ ملايين نسمة؛
وهم أكبر أقلية في العراق وتركيا. ومن أهمّ المدن الكردية إربيل،
السليمانية، الموصل، وكركوك في العراق.

أصل الأكراد غير معروف، ولكن يُعتقد أنّهم من أصل هندي-أوروبي،
والدليل على ذلك أن لغتهم قريبة من اللغة الفارسية. والأكراد مسلمون
سنّيون، وقد دخلوا الإسلام في القرن السابع الميلادي.

علاقة الأكراد بالدول التي يعيشون فيها ليست جيدة لأنهم يريدون
الإستقلال ويحاربون من أجله. ففي تركيا مثلاً يُسمّى الأكراد "أتراك الجبال"،
لأن الحكومة التركية لا تعترف بهم، وكانت لا تسمح لهم باستعمال لغتهم.
وفي العراق حاربتهم الحكومة مدة طويلة ودمّرت الكثير من قراهم.

فشلت كل محاولات الأكراد للاستقلال الا مرة واحدة؛ ففي سنة ١٩٤٦ تأسّست دولة "مهراباد" الكردية في ايران بمساعدة سوفييتية، ولكن الدولة استمرت سنة واحدة فقط.

من أشهر رجال الأكراد صلاح الدين الأيوبي القائد المسلم المعروف الذي انتصر على الصليبيين في معركة حطين سنة ١١٨٧. ومن أشهر رجالهم في القرن العشرين مصطفى البرزاني الذي أسّس الحزب الديمقراطي الكردي سنة ١٩٥٨ وقاد الأكراد في حربهم مع الحكومة العراقية من أجل الاستقلال.

أسئلة

1. Where do the Kurds live?

_____

2. What is the origin of the Kurds believed to be?

_____

3. When did the Kurds become Muslim?

_____

4. What characterizes the relationship between the Kurds and the government they live under? Why?

_____

5. How are the Kurds treated in Turkey? Explain.

_____

6. a. When did the Kurds have their own state?

_____

   b. What was the state called?

_____

   c. How long did it last?

_____

   d. Where was it located?

_____

7. Who is Mustafa Barazani?

_____

كلمات جديدة

origin	أصل	to live	عاش (يعيش)
proof, evidence	دَليل	to believe	أعتقَد (يعتقد)
not	ليس = مش	relationship	عَلاقَة
because	لأنّ	good	جيّد=كويس
for the sake of	مِن أجل = على شان	to want	أراد (يريد) = بدّ...
to recognize	اعترف (يعترف) بـ	to name, call	سمّى (يسمّي)
using	استعمال	to allow	سمح (يسمَح)
villages	قُرى (م. قرية)	to fight	حارَب
attempt	مُحاوَلة	to fail	فَشل
to continue	استمرّ	help	مُساعَدة
		only	فقط = بـسّ
		to defeat, be victorious over	انتصر على
		the Crusaders	الصليبيّين
battle	مَعركة	(political) party	حِزب
to lead	قاد		

قواعد

Negation with ليس and غير

Nonverbal elements are negated in MSA by using ليس or غــــير. (Remember that such elements are negated by using مـش in Levantine.) غــــير is used only with adjectives, and لــــيس is used with adjectives, nouns, and prepositional phrases:

العنوان غير معروف.   "The address is not known, unknown."

تركيا ليست عربية.   "Turkey is not Arab."

طرابلس ليست في سوريا.   "Tripoli is not in Syria."

نجد ليست مدينة، هي صحراء.   "Najd is not a city; it is a desert."

Pronouns Attached to Conjunctions

The same set of pronouns that are used to indicate possession in nouns can be suffixed to conjunctions like لكنّ "but," لأنّ "because," and إنّ and أنّ, both of which are translated as "that." The pronoun in this case functions as the subject of a clause:

أصل الأكراد غير معروف، ولكن يُعتَقَد أنّهم (أنّهم) من أصل هندي-أوروبي.

"The origin of the Kurds is not known, but it is believed that <u>they</u> are of Indo-European origin."

علاقة الأكراد بالدول التي يعيشون فيها ليست جيدة لأنّهم (لأنّهم) يريدون الإستقلال.

"The relationship of the Kurds with the states in which they live is not good because <u>they</u> want independence."

The following table shows the conjunction لأنّ with the full set of pronouns attached to it. إنّ, لكنّ and أنّ, are treated the same way. (The forms are given in their MSA and Levantine pronunciations. Some MSA forms, i.e., dual and feminine plural, are not listed because they are not likely to be encountered in this book.)

<u>MSA</u>	<u>Levantine</u>	
لأنَّهُ	لأنّه	"because he"
لأنَّها	لأنّها	"because she"
لأنَّهُم	لأنّهُم	"because they, m."
لأنَّكَ	لأنّك	"because you, m.s."
لأنَّكِ	لأنّك	"because you, f.s."
لأنَّكُم	لأنّكُم	"because you, m.pl."
لأنّي، لأنّني	لأنّي	"because I"
لأنّنا	لأنّا	"because we"

تمرين
اقرأ واكتب

Give the singular form of each of the following words:

جَوامـع
بُنـوك
أسـواق
علامـات
مـوادّ
مُستمعين
قُرى

اسمع

أسئلة

1. Who spoke with Sharif yesterday?

_____

2. Where was he?

_____

3. Where did he come from yesterday?

_____

4. What was his problem?

_____

5. Where was the money?

_____

6. Does he know people in Canada?

_____

كلمات جديدة

شنطة يَد   handbag

لا سـايح ولا موظف. أنا طالب في الجامعة الاردنية.

أسئلة

1. Where are Dan and Jalal going?

_____

2. When did Dan arrive in Jordan?

_____

3. What does Dan study?

_____

كلمات جديدة

tourist	سايح	you (formal)	حَضرتك
employee	مُوظّف	job	وَظيفة
		by the way	على فِكرَة

مصر (١)

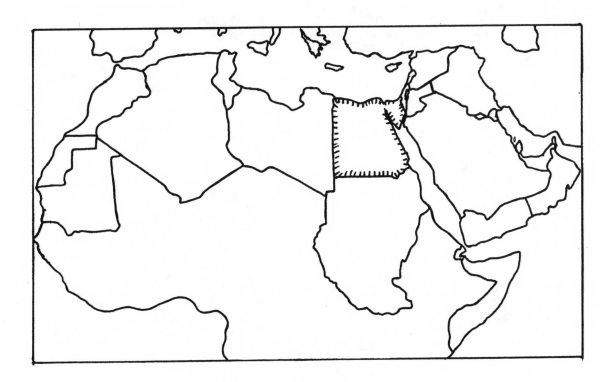

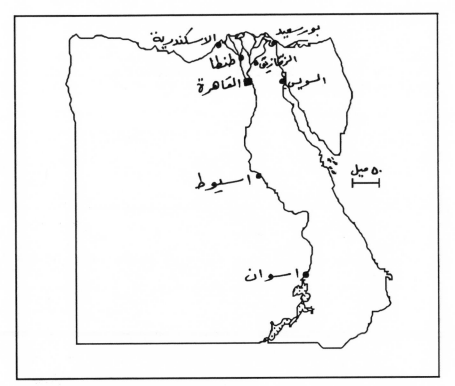

جمهورية مصر العربية	الإسم الكامل
٣٦٨ الف ميل مربع	المساحة
٥٥ مليون نسمة	عدد السكان
القاهرة (١٠ ملايين)، الإسكندرية، أسوان	المدن الرئيسية
العربية	اللغات
الإسلام (٩٠٪)، المسيحية (١٠٪)	الدين
الرئيس محمد حسني مبارك	اسم الحاكم
١٩٢٢	سنة الاستقلال
الجنيه المصري	العملة
٧٠٠ دولار أمريكي	الدخل السنوي للفرد

تقع جمهورية مصر العربية في شمال شرق إفريقيا. يحدّها من الغرب ليبيا ومن الجنوب السودان ومن الشرق البحر الأحمر وإسرائيل، ومن الشمال البحر الأبيض المتوسط. مصر أكبر دولة عربية بعدد السكان: يزيد عدد سكانها على ٥٥ مليون نسمة. مساحة مصر حوالي مليون كيلومتر مربّع، ولكن ٩٧٪ من أرضها صحراء. ويعيش أكثر المصريين في مساحة صغيرة بالقرب من نهر النيل، وأرض هذه المنطقة من أخصب الأرض في العالم.

يرجع تاريخ مصر الى سنة ٤٠٠٠ ق.م. وتأسست الإمبراطورية المصرية بين القرن السادس عشر والقرن الثالث عشر ق.م. احتلّ الفرس مصر سنة ٥٢٥ ق.م. واحتلها الإسكندر الكبير سنة ٣٣٢ ق.م. وبعده حكمت مصر عائلة "بطليموس"، وبعد انتهاء حكم عائلة بطليموس صارت مصر جزءاً من الإمبراطورية الرومانية.

دخل العرب المسلمون مصر سنة ٦٤١ ميلادية وصارت جزءاً من الدولة العربية الإسلامية، وفي سنة ١٥١٧ صارت مصر جزءاً من الإمبراطورية العثمانية.

احتلّ القائد الفرنسي نابليون مصر سنة ١٧٩٨ وبقي الفرنسيون فيها ثلاث سنوات. وفي سنة ١٨٠٥ م. صار محمّد علي حاكماً لمصر. كان محمد علي ضابطاً البانياً في الجيش التركي.

أرادت بريطانيا احتلال مصر بسبب موقعها الإستراتيجي على الطريق الى الهند، وخصوصاً بعد فتح قناة السويس سنة ١٨٦٩، واحتلها الجيش البريطاني سنة ١٨٨٢.

Indicate whether each of the following statements is true or false.
1. In terms of population, Egypt is the largest Arab country._____
2. Most Egyptians live in the desert._____
3. Some of Egypt's land is among the most fertile in the world._____
4. The Egyptian Empire was established between the sixteenth and thirteenth centuries B.C._____
5. Egypt was part of the Roman Empire._____
6. The Muslim Arabs ruled Egypt until it became part of the Ottoman Empire._____
7. Egypt became part of the Ottoman Empire in 1798._____
8. Muhammad Ali was a Turkish officer in Napoleon's army._____
9. The British army occupied Egypt in 1869. _____

كلمات جديدة

to occupy	احتلّ	to be founded	تأسّس
to remain	بَقِي=ظلّ	Ptolemy	بطليموس
army	جيش	officer	ضابط
because of	بسبب	occupation	احتلال
strategic	استراتيجي	location	موقع
India	الهند	road, way	طريق
		the Suez Canal	قناة السويس

تمارين

١. اكتب

Fill in the blanks in the following.

تقع ــــــ مصر العربية في ــــــ شرق إفريقيا. يحدّها من
ــــــ ليبيا ومن الجنوب السودان ومن الشرق ــــــ ــــــ
وإسرائيل، ومن الشمال ــــــ ــــــ ــــــ ــــــ مصر أكبر دولة
عربية بـ ــــــ ــــــ: يزيد عدد سكانها على ٥٥ مليون ــــــ
ــــــ مصر حوالي مليون كيلومتر ــــــ، ولكن ٩٧٪ من أرضها
ــــــ ويعيش أكثر المصريين في مساحة ــــــ بالقرب من ــــــ
النيل، وأرض هذه المنطقة من أخصب الأرض في ــــــ.

٢. اكتب

Classify the following verbs into different types: *sound, hollow, lame, assimilated,* or *doubled.*

وجد، ضاع، دخل، قعد، ركب، زار، نزل، سلم، مرّ، ذكر، بنى

٣. املاء

حلب مدينة كبيرة في شمال سوريا. هي بعيدة عن العاصمة دمشق
وقريبة من تركيا. الطقس في حلب بارد في الشتاء.

الدرس رقم ٣٦

أسئلة

1. Did Muhammad talk to the police?

_____

2. Did he talk to his embassy?

_____

3. Where is he going?

_____

4. What did he want?

_____

كلمات جديدة

شُرطَة   police   رجّع (يرجّع)   to return (something)

حوار

- درست البكالوريوس في جامعة كورنيل؟
- لا، في جامعة صغيرة في ولاية كولورادو.

أسئلة

1. What degree is Dan studying for now?

_____

2. Where did Dan get his B.A. degree?

_____

3. What was his undergraduate major?

_____

4. What is his major now?

_____

5. How many Arab students are at Cornell?

_____

كلمات جديدة

M.A. degree	ماجستير	B.A. degree	بكالوريوس
studies	دراسات	field of specialization	تَخصّص

٢١٥

اقرأ

مصر (٢)

استقلّت مصر عن بريطانيا سنة ١٩٢٢، ولكنّ البريطانيّين احتفظوا بقناة السويس. وفي سنة ١٩٥٢ قام الجيش المصري بانقلاب عسكري، وانتهت الملكية وصارت مصر جمهورية. كان آخر ملك مصري هو الملك فاروق وهو من عائلة محمد علي.

وفي سنة ١٩٥٦ أمّم الرئيس المصري جمال عبد الناصر قناة السويس وطرد الجيش البريطاني من مصر، فهجمت بريطانيا وفرنسا وإسرائيل على مصر واحتل الجيش الإسرائيلي قطاع غزّة وسيناء وقصفت الطائرات البريطانية والفرنسية المطارات المصرية. تدخّلت الولايات المتحدة والاتحاد السوفييتي وانتهت الحرب وانسحب الجيش الإسرائيلي من قطاع غزّة وسيناء.

وفي سنة ١٩٥٨ اتحدت مصر وسوريا وصارت الدولتان دولة واحدة اسمها "الجمهورية العربية المتّحدة"، ولكنّ سوريا انسحبت سنة ١٩٦١.

وفي سنة ١٩٦٧ قامت حرب بين الدول العربية وإسرائيل، وخسرت الدول العربية الحرب واحتلت إسرائيل قطاع غزّة وسيناء من مصر والضفة الغربية من الأردن والجولان من سوريا. ونتج عن الحرب إغلاق قناة السويس.

وفي ٦/ ١٠/ ١٩٧٣ قـامت حـرب أخـرى بـين العـرب وإسـرائيـل، وانسـحب الجيش الإسرائيلي من منطقة صغيـرة في سيناء وفُتـحت قناة السـويس.

وفي سنـة ١٩٧٧ زارالرئيس المصـري أنور السـادات القـدس وبدأت محـادثات سـلام بـين مصـر وإسرائيل بمساعدة الرئيس الأمريكي "جمي كارتر". وفي ٢٦/٤/ ١٩٧٩ وقّع الرئيس أنور السـادات و"مناحم بيجن" رئيس وزراء اسرائيل اتفاقية سلام بين مصر وإسرائيل. وفي ٦/١٠/ ١٩٨١ قُتل الرئيس المصري أنور السادات، وصار حسني مبارك رئيساً.

اسئلة

1. What did the British Army keep after Egypt became independent?
_____

2. What is the name of the last Egyptian monarch? When was he deposed?
_____

3. When did Jamal Abdul-Nasser nationalize the Suez Canal?
_____

4. What happened as a result of that?
_____

5. What is the United Arab Republic?
_____

6. How many wars did Egypt and Israel fight, according to the passage?
_____

7. What did Egypt lose in the 1967 war?
_____

8. What did President Anwar Sadat do in 1977?
_____

9. When was the Egyptian-Israeli peace treaty signed?
_____

كلمات جديدة

to keep	احتفظ (يحتفظ) بـ	to undertake	قام ـــــ بـ
military coup	انقلاب عَسكري	to come to an end	انتهى
monarchy	مَلَكيّة	to nationalize	أمّم
to expel	طرَد	to attack	هَجَم
the Gaza Strip	قطاع غزة	to shell, bombard	قصفَ
plane	طائرة=طيّارة	to intervene	تدخّل
the Soviet Union	الاتحاد السوفييتي	to withdraw	انسحب
to be united	اتّحد	to erupt, break out	قام (يقوم)
to lose	خَسِر	to result	نتَج
closing	إغلاق	discussions, talks	محادثات
help	مُساعدة	to sign	وقّع (يوقّع)
prime minister	رئيس وزراء	peace agreement	اتفاقيّة سلام
was killed	قُتِل		

أغنية

سافر مع السلامة (فريد الأطرش)

سافر مع السلامة!
ترجع لنا بالسلامة
ونشوفك بالسلامة

اكتب جوابات يا أعزّ حبيب
وابعث سلامات اطفي لي لهيبي
يمكن تطمّني
وانت بعيد عني.

تمارين

١. كلمات متقاطعة

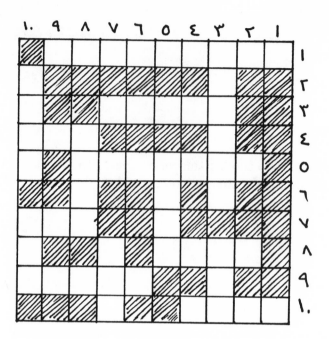

أفقي

١. قائد مسلم مشهور من أصل كردي

٣. مغنّية (singer) لبنانية مشهورة

٤. مدينة في الإمارات العربية المتحدة

٥. يأخذها الطالب من الجامعة بعد دراسة عدد من السنوات

٧. عكس صعب

٨. عكس جنوب

٩. نسافر بها لمسافات بعيدة

١٠. مسجد

عمودي

٣. نهر يمر في تركيا وسوريا والعراق؛ اسم حرف (letter) عربي

٥. شاطئ

٧. بيته عند بيتك

٨. جمع درس

١٠. عكس جديد أو حديث؛ العربية والإنجليزية والفرنسية

٢. اكتب

Classify the following verbs into different types: *sound, hollow, lame, assimilated,* or *doubled.*

حَكَم، دخَل، حدّ، وقع، قدِر، قسَم، جمَع، صار، سمَح، طلَب، ظلّ

٣. تكلّم

Create a dialogue with another student in which you ask and answer questions about your major and the courses you are taking.

اسمـع

أسئلة

1. Who talked to him on the phone?

_____

2. How much money was she willing to pay?

_____

3. When he said, "I am an engineering student, not an Arabic teacher," did she still want him to teach her?

_____

4. Did he have a lot of work to do at that time? Why?

_____

5. Where are they going to meet? When?

_____

6. How much Arabic did Cathy know?

_____

7. Does she want to learn to read Arabic?

_____

8. How often are they going to meet?

_____

كلمات جديدة

ready, willing	مُستعدّ	quickly	بسُرعة
vacation	عُطلة	to pay	دَفَع (يدفع)
library	مَكتبة	to agree	اتّفَق
		word	كلمة

‏- الدراسة في الجامعات الأمريكية غالية ولا رخيصة؟
‏- الجامعات الخاصة غالية، لكن الجامعات الحكومية أرخص.

أسئلة

1. How many universities are in America according to Dan?

_____

2. How many universities and colleges are there?

_____

3. How many universities are in Jordan?

_____

4. What is the population of Jordan?

_____

5. How much does a year at a state university cost in America?

_____

6. How much does a year at Harvard cost?

_____

كلمات جديدة

state, public	حُكومي	exactly	بالزبط
even	حتّى	it depends	بيعتَمِد

اقرأ ١

الجامعات المصرية

اسم الجامعة	سنة التأسيس	لغة التدريس	عدد الأساتذة	عدد الطلاب	عدد الكتب	نوع الجامعة
عين شمس	١٩٥٠	العربية	١٨٧٠	١٢١٥١٣	٩٢٠٠٠	حكومية
الأزهر	٩٧٠	العربية	٣٦٠٠	٩٠٠٠٠	٨٠٠٠٠	حكومية
الإسكندرية	١٩٤٢	العربية، الإنجليزية	٣١٨٠	٩٦٩٠٠	٢١٠٠٠	حكومية
أسيوط	١٩٥٧	العربية، الإنجليزية	٢٢٢٥	٤٤٦٦٠	غير معروف	حكومية
القاهرة	١٩٠٨	العربية، الإنجليزية، الفرنسية	٥٧٥٠	١١٣٦٠٠	مليون	حكومية
حلوان	١٩٧٠	العربية الإنجليزية	١١٠٠	٣٣٣٠٠	٩٢٠٠٠	حكومية
المنصورة	١٩٧٢	العربية	٩٣٠	٤٢١٤١	غير معروف	حكومية
المنوفية	١٩٧٦	العربية، الإنجليزية	٧٦٠	١٦٥٠٠	غير معروف	حكومية
المنيا	١٩٧٦	العربية، الإنجليزية	٣٤٠٠	١٦١٢٠	٨٨٥٠٠	حكومية
طنطا	١٩٧٢	العربية، الإنجليزية	٥٧٨	٣٣٧٩٥	١٩٠٠٠	حكومية
الزقازيق	١٩٧٤	العربية، الإنجليزية، الفرنسية	٢٢٣٦	٦٧٨٦٩	غير معروف	حكومية
الأمريكية	١٩١٩	الإنجليزية	١٣٨	٢٠٨٧	١٨٥٠٠٠	خاصّة

1. When were the following universities founded:

     Ain Shams _____

     al-Azhar _____

     Cairo _____

     Tanta _____

     the American University in Cairo (AUC) _____

2. What is the language of instruction at the following universities:

     al-Azhar _____

     Cairo _____

     the AUC _____

     al-Zaqaziq _____

3. How many students does each of the following universities have:

     Alexandria _____

     Asiout _____

     al-Zaqaziq _____

     al-Mansoura _____

4. How many books does each of the following universities have:

     al-Azhar _____

     Cairo _____

     Helwan _____

     al-Mansoura _____

     al-Minya _____

5. How many of the universities listed above are private? _____

الجامع الأزهر

يقع الجامع الأزهر في مدينة القاهرة في مصر، وهو من أهم مراكز التعليم في مصر والعالم الإسلامي. ويقول الكثيرون إنه أقدم جامعة في العالم، فقد بناه القائد الفاطمي جوهر الصقلي سنة ٩٧٠ ميلادية.

كان الأزهر مدرسة دينية يدرس فيها الطلاب علوم الدين الإسلامي واللغة العربية، وفي سنة ١٩٦١ فُتحت فيه ثلاث كلّيّات جديدة هي كليات الطب والهندسة والتجارة، وصار الأزهر جامعة حديثة.

عدد الطلّاب في الأزهر حوالي ٩٠ ألف طالب وعدد الأساتذة حوالي ٣٦٠٠ أستاذاً. ولكن مكتبة الأزهر صغيرة جداً: عدد الكتب فيها حوالي ٨٠ ألف كتاب فقط.

لغة التدريس في الأزهر هي اللغة العربية ويجيء له الطلاب المسلمون من كل بلاد العالم وخاصة من إفريقيا وآسيا.

أسئلة

1. When was a school of medicine opened at al-Azhar?

_____

2. Where do students come from to study at al-Azhar?

_____

language	لُغة	founding	تأسيس
type	نوع	teaching, instruction	تَدريس
religious	ديني	private	خاصّ
especially	خاصّةً = خصوصاً	modern	حَديث

قواعد

Plural Object Suffixes

The same set of pronominal suffixes used to indicate possession in nouns is used to refer to the objects of verbs. You have already seen the singular forms of these pronouns suffixed to certain verbs like سأل–سألها . (You may also recall that in the first person singular an ن is added before the object pronoun: سألني.) The following examples show how the plural object pronoun are attached to the verb:

سألهم	"He asked them."
سألكم	"He asked you, pl."
سألنا	"He asked us."
سألتهم	"I asked them."
سألتكم	"I asked you, pl."
يسألوهم	"They ask them."
يسألوكم	"They ask you, pl."
يسألونا	"They ask us."

تمارين

١. اكتب

Fill in the blanks in the following.

يقع ــــــــ ــــــــ الأزهر في ــــــــ ــــــــ القاهرة في مصر، وهو من أهم مراكز التعليم في مصر ــــــــ الإسلامي. ويقول الكثيرون إنه أقدم ــــــــ في العالم، فقد بناه ــــــــ الفاطمي جوهر الصقلي سنة ٩٧٠ ــــــــ.

كان الأزهر ــــــــ ــــــــ ــــــــ يدرس فيها الطلاب علوم ــــــــ الإسلامي ــــــــ العربية، وفي سنة ١٩٦١ فتحت فيه ثلاث كليات ــــــــ هي كليات الطب ــــــــ والتجارة، وصار الأزهر جامعة ــــــــ.

عدد ــــــــ في الأزهر حوالي ٩٠ ألف طالب و ــــــــ الأساتذة حوالي ٣٦٠٠ أستاذاً. ولكن مكتبة ــــــــ ــــــــ صغيرة جداً: عدد الكتب فيها ــــــــ ٨٠ ألف ــــــــ ــــــــ فقط.

٢. اقرأ واكتب

Rewrite the following words, grouping them into related families. For each family identify the root and give its general meaning in English.

حاكم، تدريس، مَزرعة، خاصٌّ، دخول، عمل، معروف، موظّف، سمع، اجتماع، مزارع، مجموع، زراعة، جمع، مستمع، خاصّة، وظيفة، اعترف، دراسة، استعمال، دخل، تخصّص، جامع، دراسات، حكومي، خصوصاً، درس

٣. تكلّم

Create a dialogue with another student in which one criticizes the school you go to and the other defends it.

Translate the following into Arabic:

1. They took you, pl.

_____

2. They visit us.

_____

3. We asked them.

_____

4. You, pl. found us.

_____

5. They lost her.

_____

6. We study it, f.

_____

٥. املاء

أنا متـزوّج وعندي ولد وبنت. أسكن مع زوجتي وابني وبنتي في
بيت في جنوب هذه المدينة. بيتنا صغير، فيـه ثلاث غرف نـوم وغرفة جلوس
ومطبخ وحمام واحد. أجرة بيتي ١٠٠ دينار في الشهر.

اسـمـع

أسئلة

1. How did the first week go?
_____

2. Why was he happy?
_____

3. How did the second week go?
_____

4. What did Cathy say when she called the third week?
_____

5. What did Cathy's Egyptian friend tell her?
_____

كلمات جديدة

wrong	غَلَط	what happened?	ايش صار
lessons	دُروس (م. درس)	end	نِهاية

أسئلة

1. What has Dan seen in Jordan?
_____

2. Did he like Amman?
_____

3. Did Dan like the Roman amphitheater?
_____

4. Which places should Dan see?
_____

كلمات جديدة

		to please	أعجب
antiquities	آثار	Roman amphitheater	المدرّج الروماني
beautiful (sweet)	حِلو	to hear	سمِع
		to swim	سبَح (يسبَح)

اقرأ

جمال عبد الناصر

وُلد الرئيس المصري جمال عبد الناصر في ١٩١٨ /١/١٥ في حَيّ
فقير في مدينة الإسكندرية. كان أبوه موظفاً في البريد. ذهب وهو صغير
الى القاهرة وسكن في بيت خاله ودخل المدرسة. وبعد المدرسة الثانوية دخل
الأكاديمية الملكية العسكرية وصار ضابطاً.

وفي الجيش التقى بثلاثة ضبّاط هم زكريا محيي الدين وأنور
السادات وعبد الحكيم عامر، وأسّس الضبّاط الأربعة منظمة سرّية اسمها
"الضبّاط الأحرار"، وكان هدف المنظمة إخراج الإنجليز والعائلة المالكة من
مصر.

وفي ١٩٥٢ /٧/٢٣ قام جمال عبدالناصر و٨٩ ضابطاً في منظمة
الضباط الأحرار بانقلاب عسكري. وحكم مصر مجلس ثورة بقيادة محمد
نجيب. ولكن الرئيس الحقيقي كان جمال عبد الناصر. وفي سنة ١٩٥٤ صار
جمال عبد الناصر رئيس الوزراء.

وفي سنة ١٩٥٦ أمّم جمال عبد الناصر قناة السويس فهجمت
بريطانيا وفرنسا وإسرائيل على مصر، واحتلّت اسرائيل قطاع غزّة
وسيناء، وقصفت الطائرات الفرنسية والبريطانية المطارات العسكرية

المصرية. وبعد هذه الحرب صار جمال عبد الناصر بطلاً في نظر العرب.

وفي سنة ١٩٥٨ اتحدت سوريا ومصر، وكان عبد الناصر يأمل أن تصبح كل البلاد العربية دولة واحدة، ولكن سوريا انسحبت من الوحدة سنة ١٩٦١.

من أهم أعمال جمال عبد الناصر بناء السد العالي بمساعدة سوفييتية، تحسين حياة الفلاحين المصريين، تصنيع مصر، تحديد مِلكِيّة الأرض، وتحسين وضع المرأة المصرية.

مات جمال عبد الناصر في ١٩٧٠ /٢٨/٩.

كان جمال عبد الناصر رجلاً لطيفاً وبسيطاً في حياته الشخصيّة، وكانت له شعبية كبيرة في كل بلاد العالم العربي وبلاد العالم الثالث، على الرغم من فشله في حرب ١٩٥٦ وحرب ١٩٦٧ وفشله في توحيد العالم العربي.

اسئلة

1. Where was Jamal Abdul-Nasser born?
_____

2. Where did he live when he went to Cairo?
_____

3. Who did he meet in the army?
_____

4. What was the goal of the "Free Officers"?
_____

5. What happened on July 23, 1952?
_____

6. What happened in 1954, 1956, 1958?
_____
_____
_____

7. What are some of Nasser's achievements in Egypt?
_____

8. Was Jamal Abdul-Nasser popular in the Arab world?
_____

9. Was he successful in unifying the Arabs?
_____

كلمات جديدة

neighborhood, quarter of a city	حيّ = حارة
post office	بريد
to go	ذَهَب = راح
while (he was) young (see note below)	وهو صغير
maternal uncle	خال

the Royal Academy	الأكاديمية الملكية	secondary school	المدرسة الثانوية
organization	منظّمة	officers	ضُبّاط (م. ضابط)
free	أحرار (جمع حُرّ)	secret	سرّي
the royal family	العائلة المالكة	goal	هدَف
revolution	ثورة	council	مَجلس
hero	بَطَل	real	حَقيقي
to hope	أمِل (يأمَل)	in the eyes of	في نظر
building	بناء	to become	أصبح (يصبح)
improving	تحسين	the High Dam	السدّ العالي
peasant	فلّاح	life	حياة
limiting	تحديد	industrialization	تَصنيع
woman	مَرأة	situation	وَضع
man	رَجُل	to die	مات
simple	بسيط	kind, gentle	لَطيف
popularity	شعبيّة	personal, private	شَخصي
failure	فَشَل	in spite of	على الرغم من

Note

Phrases like وهو صغير are translated as "while (he was) young." This type of construction is referred to in Arabic grammar as حال "circumstantial clause," and the و in it is translated as "while."

Roots, Patterns, and Using the Dictionary

Consider the following Arabic words:

كاتِب	"writer, clerk"
كتاب	"a book"
مَكتَب	"an office"
مَكتوب	"written"

All these words have three consonants in common (كـتـب) and share the general meaning of writing: a *clerk* is a person who writes, a *book* is is something that has been written, an *office* is a place where people write, and *written* indicates that something has been the object of writing.

The consonants (كـتـب) ك ت ب in this order, which are shared by all the words above, are called the root. Most roots in Arabic consist of three consonants, but a few contain two or four consonants. To facilitate discussion of roots and words derived from them, the skeleton فعل is used to represent any root:

ف stands for the first consonant, ع for the second, and ل for the third consonant. Additional sounds are added to the root to create words:

كتب = فعل	
كاتب = فاعل	ا
كتاب = فعال	ا
مكتب = مفعل	م
مكتوب = مفعول	م-و

The words created by the addition of certain sounds express new shades or extensions of the basic meaning. They are formed according to a limited number of patterns. A pattern may indicate place, actor, instrument, recipient of an action, etc. For example, a noun with the pattern *mafʕal* (مَطعَم) generally indicates a place where the action of the corresponding root takes place, an adjective with the pattern *mafʕuul* (مفعول) implies a recipient of an action (or passive participle), etc.

In order to look up words in the dictionary, you need to be able to identify their root. All words that are derived from the same root are generally listed under that root. Recognizing roots of words is a skill that takes time and practice, but as you learn more Arabic you will find it easier to recognize roots. Rules and explanations help, but the skill is developed mainly through practice with the language itself.

Relative Adjectives: النسبة

Adjectives referring to nationalities, countries, cities, and places in general are formed by suffixing the ending ي (f., يّة) to the noun from which they are derived. If the noun ends in a vowel or تاء مـربـوطة, these letters are dropped when the adjectival suffix is added:

مصر-مصري، مصريّة
فرنسا-فـرنسي، فرنسيّة
السعودية-سعودي، سعوديّة
بيروت-بيروتي، بيروتيّة

تمارين

١. اقرأ واكتب

Give the singular form of each of the following words.

	ضبّاط		زيارات
	دراسات		طائرات
	فلّاحين		موظّفين
			رجال

٢. اكتب

For the following words, identify the three-consonant root and show which letters are added to the root to create the word. Example:

م-و   جمع   مجموع

كتـاب، أسـبوع، ربيـع، سفـارة، مكتـوب، مـشـغـول، سـافـر، اشتـغـل، مـفتـاح، استقبل، موقِف، محجوز، مكتبة

٣. اكتب

Identify the seven patterns the following words belong to:

استقبل، تحديد، كاتِب، طُلّاب، احتـفظ، مكتـوب، رجّع، تعليم، قائد، اشتـغل، مجموع، سكّان، جامِع، استمـع، مشغول، تأسيس، اجتمـع، استعمل، علّم، طالب

٢٣٦

اسـمـع

أسئلة

1. How old was Hassan when he started school?

_____

2. Was this the first time that Hassan wore shoes?

_____

3. Where did Hassan go to school?

_____

4. How far away was the school that Hassan attended?

_____

5. Who did Hassan go to school with?

_____

6. What did Hassan ask his brother and cousins to do?

_____

7. Did his brother agree to that? Why?

_____

كلمات جديدة

pants	بَنطلون	shirt	قَميص
wear	لَبِس (يلبس)	shoes	كُندرة
difficult	صَعب	mountainous	جبَلي
to start	بدا	new	جديد
to hurt	أوجع (يوجع)	feet, legs	رِجلين (م. رِجل)
to rest	استراح (يستريح)	time	وَقت

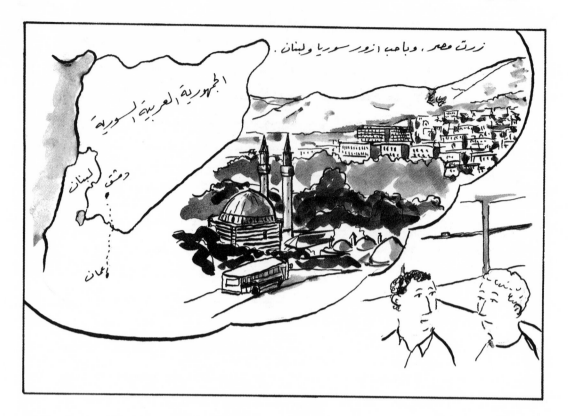

حوار

أسئلة

1. Which Arab country or countries has Dan visited besides Jordan?

_____

2. Which countries would he like to visit?

_____

3. How far is Damascus from Irbid by car?

_____

4. Does Dan have an entry visa to Syria?

_____

5. Is there a bus service between Amman and Damascus?

_____

كلمات جديدة

visit	زيارة	to visit	زار (يزور)
		it depends ("you and your luck")	انت ونَصيبك
right away	على طول	sometimes	أحياناً
		entry visa	تأشيرة دُخول

٢٣٩

اقرأ ١

نوال السعداوي

نوال السعداوي كاتبة وطبيبة مصريّة مشهورة. وُلدت سنة ١٩٣٠ في قرية "كُفر طَلحة". درست الطبّ في "القصر العيني" في القاهرة وحصلت على شهادة البكالوريوس وأصبحت طبيبة، ثم حصلت على شهادة الماجستير في الصحة العامة من جامعة "كولومبيا" في الولايات المتحدة، وعملت في مستشفى القصر العيني، وبعد ذلك أصبحت مديرة الصحة العامة في مصر.

في سنة ١٩٧٢ نشرت نوال السعداوي كتـاب "المرأة والجنس"، وأغضب ذلك السلطات الدينية والسياسية، التي ضغطت على وزارة الصحة لطردها من وظيفتها. كذلك فقدت وظيفة محرّرة مجلّة "الصحة" ومساعدة السكرتير العام لنقابة الأطبّاء المصريين. ومن سنة ١٩٧٣ الى سنة ١٩٧٦ عملت باحثة في كلية الطب في جامعة عين شمس في القاهرة، ودرست المشاكل النفسية التي تعاني منها المرأة، ومن ١٩٧٩ الى ١٩٨٠ عملت مستشارة للأمم المتحدة في إفريقيا والشرق الأوسط. وفي سنة ١٩٨٠، وبعد حرب طويلة مع الحكومة، سجنها الرئيس أنور السادات.

استمرت نوال السعداوي في الكتابة والدفاع عن حقوق المرأة وحريتها الفكرية والاجتماعية في السجن وبعد خروجها منه، وزادت شهرتها داخل مصر وخارجها. وقد كتبت أكثر من ١٦ كتاباً، من أشهرها "المرأة والجنس"، "المرأة والصراع النفسي"، "الأنثى هي الأصل"، "أنا المرأة"، "سقوط الإمام"، "رحلاتي حول العالم"، "الباحثة عن الحب"، "الخيط والجدار"، و"مذكّرات طفلة اسمها سعاد". وتُرجِمت بعض كتبها الى لغات أجنبية. وفي سنة ١٩٨٢ أسّست منظمة اسمها "منظمة المرأة العربية الجديدة".

نوال السعداوي متـزوجة ولها ولدان، وتسكن في مدينة الجيـزة المصرية، وتقضي وقتها في الكتابة والتحدث عن مشاكل المرأة.

1. Where did Nawal el-Saadawi go to school?
_____

2. What did she do between the years 1973 and 1976?
_____

3. How many books has she written?
_____

4. Who jailed her? Why?
_____

5. What did she found in 1982?
_____

كلمات جديدة

certificate, degree	شـهادة	to obtain	حصل على
to publish	نَشَر	health	صِحّة
to anger	أغضب	Women and Sex	المرأة والجنس
to pressure	ضَغط	authority	سُلطة
editor	مُحرّر	to lose	فَقد
association	نقابة	magazine	مَجلّة
researcher	باحث	doctors, physicians	أطبّاء (م.طبيب)
to suffer	عانى (يعاني)	psychological	نفسي
the United Nations	الأمم المتحدة	consultant, advisor	مستشار
defense	دفاع	to jail	سَجَن
freedom	حُرّيّة	rights	حُقوق (حق)
jail	سِجن	intellectual	فكري
to translate	تَرجَم	fame, reputation	شُهرَة
		speaking	تحدُّث

اقرأ ٢

الساعة الثالثة والربع ولا أزال أمامي الوقت. طلبت كوباً كبيراً من البيرة وشرائح رقيقة من البطاطس المحمّرة. رائحة البيرة وملمسها المثلج في جوفي يملآني بالانتعاش. اترك جسمي يسترخي أكثر في المقعد، وأغمض عيني.

اشعة الشمس أحسها دافئة فوق جفني. أفتح عيني فجأة باندهاش. أين أنا؟ وأدرك أنني جالسة في المقعد على رصيف المقهى. جالسة وحدي وأمامي كوب ضخم من البيرة، والناس تمر، والرجال يمرون، ولا أحد يقذفني بكلمة أو يرمقني بنظرة.

لم أستمتع بجلسة في مقاهي الوطن.. فالمقاهي في بلادنا للرجال. يجلسون على المقاعد، ويرمقون النساء السائرات، من الأمام ومن الخلف. من الرأس حتى الصدر، ثم تدور عيونهم لتفحص السيقان من الخلف والردفين.

وفي يوم جلست في المقهى المواجه لوزارة المالية في ميدان لاظوغلي. كانت لي بعض الأوراق في الوزارة وتأخر الموظف المسئول وقررت انتظاره في المقهى. طلبت كوباً من الشاي وجلست. لكن عيون الرجال ظلت ترمقني، من داخل المقهى وخارجها. ثم اقترب مني رجل وجلس الى المنضدة المجاورة لي وهمس ببضع كلمات لم أسمعها. وسألته بدهشة: ماذا تريد؟

ولم أكن أعرف حينئذ أن مثل هذا السؤال يعد في نظر الرجال قبولاً لفتح الحوار أو على الأقل عدم الرفض. فاذا به ينتقل بسرعة الى المقعد المجاور لي ويقول بصوت لزج: تشرب ايه يا جميل؟ ولم أستطع التخلص منه الا حين رفعت صوتي الغاضب عالياً، وبدأ الرجال الجالسون في المقهى يضحكون ويقهقهون، ووجدتني أترك كوب الشاي دون أن أكمله وخرجت مسرعة من المقهى والعيون تلاحقني ومعها النكات والقفشات النابية.

ولم يكن في إمكاني التنزه على شاطئ النيل دون أن يتبعني رجل يهمس بصوت قبيح كالفحيح، أو يرفع يده ويلمس ذراعي أو صدري حين يكون الطريق خالياً من المارة.

ولم أعد أجلس في المقاهي، أو أتنزه على الشاطئ. وأدركت أن المرأة ليس لها مكان للنزهة في بلادنا الا اذا سار الى جوارها زوج أو أخ أو أي رجل آخر.

إن وجود الرجل الآخر الى جوارها يعني على الفور أنها ليست وحيدة، وأن هناك رجل يملكها. وليس للرجال الآخرين أن يعتدوا على امرأة مملوكة لرجل آخر.

أما المرأة الوحيدة فهي غير مملوكة لأحد، وبالتالي تصبح في نظر الرجال ملكية عامة وليست ملكية خاصة، والاعتداء عليها غير ممنوع، سواء بالنظر أو اللمس.

(نوال السعداوي، رحلاتي حول العالم صص. ٤٩-٥٠.)

(Translation)

It is 3:15 and I still have time. I ordered a large glass of beer and thin potato chips. The smell of the beer and its icy feel inside me thoroughly refresh me. I let my body relax more in the chair, and I close my eyes.

I feel the rays of the sun warm on my eyelids. Suddenly I open my eyes, surprised. Where am I? I realize that I am sitting in the chair on the sidewalk of the cafe, sitting by myself. In front of me is a large glass of beer; people are passing by; men are passing by; no one throws a word or a look at me.

I never enjoyed sitting in a cafe in my homeland.Cafes in our country are for the men. They sit in the chairs and stare at the women walking by, from the front and the back, from the head to the breasts, then their eyes move around to examine the legs from the back and the rumps.

One day I sat in the cafe facing the Ministry of Finance in Lazoghli Square. I had some papers in the Ministry and the employee was late. I decided to wait for him in the cafe. I ordered a cup of tea and sat down. But the eyes of the men kept staring at me, from inside and outside of the cafe. Then a man came closer and sat at the table next to mine and whispered a few words that I did not hear. I asked him in surprise: "What do you want?"

I did not know then that such a question is considered an acceptance to open a dialogue or at least as not a rejection. The man quickly moved to the chair next to me and said in a sticky voice: "What would like to drink, beauty?" I could not get rid of him until I raised my angry voice high, and the men sitting in the cafe started to laugh boisterously. I left my cup of tea without finishing it, and I left the cafe quickly. The eyes were pursuing me together with rude comments and jokes.

I could not take a walk by the Nile without a man following me and whispering something to me in an ugly hissing, or touching my arm or breast when there were no passersby on the road.

I stopped sitting in the cafes and taking walks on the beach. I realized that there is no place for a woman to enjoy herself in our country unless a husband or a brother or another man walks beside her.

The presence of the man next to her automatically means that she is not alone, that a man owns her. Other men cannot encroach on a woman owned by another man.

As for the woman who is by herself, she is not owned by anyone and consequently becomes in the eyes of men public and not private property; encroaching on her through staring or touching is not prohibited.

Forms of the Verb

Arabic verbs are grouped into fifteen patterns or forms. Only eight of these will be discussed in this book because of the relative infrequency of the other seven. The first form (Form I) is the simplest; it consists of the basic elements of the verb with no vowel or consonant modifications. Examples of Form I verbs are كتب، شـرب، أكل، كـان، درس، ركب، وصل، وجـد، حـجـز. Changing the tense and/or the person of the verb does not change its form. So يـحـجـز، تاكل، يكتبـوا, etc. are still Form I verbs.

Other forms are constructed by modifying the structure of Form I in specific ways, such as doubling the second consonant, inserting ا between the first and second consonants of the root, adding a prefix, or a combination of these. Certain meanings are generally associated with the different forms: Form II has a causative, repetitive, or intensifying meaning; Form VII has a passive meaning; and so on. It should be emphasized, however, that there are many exceptions to this generalization.

Knowledge of verb forms is helpful in learning Arabic in a number of ways. For example, if you want to look up the word استـقبـل in the dictionary, you will have to know that it derives from the root قـبـل by adding the prefix اسـت and that it is a Form X verb. Try looking it up in your dictionary. Note that the dictionary will not have استـقبـل but will list its number (X) instead.

Knowledge of the verb forms is also helpful in predicting the meanings of new words of which you already know a relative. For instance, if you know the Arabic word علّم "he taught" and you see the word تعلّم for the first time, you can predict that its meaning will most likely be *he taught himself*, because you know the prefix تـ that is added to Form II verbs indicates reflexive meaning. You will also be able to predict the meaning of the word تعليـم on the basis of your knowledge of علّم because it is the verbal noun that is derived from the Form II verb following a regular pattern.

Many regularities of the language can be captured by an examination of the verb forms, their modifications, and their derivations. Some modifications and derivations are more useful than others in a first-year Arabic course simply because of the frequency of their occurrence or the fact that a certain recurrent pattern can be understood by stating a simple rule. The features of the forms that I believe are particularly useful at this stage are the perfect and imperfect conjugations of all eight forms presented, the active and passive participle patterns of Form I, and the verbal nouns of Forms II, IV, VII, VIII, and X. (A verbal noun is a noun derived from a verb, as in English *go/going*; e.g., *Going there is easy*.)

Form I

Of all forms used in Arabic, Form I is considered the least regular in shape, modifications, and the general meanings associated with it. A major problem faced in deriving the imperfect from the perfect of Form I is the unpredictability of the vowels of the verb in the imperfect. For example, the stem vowel (the vowel between the second and third consonants of the root) of يكتُب is ُ (yaktub), that of يعـرف is (yaʕ rif), and that of يفـتَح is َ (yaftaḥ). For hollow and lame verbs, the long vowel of the imperfect (in second or third position of the three-consonant skeleton) may be و, ي, or ا: يروح يطير ينام.

There are regularities, to be sure, but for now it might be easier for the learner to remember the vowel that goes with each verb.

The only regular behavior of Form I verbs that may be useful at this stage is the derivation of the active and passive participle patterns. We have already heard and seen a number of these participles. The active participle, which follows the فـــاعـل (faaʕil) pattern, generally refers to the doer of an action, and the passive participle, which follows the مـــفـعــول (mafʕuul) pattern, generally refers to the recipient.

Active Participles		Passive Participles	
ساكِن	residing, inhabitant	مَوجود	found, present
كاتِب	clerk, writer	مَكتوب	written
رايِح	going	مَولود	born
قادِم	coming	مَشغول	(made) busy

The Derived Forms

The forms that will be discussed in addition to Form I are II-X with the exception of IV and IX.

Forms II-X are more regular in shape and derivations. The meanings associated with each of them are more predictable than Form I verbs, but keep in mind that there are still a great many exceptions. (Predictable in this case means that if we know a certain form of the verb, we can tell the shape of its derivatives and form an idea about their individual meanings.)

Form II

Shape: faꟻꟻal (Double the middle consonant of the root.) In writing, this is indicated by a شدّة (ّ) over the doubled consonant.

ذكر   "to remember"   ذكّر   "to remind, to make someone remember"

Meaning: As the example shows, the meaning associated with this form is transitive/causative, i.e., to make or cause someone to remember. Other meanings associated with this form include repetitiveness and intensification.

Imperfect form: يـفعّل (yufaꟻꟻil)

Verbal noun: تفعيل (tafꟻiil)

Examples:

رجّع-يرجّع   "to return something" (compare with رجع "to return")

ضيّع-يضيّع   "to lose"   (compare with ضاع-root ضَيَع"to be lost")

صدّر-يصدّر   "to export"   (compare with صدر "to come out, be issued")

Form V

Shape: This form is constructed by adding the prefix تـ to Form II verbs.

علّم   "to teach"   تعلّم   "to learn, teach oneself"

Meaning: Reflexive of II.

Imperfect form: يتفعّل (yatafaꟻꟻal)

Examples:

تأسّس-يتأسّس   "to be founded"

تذكّر-يتذكّر   "to remember, to be reminded"

تزوّج-يتزوّج   "to get married"

تمارين

١. اكتب

Identify the root and the verb form in the following:

(هي) فتحت، رجّع، يُصدّر، تأسّس، يتزوّج، وصل، فتّش، قال، تتكوّن، يُفكّر، أمّم، وقع، يتحدّث

٢. اكتب

Fill in the blanks in the following table. Ignore the ones marked by an x.

	Imperfect	Active Participle	Passive Participle	Verbal Noun
عرف				x
كتب				x
شهر	x	x		x
طلب				x
قدّس		x	x	
شغل				x
علّم		x	x	
حكم				
أسّس	x	x	x	

٣. اقرأ

Match each of the words in the first column with its opposite in the second. There is one extra word in the first column.

لوحدهم	غني
انتهى	مع بعض
فقير	قديم
وجد	جميل
حديث	بدأ
بداية	فقد
	نهاية

٤. املاء

الإسكندريّة مدينة كبيرة في شمال مصر. هي ثاني مدينة في مصر بعد القاهرة. في الإسكندرية جامعة كبيرة اسمها جامعة الإسكندرية.

٢٤٧

الدرس رقم ٤٠.

اسمع

أسئلة

1. What time did school end?

_____

2. What did Hassan ask the other children to do?

_____

3. What did the other children do when Hassan started crying?

_____

كلمات جديدة

to cry	بَكى (يبكي)	to end	انتَهى

أسئلة

1. Why is Um Sharif worried?
_____

2. Why did Sharif go to America, according to Abu Sharif?
_____

3.What do the people who go to America do, according to Um Sharif?
_____

4. Is Abu Sharif worried?
_____

5. What did Um Sharif ask Abu Sharif to do?
_____

6. What did she want Sharif to beware of?
_____

7. Who is Nada?
_____

8. Who is Huda?
_____

9. When is Abu Sharif going to write a letter?
_____

كلمات جديدة

talk	كَلام
true	صَحيح

اسمع من هون وطيّر من هون
don't pay attention ("hear from here [one ear] and let fly from here [the other ear]")

mind	عَقل
young man	شابّ
beware, be careful	دير بالك
female cousin (mother's side)	بنت خال
educated	متعلّم
from a good family	بنت ناس
get up	قوم
crazy	مجنون
the middle of the night	نُصّ الليل
daughter of good people	بنت الحلال
good night	تصبح على خير

تكلّم

Create a dialogue with another student in which one of you is Um Sharif and the other Sharif. Um Sharif is warning her son against marrying an American and is urging him to come back and marry one of his cousins.

السودان

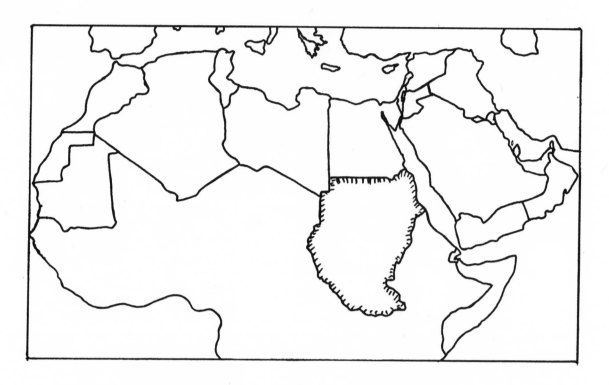

الإسم الكامل	جمهورية السودان
المساحة	٩٦٧ . ٤٩١ ميل مربع (٢ . ٥٠٥ . ٨,٢ كيلومتر مربع)
عدد السكان	٢٠,٢ مليون نسمة
المدن الرئيسية	الخرطوم (العاصمة،٠٠٠ . ٨١٧ نسمة)، أم درمان، (٠٠٠ . ٥٢٧)، بورسودان (٢٠٧ . ٠٠٠)
اللغات	العربية ولغات القبائل الإفريقية
الدين	الإسلام (٧٣٪)، عبادة الطبيعة (١٨٪)، المسيحية (٩٪)
اسم الحاكم	البريغادير عمر حسن بشير
سنة الاستقلال	١٩٥٦
العملة	الجنيه السوداني
الدخل السنوي للفرد	٣٤٠ دولار

السودان دولة عربية في شمال شرق إفريقيا، وهي أكبر دولة في العالم العربي وفي إفريقيا في المساحة. يحدّها من الشرق البحر الأحمر وإثيوبيا، ومن الشمال مصر وليبيا، ومن الغرب تشاد وجمهورية إفريقيا الوسطى، ومن الجنوب كينيا وأوغندا وزائير. طول السودان من الشمال الى الجنوب حوالي ١٢٠٠ ميل (١٩٣١ كيلومتر) ومن الشرق الى الغرب ١٠٠٠ ميل (١٦,٩ كيلومتر). يمر نهر النيل وكثير من فروعه من السودان.

تأسّست في السودان مملكة قويّة في زمن الرومان وكانت عاصمتها مدينة دنقلة، ودخلت المسيحية السودان في القرن السادس واتحدت مع اثيوبيا في مقاومة الدين الإسلامي حتى القرن الرابع عشر. وبعد ذلك انقسم السودان الى عدة دول صغيرة حتى احتلّه محمد علي باشا حاكم مصر سنة ١٨٢٠-١٨٢٢.

انسحب الجيش المصري من السودان بعد الثورة المهديّة التي بدأت سنة ١٨٨١، ولكن المصريين رجعوا مرة ثانية مع البريطانيين سنة ١٨٩٦-١٨٩٨ وصار السودان جزءاً من الإمبراطورية البريطانية.

وفي سنة ١٩٥٣ وافقت بريطانيا ومصر على إعطاء الحكم الذاتي للسودان وأعلن البرلمان السوداني استقلال السودان في يناير ١٩٥٦.

وفي سنة ١٩٦٩ قام جعفر النميري، الذي كان ضابطاً في الجيش السوداني، بانقلاب عسكري ونصّب نفسه رئيس وزراء. وفي سنة ١٩٧١ صار رئيس الجمهورية.

ومن سنة ١٩٧١ الى سنة ١٩٨٥ قامت عدة انقلابات عسكرية ضدّ النميري وفشلت. وفي سنة ١٩٨٥ نجح وزير الدفاع عبد الرحمن سوار الذهب في انقلاب عسكري عندما كان النميري يزور الولايات المتحدة ولم يرجع النميري الى السودان حتى الآن.

من أهم المشاكل في السودان الحرب الأهليّة في الجنوب، والفقر والمجاعة في كثير من المناطق. وقد ساعدت هذه المشاكل على قيام انقلاب عسكري آخر سنة ١٩٨٩ بقيادة البريغادير عمر حسن البشير.

أسئلة

Indicate whether each of the following statements is true or false.
1. Sudan is the largest Arab country in population. _____
2. Sudan is the largest Arab country in area. _____
3. Sudan is about 1,200 miles wide. _____
4. The capital of Sudan is Danqala. _____
5. Sudan joined Ethiopia in resisting Islam. _____
6. Christianity was introduced to Sudan in the fourteenth century. _____
7. The Mahdi revolution started in 1881. _____
8. Sudan was declared independent in 1953. _____
9. Jaafar Numeiry came to power through military means. _____
10. The civil war in the south was one of the causes of the Sudanese government's downfall in 1989. _____

كلمات جديدة

nature worship	عبادة الطبيعة	tribes	قَبائِل
strong	قوي	branches, tributaries	فُروع
fourteenth	رابع عشر	resistance	مقاوَمة
giving	إعطاء	to agree	وافَق
to announce	أعلن	self-government	حُكم ذاتي
to appoint	نصّب	parliament	بَرلمان
against	ضدّ	a number of	عدّة
poverty	فَقر	minister of defense	وزير دفاع
another	آخَر	hunger, famine	مجاعة

Form VII

Shape: This form is constructed by adding the prefix ان to Form I verbs.

قطع "to cut" انقطع "to be cut"

Meaning: Passive of I.

Imperfect form: ينفعل (yanfaʕil)

Verbal noun: انفعال (infiʕaal)

Examples:

انشغل-ينشغل "to be busy"

انسحب-ينسحِب "to withdraw"

تمارين

١. اقرأ واكتب

Identify the root and the verb form in the following:

انقسم، يحجز، ضيّع، انولد، مرّ، انسحب، تشرّف، يظلّ، يكلّف

٢. اقرأ واكتب

Make a table that shows the perfect, imperfect, and verbal noun forms of the following verbs.

انسحب، فتّش، وقّع، انقلب

٣. اكتب

Fill in the blanks in the following.

انسحب ——— المصري من السودان نتيجة ——— المهدية التي
بدأت سنة ١٨٨١، ولكن المصريين رجعوا مرة ثانية مع ——— سنة
١٨٩٦-١٨٩٨ وصار ——— جزءاً من الإمبراطورية البريطانية.

وفي سنة ١٩٥٣ وافقت بريطانيا و——— على إعطاء الحكم الذاتي
للسودان وأعلن البرلمان السوداني ——— السودان في يناير ١٩٥٦.

وفي ——— ١٩٦٩ قام جعفر النميري وهو ——— في الجيش
السوداني بانقلاب ——— ونصّب نفسه ——— وزراء. وفي سنة ١٩٧١
صار رئيس ———.

ومن سنة ١٩٧١ الى سنة ١٩٨٥ قامت عدة ——— عسكرية ضد
النميري وفشلت. وفي سنة ١٩٨٥ نجح ——— الدفاع عبد الرحمن سوار
الذهب في انقلاب ——— عندما كان النميري يزور ——— المتّحدة.

انت ونصيبك، اذا معك نلوس بتدخل على طول، واذا ما
معك نلوس امرك الى الله.

الدرس رقم ٤١

الاولاد قعدوا تحت شجرة وحسن شلح كندرته .

أسئلة

1. How long did the children sit under the tree?
_____

2. What did the man see under the tree?
_____

3. What did Hassan do when he could not find his shoes?
_____

4. Did Hassan's feet hurt that day?
_____

كلمات جديدة

to take off	شَلَح	tree	شَجَرة
to pass	مرّ	to get up	قام
		that	هذاك

٢٥٦

أسئلة

1. Does Dan like his apartment?

_____

2. When is Dan going to Irbid?

_____

3. How is Dan going to get to Abu Sharif's house from the bus station?

_____

كلمات جديدة

I will be honored	باتشرّف	to have lunch	تغدّى (يتغدّى)

اقرأ ١

الطيّب صالح

الطيّب صالح كاتب سوداني معروف. وُلد سنة ١٩٢٩ في قرية صغيرة في السودان. درس في مدرسة قريته، ثمّ درس في جامعة الخرطوم وجامعة لندن، ويعمل الآن ويسكن في لندن.

من كُتبه المشهورة "موسم الهجرة الى الشمال" (١٩٦٦) و"عرس الزين" (١٩٦٩). تركّز كتاباته على مشكلات الإفريقيين بشكل عامّ والسودانيين بشكل خاص، وخصوصاً مشكلات الشباب الذين درسوا في اوروبا ورجعوا الى بلادهم. ومن الأمثلة على ذلك قصة "سوزان وعلي".

اقرأ ٢

سوزان وعلي (الطيّب صالح)

كان اسمه علي. واسمها هي سوزان. الخرطوم. لندن. درست الفن في معهد "سليد". درس العلوم السياسية في معهد الاقتصاد بجامعة لندن.

قالت: "تزوّجني."

قال: "لا. صعب."

قالت: "لكني أحبّك."

قال: "وأنا ايضاً أحبّك. لكن..."

ومِن ثَمّ عاد الى بلده، وأخذا يتراسلان.

لكني أحبّك يا علي."

"وأنا أحبّك يا سوزان. لكن..."

ستة أشهر.

كتبت تقول: قابلت رجلاً. سأتزوّجه."

كتب يقول: "لكني أحبّك يا سوزان."

انقطعت الرسائل.

يفكّر بها في غالب الأحيان.

وتفكّر به من حين لآخر.

لكن...

كلمات جديدة

to focus on	ركّز (يركّز)	since	مُنذُ
in particular	بشكل خاصّ	in general	بشكل عامّ
institute	معهد	art	فنّ
economics	اقتصاد	political science	علوم سياسيّة
after that	من ثمّ=بعد ذلك	to love	أحبّ (يحبّ)
to start	أخذ=بدأ	to return	عاد=رجع
to meet	قابَل	to correspond	تَراسل (يتراسَل)
to stop, end	انقطَع	will, shall	سَ
most	غالب=أكثر	letters	رسائل (م. رسالة)
		times	أحيان (م. حين)=أوقات

قواعد

Form III

Shape: This form is constructed by inserting ا between the first and second consonants of the root.

قبل "to accept"   قابل "to meet"

Meaning: Associative.
Imperfect: يفاعِل (yufaaʕil)
Verbal noun: مفاعلة (mufaaʕala)

Examples:
ساعد–يساعِد   "to help"
هاجر–يهاجِر   "to emigrate"

Form VI

Shape: This form is constructed by adding the prefix ت to Form III verbs.

قابَل   "to meet someone"   تَقابَل   "to meet one another"

Meaning: Reflexive of III.

Imperfect form: يتفاعل (yatafaaʕal)

Examples:

تراسل-يتراسَل   "to correspond with each other"

تفاهم-يتفاهَم   "to communicate with each other"

تمارين

١. اكتب

Identify the root and the verb form in the following:

قابل، تكلّم، ساعد، يزيد، يحُدّ، يقدر، يتراسلون

٢. املاء

درست اللغة العربية سنتين في جامعة تكساس في اوستن، وأربعة شهور في الجامعة الأمريكية في القاهرة.

٣. تكلّم

Create a dialogue with another student in which one of you invites the other for a meal at his/her house and gives directions how to get there.

الدرس رقم ٤٢

اسمع

أسئلة

1. What was the boy wearing?

2. What did the boy say when Hassan told him that these were his shoes?

3. What did the boy's father demand in return for Hassan's shoes?

4. Why was Hassan happy (two reasons)?

كلمات جديدة

a box of chocolate	علبة شوكولاتة	to find	لِقي=وَجد
soft	طري	to become	صار

أسئلة

1. Is the post office on the right or left?

_____

2. Where is the package from?

_____

3. What did Dan want from the post office besides the package?

_____

4. How many stamps did Dan want?

_____

5. What is the total?

_____

كلمات جديدة

registered	مُسجَّل	package	طَرد
request, application	طَلَب	stamp	طوابع (م. طابع)

السعودية

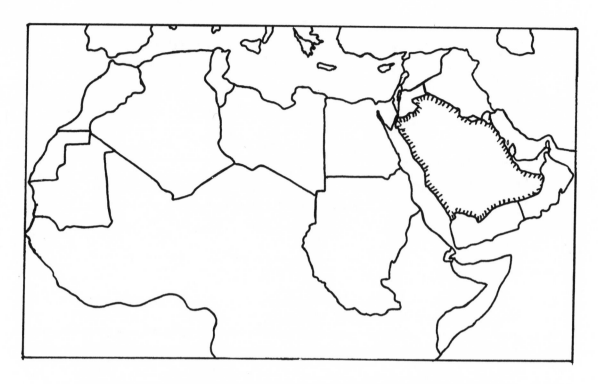

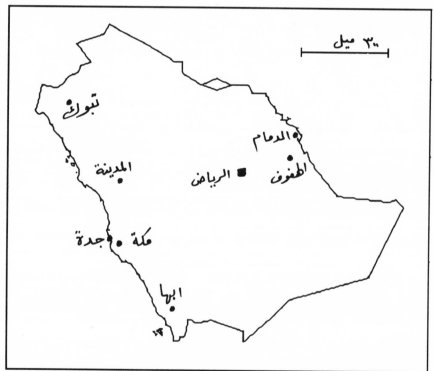

الإسم الكامل	المملكة العربية السعودية
المساحة	٨٦٥،٠٠٠ ميل مربّع (٢،٢٥٠،٠٧٠ كيلومتر مربّع)
عدد السكان	١٥ مليون نسمة
المدن الرئيسية	الرياض (العاصمة، ١،٢٥٠،٠٠٠ نسمة)، جدة (١،٥٠٠،٠٠٠)، مكة (٧٥٠،٠٠٠)
اللغات	العربية
الدين	الإسلام (١٠٠٪)
اسم الحاكم	الملك فهد بن عبد العزيز
العملة	الريال السعودي
الدخل السنوي للفرد	٥،٤٨٠ دولار أمريكي

تقع المملكة العربية السعودية في شبه الجزيرة العربية وهي أكبر دولة فيها. يحدّ السعودية من الشرق الخليج العربي والبحرين وقطر والإمارات العربية المتحدة، ومن الجنوب عُمان واليمن ومن الغرب الأردن والبحر الأحمر ومن الشمال الكويت والعراق.

تنقسم السعودية الى خمس مناطق رئيسية، أولاً: منطقة الوسط (نجد) وفيها الرياض عاصمة الدولة. ثانياً: المنطقة الغربية (الحجاز) ومن المدن الكبيرة فيها جدة ومكّة المكرّمة والمدينة المنوّرة. ثالثاً: المنطقة الشرقية (الإحساء) ومن مدنها الدمّام والخبر والظهران. رابعاً: المنطقة الجنوبية (عسير) وعاصمتها أبها. وأخيراً المنطقة الشمالية ومن المدن الكبيرة فيها مدينة تبوك.

عدد سكّان السعودية حوالي ١٥ مليون نسمة ومساحتها حوالي ٨٦٥ الف ميل مربع. السعودية مملكة يحكمها الملك فهد بن عبد العزيز، الذي صار ملكاً سنة ١٩٨١ ميلادية.

أكثر أرض السعودية صحراوية غير صالحة للزراعة والسكن. والمناطق الصحراوية حارّة في الصيف وباردة في الشتاء. وقد تصل درجة الحرارة في بعض المناطق الصحراوية في الصيف الى ١٢٠ درجة فهرنهايت. ومن أكبر الصحاري في السعودية صحراء النفوذ في الشمال، وصحراء الربع الخالي في الجنوب الشرقي. وتقع أكثر المناطق الجبلية في الغرب (الحجاز) والجنوب (عسير).

كانت السعودية دولة فقيرة حتى اكتُشف فيها البترول سنة ١٩٣٦، وهي الآن من أغنى الدول العربية.

1. What borders Saudi Arabia from the west?

_____

2. What is the total area of Saudi Arabia (in square miles)?

_____

3. Into how many areas or provinces is Saudi Arabia divided? What are their names?

_____

4. What is the capital of Assir?

_____

5. What are some of the major cities in the Western Province?

_____

6. What is the name of the king of Saudi Arabia? How long has he been ruling?

_____

7. Where is the Empty Quarter desert located?

_____

8. When was oil discovered in Saudi Arabia?

_____

كلمات جديدة

finally	أخيراً	peninsula	شبه جزيرة
living, habitation	سكَن	not good, unsuitable	غير صالح
was discovered	اكتُشف	some	بعض

تمارين

١. اكتب

Fill in the blanks in the following.

تنقسم السعودية الى خمس ــــــــــ رئيسية، أولاً: منطقة الوسط (نجد) وفيها الرياض عاصمة الدولة. ــــــــــ: المنطقة ــــــــــ (الحجاز) ومن المدن الكبيرة فيها جدة ومكة المكرمة والمدينة المنورة. ثالثاً: ــــــــــ الشرقية (الإحساء) ومن مدنها الدمام والخبر والظهران. ــــــــــ: ــــــــــ الجنوبية (عسير) وعاصمتها أبها. وأخيراً المنطقة ــــــــــ ومن المدن الكبيرة فيها مدينة تبوك.

عدد ــــــــــ السعودية حوالي ١٥ مليون ــــــــــ ومساحتها حوالي ٨٦٥ الف ميل ــــــــــ السعودية مملكة يحكمها ــــــــــ فهد بن عبد العزيز الذي صار ملكاً ــــــــــ ١٩٨١ ميلادية.

Create a dialogue with another student in which one of you is a postal worker and the other is buying stamps and/or sending a letter to another country.

اسـمع

أسئلة

1. Where did James Baker go?
_____

2. Where did he stay?
_____

3. What did he eat the first day?
_____

4. What did he eat the second day?
_____

5. What did President Bush ask Baker?
_____

6. What food did Baker like in particular?
_____

كلمات جديدة

to stay (in a hotel)	نزل	secretary of state	وزير خارجيّة
		fava beans	فول

حوار

أسئلة

1. How long is the snow season in Ithaca?

_____

2. How is the weather in the summer?

_____

3. How is it in the spring?

_____

كلمات جديدة

green	أخضَر	heat	حَرّ
moderate	مُعتدِل	flowers	زُهور

اقرأ

مكّة المُكرّمة

الكعبة في الليل

تقع مدينة مكّة في غرب المملكة العربية السعودية، وتبعد عن البحر الأحمر حوالي ٥٠ ميلاً. عدد سكانها حوالي ٧٥٠،٠٠٠ نسمة.

مكة مدينة مقدّسة عند المسلمين لأنها مكان ولادة النبي محمد مؤسس الدين الإسلامي، وفيها تقع الكعبة والمسجد الحرام. يعتقد المسلمون أنّ النبيّ إبراهيم بنى الكعبة، والكعبة داخل المسجد الحرام، وهو من أكبر المساجد في العالم.

لا نعرف الكثير عن تاريخ مكّة القديم ولكن نعرف أنّها كانت مركزاً تجاريّاً هامّاً في سنة ٤٠٠ م.

وُلد النبي محمد في مكة سنة ٥٧٠، ولكنّه هاجر منها سنة ٦٢٢ لأنّ أهل مكّة لم يعترفوا بالدين الجديد. وبعد ثماني سنوات رجع الى مكة مُنتصراً وكسر الأصنام التي كانت في الكعبة وصارت مكة العاصمة السياسية والدينية للدولة الإسلامية، ولكن بعد وقت قصير صارت دمشق العاصمة السياسية للدولة وبقيت مكة العاصمة الدينية. وفي سنة ١٥١٧ صارت مكة جزءاً من الإمبراطورية العثمانية. وبقيت كذلك حتى سنة ١٩١٦

عندما أعلن حاكمها الشريف حسين بن علي استقلال الحجاز عن تركيا، وكانت مكّة عاصمة الحجاز. وفي سنة ١٩٢٤ دخل عبدالعزيز بن سعود مكة وصارت جزءاً من المملكة العربية السعودية.

ويزور مكة أكثر من مليون شخص في كل سنة للحجّ.

أسئلة

1. How far is Makka from the Red Sea?

_____

2. Where is the Kaaba located?

_____

3. When was the Prophet Muhammad born?

_____

4. When did the Prophet Muhammad return to Makka from Madina?

_____

5. What happened to Makka in 1517, 1916, and 1924?

_____

6. How many pilgrims visit Makka every year?

_____

كلمات جديدة

founder	مُؤسِّس	sacred, holy	مُقدّس
to break	كَسَر	victorious	مُنتصِر
short	قَصير	idols	أصنام
pilgrimage	حَجّ	person	شَخص

٢٧٠

أغنية
القلب يعشق كل جميل (أم كلثوم)

مكَّة وفيها جبال النور
طالَّة على البيت المعمور
دخلنا باب السلام
غمر قلوبنا السلام
بعفو رب غفور

فوقنا حمام الحِمى
عدد نجوم السما
طاير علينا يطوف
ألوف تتابع ألوف
طاير يغني الضيوف
بالعفو والمرحمة
واللي نصب سيره
واحد ما فيش غيره
دعاني لبِّيته
لحدِّ باب بيته
وامَّا تجلَّى لي
في الدمع ناجيته.

تمارين

١. اقرأ واكتب

Rewrite the following, grouping them into families of related words. For each family identify the root and give its general meaning in English.

مُؤَسِّس، سعر، ملحمة، أسّس، القدس، علوم، مملكة، حديث، ملابس، رسالة، متزوّج، طالب، معلّم، مالكة، تسعيرة، لحّام، تحدّث، لبس، تراسل، تزوّج، طلب، متعلّم، مقدّس، تأسيس، علم، زوج، رسائل، محادثات، لحم، أسعار، مَلَكِيّة

٢. املاء

إربد مدينة كبيرة في شمال الأردن. هي ثاني مدينة بعد عمان العاصمة. الطقس في إربد بارد في الشتاء وحار في الصيف. في إربد جامعة كبيرة اسمها جامعة اليرموك. في جامعة اليرموك ١٢ الف طالب و٥٠٠ أستاذ تقريباً.

٣. تكلّم

Tell the other students in the class in some detail what the weather is like where you come from.

الدرس رقم ٤٤

اسمع

أسئلة

1. Had President Bush eaten Arab food before?

2. What did President Bush request when he visited Egypt?

3. Why?

4. What did the president have for breakfast?

5. What did he have for lunch?

6. What did he have for dinner?

7. Did he have breakfast with the family the following day?

كلمات جديدة

to meet	اجتمع	to live	عاش (يعيش)
to look	تطلّع	to discuss	بحث
		excellency	سِيادة

حوار

أسئلة

1. What help did Abu Sharif request from Dan?

_____

2. Why does Dan have to return to Amman?

_____

3. When is Dan going to give Suad an English lesson?

_____

كلمات جديدة

weak	ضعيف	help	مُساعَدة
to help	ساعَد (يُساعِد)	as you know	مثل ما بتعرف
truly	فعلاً	ready, willing	مُستَعِدّ

٢٧٥

اقرأ

البترول في السعودية

الحي الصناعي في مدينة ينبع

تحتوي منطقة الشرق الأوسط وشمال إفريقيا على ٦١.٤٪ من بترول العالم. من أهم الدول المنتجة للبترول في هذه المنطقة: السعودية، ايران، العراق، ليبيا، الجزائر، الكويت، والإمارات العربية المتحدة.

تكاليف إنتاج البترول في الشرق الأوسط وشمال إفريقيا أرخص من المناطق الأخرى في العالم لأنه موجود في آبار كبيرة جداً وقريب من سطح الأرض. مثلاً قد يصل إنتاج البئر الواحد في السعودية الى أكثر من ١٥ ألف برميل في اليوم، بينما متوسط إنتاج البئر الأمريكي حوالي ١٧ برميلاً فقط.

تحتوي السعودية وحدها على ١٦٩ بليون برميل او حوالي ٢٣.٩٪ من بترول العالم، وفيها بئر اسمه بئر "الغوّار" يحتوي على ضعف بترول الولايات المتحدة كلها. والسعودية أكبر مُنتج ومُصدّر للبترول في منطقة الشرق الأوسط وشمال إفريقيا.

بدأ انتاج البترول في السعودية سنة ١٩٣٦، وإنتاجها أكثر من أربعة ملايين برميلاً في اليوم، أي حوالي ٨.١٪ من الإنتاج العالمي.

يوجـد أكثـر البتـرول فـي السعـوديـة فـي المنطقـة الشرقيـة، وتعمـل شـركات كثيـرة من أمـريكا واوروبـا فـي صناعـة البتـرول وتصـديـره، وخـاصـةً شـركـة الـزيت العـربيـة الأمـريكيـة (أرامكـو). ويعمـل الكثيـر مـن السعـوديـين والأجـانـب فـي هـذه الصنـاعـة. وتُعتـبَـر مـدينـة الظهران عـاصمـة البتـرول فـي السعـوديـة، وهـي مـركـز شـركـة أرامكـو.

تصـدّر السعـوديـة أكثـر بتـرولهـا الى اليـابـان ودول اوروبـا الغـربيـة والولايـات المتحـدة.

أسئلة

Indicate whether each of the following statements is true or false.
1. The Middle East and North Africa contain more than half of the world's oil reserves. _____
2. Oil is cheaper to produce in the Middle East than in America. _____
3. Saudi Arabia is the second largest producer and exporter of oil in the Middle East. _____
4. Saudi Arabia produces 8.1 million barrels of oil a day. _____
5. Dhahran is the oil capital of Saudi Arabia. _____
6. Saudi Arabia exports some of its oil to the United States. _____

كلمات جديدة

producer	مُنتِج	to contain	احتوى (يحتوي) على
production	إنتـاج	costs	تكـاليف
well	بئـر (آبـار)	existing, present	مَوجـود
barrel	بـرميـل	very	جـدّاً
whereas	بينمـا	surface	سطح
only	فقط=بَس	average	متوسّـط
exporter	مُصـدّر	twice as much, double	ضعف
is found	يوجَد	or, in other words	أيْ
is considered	يُعتَبَر	exporting	تصـدير

تمارين

١. اطبخ (الحمّص)

اخلط واطحن

حمّص	علبة (١٥ اونصة)
عصير ليمون	ثلث (١/٣) كوب
طحينة	ثلث (١/٣) كوب
ملح	نصف ملعقة
ثوم	فصّ واحد
زيت زيتون	ملعقة كبيرة
ماء الحمص	حوالي ملعقة كبيرة

ضع الخليط على صحن وضع عليه "بابريكا" وبقدونس وزيت زيتون.

٢. إقرأ—شعر (نزار قبّاني)

عدّي على أصابع اليدين ما يأتي
فأوّلاً حبيبتي أنتِ
وثانياً حبيبتي أنتِ
وثالثاً ورابعاً وخامساً وسادساً
وسابعاً وثامناً وتاسعاً وعاشراً
حبيبتي أنتِ.

٣. اقرأ واكتب

Give the plural form of each of the following words.

مَجلّة
طَبيب
عِلم
رِسالة
طابِع

٤. تكلّم

Create a dialogue with another student in which one of you is preparing for an exam in Arabic and asks the other for help.

الدرس رقم ٤٥

اسمـع

طيب يا أخي ممكن للبيت بابين
وأنا طلعت من الباب الثاني.

أسئلة

1. What did Juha tell his wife?

_____

2. What did the man want?

_____

3. Did the man see Juha when he entered the house?

_____

4. What did Juha say when the man did not believe his wife?

_____

كلمات جديدة

standing	واقف	to knock	دَقّ (يدُقّ)
to shout	صاح	to continue	استمرّ
		inside	داخل

٢٧٩

أسئلة

1. How many subjects are on the Tawjihi exam?

_____

2. How many subjects is Suad worried about?

_____

3. How can Dan help Suad with her English?

_____

4. What is Dan good at?

_____

كلمات جديدة

grammar	قَواعِد	afraid, worried	خايِف
math	رياضيّات	writing	كِتابة
physical education	رياضة	science	عُلوم

اليمن

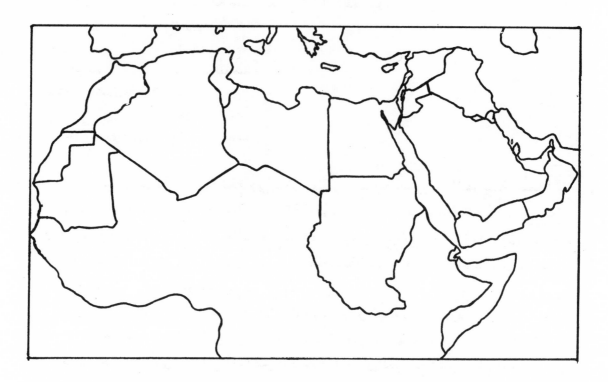

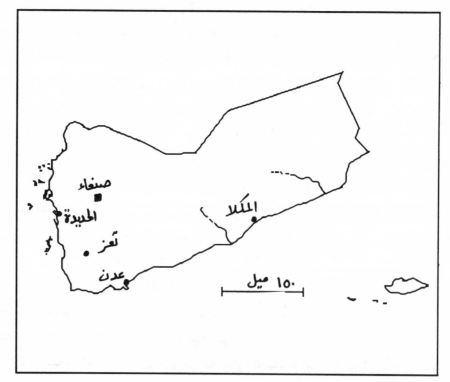

الإسم الكامل	الجمهورية اليمنية
المساحة	٢٠٣،٨٥٠ ميل مربع (٥٢٧،٩٧٠ كيلومتر مربع)
عدد السكان	٩،٨ مليون نسمة
المدن الرئيسية	صنعاء (العاصمة)، عدن، المكلّا، الحديّدة، تعز
اللغات	العربية
الدين	الإسلام
اسم الحاكم	علي عبدالله صالح
سنة الاستقلال	١٩١٣
العملة	الريال
الدخل السنوي للفرد	٥٦٢ دولار أمريكي

اليمن دولة عربية تقع في جنوب غرب شبه الجزيرة العربية. يحدها من الشرق عُمان، ومن الشمال المملكة العربية السعودية ومن الجنوب البحر العربي ومن الغرب البحر الأحمر. مساحة اليمن حوالي ٢٠٣،٨٥٠ ميل مربع وعدد سكانه حوالي ٩،٨ مليون نسمة. عاصمة اليمن مدينة صنعاء وتقع في غرب الدولة. اللغة الرسمية في اليمن هي اللغة العربية وأكثر الناس في اليمن مسلمون، وهناك أقلّيات من الأوروبيين والهنود واليهود.

يختلف الطقس في اليمن من منطقة الى منطقة؛ في منطقة الساحل الطقس حار جداً، ولكن في المناطق الجبلية الطقس لطيف أكثر أيام السنة.

أكثر الناس في اليمن يشتغلون بالزراعة. وفي اليمن منطقتان زراعيتان: المنطقة المنخفضة والمنطقة الجبلية. في المنطقة المنخفضة يزرع اليمنيون القمح والقطن وشجر النخيل والقهوة. أرض المنطقة الجبلية خصبة ويزرعون فيها الخضار والفواكه والقات.

اكتُشف البترول في اليمن سنة ١٩٨٤، وفي هذه الأيام يصدّر اليمن البترول الى اوروبا.

كان اليمن في الزمن القديم مركزاً مهماً للتجارة بين الشرق والغرب وخاصة تجارة التوابل، وقامت فيه ممالك كثيرة منها مملكة سبأ ومملكة حميَر. احتلّ المصريون اليمن حوالي سنة ١٦٠٠ ق.م.، وبعد ذلك دخله الأحباش (الإثيوبيون) والرومان. دخل الإسلام اليمن سنة ٦٢٨ م. وصار اليمن جزءاً من الدولة الإسلامية. وفي القرن السادس عشر دخله الأتراك العثمانيون ولكنه كان في الواقع مستقلاً حتى سنة ١٨١٩ عندما دخله محمد علي حاكم مصر. وفي سنة ١٩١٣ حصل على حكم ذاتي. واستقل بعد الحرب العالمية الاولى ودخل الجامعة العربية في سنة ١٩٤٥.

وفي سنة ١٩٦٢ قامت مجموعة من الضباط بانقلاب عسكري ضد إمام اليمن وأعلنت جمهورية. وساعدت مصر بقيادة جمال عبد الناصر الضباط

الجمهوريين وساعدَت السعودية والأردن الملكيين بقيادة الإمام، وقامت حرب أهلية. وبعد حرب الأيام الستة بين العرب وإسرائيل سنة ١٩٦٧ انسحب الجيش المصري من اليمن. انتهت الحرب الأهلية سنة ١٩٦٩.

وفي شهر مايو (أيّار) سنة ١٩٩٠ تأسّست الجمهورية اليمنية عندما توحّد اليمن الشمالي واليمن الجنوبي. وقد كان اليمن الجنوبي تحت حكم بريطانيا من سنة ١٨٣٩ حتى استقلاله سنة ١٩٦٧.

أسئلة

1. What borders Yemen on the south?

_____

2. What is the population of Yemen?

_____

3. What is the per capita income?

_____

4. What minorities are found in Yemen?

_____

5. How is the weather in the mountainous areas in Yemen?

_____

6. What kind of crops do Yemenis grow in the low areas?

_____

7. Does Yemen export oil?

_____

8. Yemen was invaded by Egypt twice. When did the two invasions occur?

_____

9. When did Islam come to Yemen?

_____

10. When did Yemen gain self-government from the Ottoman Turks?

_____

11. When did Yemen become a member of the Arab League?

_____

12. What happened in 1962?

_____

13. Who helped the royalists against the republicans?

_____

14. When did the civil war end?

_____

15. When did the two Yemens unite?

_____

كلمات جديدة

Indians	هُنود	official	رَسمي
low	مُنخفِض	nice, pleasant	لَطيف
cotton	قُطن	wheat	قَمح
qat	قات	palm trees	شَجر النخيل
kingdom	مملكة (ممالك)	spices	تَوابِل
to obtain	حَصل على	in reality	في الواقع
relationship	عَلاقة	the Arab League	الجامعة العربية
		to be united	تَوحّد

قواعد

Form VIII

Shape: This form is constructed by adding ا before the first letter of the root and ت after it.

حفظ   "to keep"   احتفظ   "to keep for oneself"

Meaning: Reflexive of I.

Imperfect form: يفتَعِل (yafta3il)

Verbal noun: افتعال (ifti3aal)

Examples:

انتظر-ينتَظِر   "to wait"

اهتمّ-يهتَمّ   "to be interested"

انتهى-ينتَهي   "to be finished"

اعتَبر-يعتبِر   "to consider"

When an assimilated verb (وقف، وصل، وجد) is changed into Form VIII, the initial و assimilates to the ت of the form, resulting in a doubled تّ:

وصل "to arrive" + اتّصل (ittaṣal)   "to contact" (from اوتصل [iwtaṣal])

٢٨٤

تمارين

١. اكتب

Identify the root and the verb form in the following:

يختلف، ترك، تحتوي، يطلب، يشتغل، يبدأ، ، التقى، اتّحد، ، تخصّص، اكتشف، احتلّ، سافر

٢. اكتب

Fill in the blanks in the following:

كان اليمن في الزمن ـــــــ مركزاً مهماً للتجارة بين الشرق وـــــــ وخاصة تجارة التوابل، وقامت فيه ممالك ـــــــ منها مملكة سبأ ـــــــ حِميَر.

احتلّ المصريون ـــــــ حوالي سنة ١٦٠٠ ق.م.، وبعد ذلك دخله الأحباش (الإثيوبيون) والرومان. ـــــــ الإسلام اليمن سنة ٦٢٨ م. وصار اليمن ـــــــ من الدولة الإسلامية. وفي ـــــــ السادس عشر دخله الأتراك العثمانيون ولكنه كان في الواقع مستقلاً حتى ـــــــ ١٨١٩ عندما دخله محمد علي ـــــــ ـــــــ ـــــــ. وفي سنة ١٩١٣ حصل على ـــــــ ـــــــ واستقل بعد ـــــــ ـــــــ ـــــــ الاولى ودخل ـــــــ العربية ١٩٤٥.

٣. اكتب

Write a short paragraph about Beirut. The following words may be useful.

بيروت، لبنان، كبيرة، عاصمة، غرب، البحر الأبيض المتوسّط، الشتاء، الصيف، حارّ، بارد

٤. تكلّم

Create a dialogue with another student in which you discuss an upcoming exam. Ask your teacher for the meanings of words you need to know in Arabic, such as the names of different subjects and different types of exams.

الدرس رقم ٤٦

اسمـع

أسئلة

1. How much meat did Juha buy?

_____

2. What happened to the meat while Juha was at work?

_____

3. What did Juha's wife bring for him to eat?

_____

4. According to Juha's wife, what happened to the meat?

_____

5. What did Juha do to prove that his wife was lying?

_____

٢٨٦

كلمات جديدة

weight	وَزْن	cat	قطّة
all	كُل	to finish	خَلَص
scale	ميزان	to bring	جاب
		to weigh	وَزَن

حوار

أسئلة

1. When did they decide to go?

_____

2. Where are they going to meet?

_____

3. What time?

_____

كلمات جديدة

قُدّام   in front of   noon   ظُهر

اقرأ

مملكة سَبَأ

سدّ مأرب

كان في بلاد اليمن في القديم ثلاث ممالك هي: سَبَأ ومَنَأ وحِميَر. تأسّست مملكة سبأ في منتصف القرن الثامن قبل الميلاد، واستمرّت الى سنة ١١٥ ق.م. وقد ذُكرت لأوّل مرّة في كتابات المؤرّخين اليونانيين في النصف الثاني من القرن الثالث قبل الميلاد.

كانت عاصمة مملكة سبأ مدينة مأرب. وتقع مدينة مأرب على بعد حوالي ١٠٠ كم شرق صنعاء عاصمة اليمن على ارتفاع ١٢٠٠ متر. وهي مشهورة بِسَبَب سدّ مأرب الذي بُني لجمع ماء المطر في بحيرة اصطناعية بين الجبال. وقد بُنيت بعض أجزائه في القرن السابع ق.م. ويُعتبر أعجوبةَ هندسيّة.

وصلت مملكة سبأ درجة عالية من الحضارة وخاصة في الزراعة والتجارة، وقد ساعد في ذلك كثرة المطر والموقع الاستراتيجي على طريق الهند والقرب من البحر.

وقد احتكر أهل سبأ تجارة التوابل في البر والبحر في الفترة بين
٥٠٠ و ٢٠٠ ق.م. وكانت تجارة التوابل تمرّ بالبحر الأحمر والمحيط الهندي
وفي طُرُق برّيّة في شبه الجزيرة العربية وبلاد الشام.

أسئلة

1. When was the kingdom of Saba' mentioned for the first time by the Greek historians?

_____

2. When was the kingdom founded?

_____

3. How long did it last?

_____

4. What was its capital?

_____

5. What is the Ma'rib Dam?

_____

6. What helped the kingdom of Saba' reach a high degree of civilization?

_____

7. Where were the spice trade routes at the time of the Saba' kingdom?

_____

كلمات جديدة

to be mentioned	ذُكِر	middle of	مُنتَصَف
because of	بِسَبَب	historian	مؤرِّخ
water	ماء=ميّة	collecting	جَمْع
artificial	اصطناعي	lake	بُحَيرَة
		parts	أجزاء (م. جزء)
		engineering wonder, feat	أعجوبة هندسية
to monopolize	احتَكر	civilization	حَضارة
period, era	فَترَة	land	بَرّ
roads	طُرُق (م. طَريق)	ocean	مُحيط

بلاد الشام=سوريا Greater Syria

٢٩٠

Form X

Shape: To obtain Form X, the prefix است is added to the root consonants.

عمل   "to do, work"   استعمَل   "to use, put to work"

Meaning: Causative/reflexive of I.

Imperfect form: يستفعِل (yastafʕil)

Verbal noun: استِفعال (istifʕaal)

Examples:

استقبَل-يستقبِل   "to meet, welcome"

استقلّ-يستقلّ   "to be independent"

استمرّ-يستمرّ   "to continue"

استورَد-يستورِد   "to import"

تمارين

١. اكتب

Identify the root and the verb form in the following:

استمرّ، يَحكُم، بَنى، استقلّ، وافَق، تغدّى، استقبَل، ركّز

٢. اقرأ

عزيزتي آن لاندرز:

أنا ربّة بيت، عمري ٣٠ سنة وعندي بنتان جميلتان وزوج ممتاز، ونتوقّع مولوداً بعد ثمانية أسابيع.

هذا الصباح جاء زوجي ومعه هديّة جميلة للعائلة: ثلاثة أرطال من لحم البقر. قرّرت أن أطبخها قبل رجوعه من العمل حتى تكون جاهزة عندما يرجع. كانت هذه أول مرّة نشتري لحم بقر من مدة طويلة. انتهيت من طبخ اللحم الساعة الرابعة فأخرجته من الفرن ووضعته على طبق حتى يبرد قليلاً.

كان منظره مغرياً جداً فقررت أن أذوق طعمه. لا أقدر يا آن أن أشرح لك ماذا حدث بعد ذلك، فكأنني أصبحت مجنونة، لم أقدر أن أتوقف عن أكل اللحم حتى أكلته كلّه. بعد ذلك شعرت بذنب كبير وكدتُ أبكي، وأحسست أنّني مثل الجرذ عندما حضّرت عشاء بديلاً من التونا.

قولي لي يا آن لماذا عملتُ هذا العمل الحقير؟

شرِهة من تكساس

عزيزتي شرهة تكساس:

أحياناً يتطور عند النساء الحوامل شعور قوي مفاجئ لأكل طعام لم يأكلنه منذ مدة طويلة، فيأكلن كميات كبيرة منه. أعتقد أن هذا ما حدث لك. لا تطبخي لحم البقر مُسبقاً قبل ولادة مولودك!

٣. اطبخ

أ. مجدّرة

عدس	كوبين
ماء	٥ أكواب
بوليون لحم البقر	ملعقتين صغيرتين
رز	كوب واحد
بصل	راس واحد مفروم
زيت زيتون	حوالي ملعقتين كبيرتين
بهار	نصف ملعقة صغيرة
كمّون	نصف ملعقة صغيرة
ملح	ملعقة صغيرة
فلفل أسود	ربع (١/٤) ملعقة صغيرة

اغلِ العدس و٤ أكواب ماء وبوليون لحم البقر في طنجرة، عند الغليان اطبخ على نار خفيفة ١٢ دقيقة.

اقلِ البصل بزيت الزيتون قليلاً.

اخلط البصل (وزيت الزيتون) والرز والبهارات وكوب واحد من الماء مع العدس، اطبخ على نار خفيفة حوالي ربع ساعة.

ب. سلطة خيار ولبن (للأكل مع المجدّرة)

اخلط

لبن		كوبين
خيار	واحد	(مقشور ومفروم)
ثوم		فص واحد كبير
ملح		نصف ملعقة

نعنع، زيت زيتون (حسب الذوق)

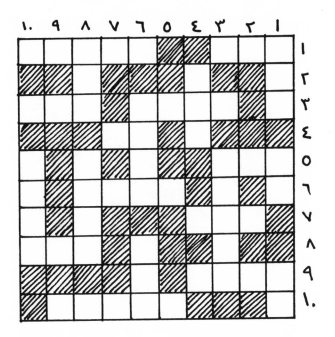

أفقي

١. أخ الأم؛ جمع طبيب

٣. كلّية من كليات الجامعة (جمع حقّ)؛ عكس خرج

٤. ليس

٥. عكس خاصّ

٦. عكس طويل

٧. عكس أعطى

٨. عكس ضعيف

٩. لون

١٠. قابل

عمودي

١. عكس عامّ؛ أخ الأب؛ ابن الأب

٣. عكس عالي

٤. ضيّع

٦. نوع من الملابس؛ نوع من الأكل

٨. دولة؛ شارع

١٠. ليس من الخارج

٥. اقرأ

دخل وزير الشؤون الاجتماعية مكتباً من مكاتب الوزارة في أحد الأيام فوجد كل الموظفين مشغولين إمّا بشرب الشاي أو بقراءة الجريدة أو الإثنين معاً، فطلب منهم أن يذهبوا الى شوارع العاصمة ويسألوا عدداً من المواطنين السؤال التالي: "هل تأكل لتعيش أم تعيش لتأكل؟" وفيما يلي نموذج من إجابات المواطنين:

-تعيش لتأكل ولّا تأكل لتعيش، ايش الفرق؟ كلّه عند العرب صابون.
-بتفكّرنا في أمريكا أو في أوروبا حتى تسأل هالسؤال، لما فيه أكل باكل، ولما ما فيه أكل بانام جوعان.
-بدّك الصحيح ولا ابن عمّه؟ بيني وبينك لما فيه أكل حتى أشبع.
-ايش هالفلسفة والكلام الفاضي؟ طبعاً كل الناس بياكلوا حتى يعيشوا.

٢٩٥

اسمع

أسئلة

1. Who visited Juha?

_____

2. What did he bring with him?

_____

3. Who came the second week?

_____

4. Who came the third week?

_____

5. What did Juha bring for the third man to eat?

_____

كلمات جديدة

gift	هَديّة	rabbit	أرنَب
bowl	صَحن	to rest	استراح
		soup, sauce	مَرَقة

أسئلة

1. How long has Dan waited?
_____

2. Why was Jalal late?
_____

3. How did Dan come from the university?
_____

4. What had Dan bought before?
_____

5. What is so strange about prices in Amman, according to Dan?
_____

كلمات جديدة

for a long time	مِن زمان	to be late	تأخّر
transport vehicle, truck	سيّارة نقل	accident	حادث
passengers	رُكّاب	to hit	ضرب
shoes	كُندَرة	ambulance	سيّارة إسعاف
shirt	قميص	gifts	هَدايا
strange	غريب	by myself	لوحدي
		next to	جنب

تكلّم

Create a dialogue with another student in which one of you invites the other to go
shopping, to the movies, or to a restaurant.

اقرأ

أحداث هامة في التاريخ العربي الإسلامي

٥٧٠	ولادة النبي محمد (صلى الله عليه وسلم)
٦١٢	بداية الدعوة للإسلام
٦٢٢	هجرة النبي محمد من مكة الى المدينة
٦٣٢	موت النبي محمد
٦٣٧-٦٤٤	فتح سوريا وفلسطين والعراق ومصر وأرمينيا وايران
٦٤٧	فتح شمال إفريقيا
٦٩١	بناء مسجد قبة الصخرة في القدس
٧١٠-٧١٤	دخول المسلمين الى اسبانيا
٧٦٢	تأسيس مدينة بغداد
٩٦٩	تأسيس مدينة القاهرة والجامع الأزهر
١٠٩٦-١٠٩٩	وصول الصليبيين الى الشرق الأوسط واحتلال القدس
١١٨٧	القائد صلاح الدين الأيوبي ينتصر على الصليبيين في معركة حطين في فلسطين
١٢٥٨	المغول يدخلون بغداد ويدمرونها
١٢٦٠	المماليك ينتصرون على المغول في معركة عين جالوت في فلسطين
١٤٥٣-١٩١٨	الإمبراطورية العثمانية
١٧٩٨-١٨٠١	نابليون يحتل مصر
١٨٠٥-١٩٥٢	حكم عائلة محمد علي في مصر
١٨٣٠	الفرنسيون يحتلّون الجزائر
١٨٦٩	فتح قناة السويس
١٨٨٢	بريطانيا تحتل مصر
١٩١٧	وعد بلفور لمساعدة اليهود في تأسيس وطن قومي في فلسطين
١٩٣٢-١٩٦٢	أكثر الدول العربية تستقل عن بريطانيا وفرنسا
١٩٤٥	تأسيس الجامعة العربية
١٩٤٨	تأسيس دولة إسرائيل على أرض فلسطين؛ أول حرب بين العرب وإسرائيل
١٩٥٢	انقلاب عسكري في مصر بقيادة جمال عبد الناصر وانتهاء الملكية

تأميم قناة السويس؛ الغزو الثلاثي (بريطانيا، فرنسا، وإسرائيل) لمصر	١٩٥٦
الوحدة بين مصر وسوريا؛ العراق يصبح جمهورية	١٩٥٨
استقلال الجزائر بعد حرب استمرت ٨ سنوات ضد فرنسا	١٩٦٢
حرب حزيران بين العرب (مصر، الأردن، سوريا) وإسرائيل	١٩٦٧
حرب أكتوبر بين العرب (مصر وسوريا) وإسرائيل	١٩٧٣
توقيع اتفاقية سلام بين مصر وإسرائيل	١٩٧٩
الغزو الإسرائيلي للبنان	١٩٨٢
الحرب العراقية الإيرانية	١٩٨.–١٩٨٨
الغزو العراقي للكويت	١٩٩.
إخراج العراق من الكويت بعد حرب عاصفة الصحراء	١٩٩١

أسئلة

1. When did the Prophet Muhammad emigrate to Madina?

_____

2. When was the Dome of the Rock built?

_____

3. When was Cairo founded?

_____

4. How long did the Ottoman Empire last?

_____

5. When did the French occupy Algeria?

_____

6. When was the Arab League founded?

_____

7. When was the Suez Canal nationalized?

_____

8. When did the October war between the Arabs and Israel take place?

_____

9. How long did the Iraq-Iran war last?

_____

10. When did Algeria become independent?

_____

	كلمات جديدة
events	أحداث
peace be upon him	صلى الله عليه وسلّم
call (to a religion)	دَعوَة
death	مَوت
opening, conquest	فَتح
the Mongols	المغول
the Mamlukes	المَماليك
invasion	غزو
three-way, three-pronged	ثُلاثي
signing	توقيع
expelling, driving out	إخراج
Desert Storm	عاصِفَة الصَحراء

تمارين

١. اقرأ

Match each of the words in the first column with their opposites in the second.
There is one extra word in the first column.

سهل	قوي	
خاصّ	جديد	
ضيّع	عامّ	
بَرد	صَعب	
ضعيف	عالي	
خارج	لقي	
مُنخفِض	حرّ	
	داخل	

٢. اكتب

Write a short paragraph about the place where you live. The following words may
be helpful.

أسكن، بيت (شقة، بيت الطلاب)، كبير (صغير)، غرفة (غرَف)، عُنوان، شارع

الدرس رقم ٤٨

اسمـع

أسئلة

1. Why did Juha go to the mosque?

_____

2. What did the people say the first week when Juha asked them if they knew what he was going to say?

_____

3. What did Juha do when he heard the answer?

_____

4. What was the answer the second and third weeks?

_____

5. What did Juha do when he heard the people's answer the third week?

_____

كلمات جديدة

to stand	وِقِف	mosque	مَسجِد=جامِع
		use	فائدة

أسئلة

1. What is the program about today?

_____

2. What was the name of the person interviewed?

_____

3. What does she do?

_____

4. How many children does she have?

_____

5. Does she own a house?

_____

6. What is her husband's monthly salary?

_____

7. How much rent does she pay?

_____

	كلمات جديدة
ladies and gentlemen	سيّداتي وسادتي
peace be upon you and God's blessings	السلام عليكم ورحمة الله وبركاته
program	بَرنامج
with the people	مع الناس
may God keep them safe	الله يخلّيهم
Ministry of Education	وزارة التربية والتعليم
money	فُلوس
tenant	مُستأجِر
to pay	دَفَع (يدفَع)
plus	زائد
high prices	غَلاء
salary	راتِب
bones	عَظم
feathers	ريش

اقرأ ١

النبي محمد

وُلد نبيّ الإسلام محمّد (صلّى الله عليه وسلّم) سنة ٥٧٠ م. في مدينة مكة، التي هي الآن في غرب المملكة العربية السعودية. مات أبوه قبل ولادته وماتت أمه عندما كان عمره ٦ سنوات. اسم أبيه عبدالله، واسم جده عبدالمطّلب، واسم عائلته "بني هاشم"، وهي من العائلات المعروفة في قبيلة قريش.

بعد موت أبيه عاش محمّد في بيت جدّه عبدالمطلب، وبعد موت جدّه عاش في بيت عمّه أبو طالب. وعندما كان شابّاً سافر مع عمّه ابو طالب الى بلاد الشام (سوريا الآن) للتجارة، وكان يذهب الى الأسواق ويستمع الى ناس من أديان مختلفة يتنقاشون في الدين.

وعندما صار عمره ٢٥ سنة بدأ يعمل في التجارة عند أرملة غنيّة اسمها خديجة، ثم تزوّجها، وكانت أكبر منه ب ١٥ سنة. ولدت خديجة ولدين وأربع بنات، ومات الولدان وهما صغيران .

كان النبي محمد يذهب الى مغارة اسمها "غار حراء" في جبل قريب من مكّة، يقضي فيها وقتاً طويلاً في التفكير. وفي ليلة من الليالي ظهر له الملاك جبريل وأخبره أن الله اختاره نبياً .

خاف محمد كثيراً، ولم يرَ جبريلاً لمدة ٣ سنوات. ولكن في سنة ٦١٣ بدأ الدعوة الى الإسلام. في البداية كان يدعو أقاربه وأصحابه، ولكن بعد وقت قصير بدأ يدعو ناساً آخرين الى الدين الجديد.

من أول الناس الذين آمنوا بدعوة النبي محمد زوجته خديجة وتاجر من مكة اسمه أبو بكر، وبعد ذلك آمن به عمر بن الخطّاب، الذي حاربه في البداية.

كان النبيّ محمد يدعو الى التوحيد، اي عبادة إله واحد، هو خالق كل شيء. واعترف بالدين اليهودي والدين المسيحي، وقال ان الدين الجديد، وهو الإسلام، مكمّل لليهودية والمسيحية.

استمر محمد في الدعوة في مكة حتى ماتت زوجته خديجة وعمه أبو طالب، وصارت الدعوة صعبة بعد موتهما وقويت مقاومة أهل قريش له لأنه كان ينتقدهم. وكانت قريش قبيلة قويّة في مكة.

في سنة ٦٢٢ هاجر النبيّ محمد من مكّة الى مدينة يثرب التي صار اسمها بعد ذلك "المدينة المنوّرة". كانت هذه هي الهجرة، وهي حدث مهم جداً في التاريخ الإسلامي، الذي يبدأ بسنة الهجرة.

استقبل أهل المدينة النبي محمد وصار أكثرهم مسلمين بعد وقت

قصير وصار محمد قائدهم الديني والسياسي.

حارب النبيّ محمد كثيراً من عادات العرب في مكّة والمدينة، وخاصة
عبادة الأصنام وعادة دفن البنات أحياء، وحدّد عدد الزوجات ونظّم الطلاق
وقانون الميراث ، ومعاملة العبيد.

اسئلة

1. When was the Prophet Muhammad born?

_____

2. What was his grandfather's name?

_____

3. How old was Muhammad when his mother died?

_____

4. Who did he work for when he was twenty-five years old?

_____

5. What is *Ghar Hiraa'*?

_____

6. What did Gabriel tell Muhammad?

_____

7. How was Muhammad's reaction?

_____

8. Who was the first man to believe in Muhammad's call to Islam?

_____

9. What was Muhammad's attitude toward Judaism and Christianity?

_____

10. What happened in 622?

_____

11. What were some of the practices that Muhammad fought in Makka and Madina?

_____

كلمات جديدة

young man	شابّ	tribe	قَبيلَة
different	مختلف	religions	أديان (م. دين)
widow	أرملة	to discuss	تناقش (يتناقش)
to spend	قضى (يقضي)	cave	مَغارة
angel	ملاك	thinking	تفكير
to tell, inform	أخبَر	Gabriel	جبريل
to be afraid	خاف	to choose	اختار
to see	رأى (يرى)=شاف	crazy	مجنون
relatives	أقارب (م. قريب)	to call upon	دعا (يدعو)
worshipping one God	تَوحيد	to believe	أمن
a god	إله	worshipping	عبادة
completing	مُكَمّل	creator	خالِق
burying	دَفن	custom	عادة
to limit	حَدّد	alive	أحياء (م. حيّ)
divorce	طَلاق	to organize, regulate	نظّم
inheritance	ميراث	law	قانون
slaves	عَبيد (م. عبد)	treatment	مَعامَلة

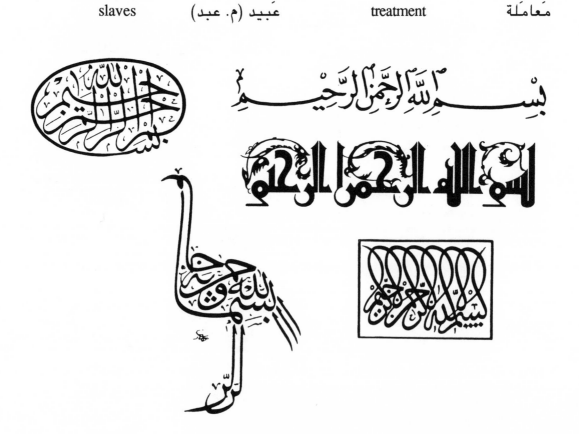

اقرأ ٢ (قرآن كريم)

بسم الله الرحمن الرحيم.

In the Name of Allah, the Beneficient, the Merciful.

إنّا أنزلناه في ليلة القدر.

Lo! We revealed it on the Night of Predestination.

وما أدراك ما ليلة القدر.

Ah, what will convey unto thee what the Night of Power is!

ليلة القدر خير من ألف شهر.

The Night of Power is better than a thousand months.

تَنزّل الملائكة والروح فيها، بإذن ربّهم من كل أمر.

The angels and the Spirit descend therein, by the permission of their Lord, with all decrees.

سلامٌ هي حتى مطلع الفجر.

(That night is) Peace until the rising of the dawn.

اقرأ ٣ (أحاديث)

١. المسلم مَن سَلِمَ الناس من يده ولسانه.

٢. لا يؤمن أحدكم حتى يحبّ لأخيه ما يحب لنفسه.

٣. أطلب العلم من المَهد الى اللَحد.

كلمات جديدة

to be safe	سَلِم	(he, that) who	مَن=مين
that which, what	ما	tongue	لِسان
grave	لَحد	cradle	مَهد

Passive Voice in فصحى

Whereas in Levantine Arabic passive meaning is generally expressed by Form VII verbs and the passive participle construction, in فصحى a verb can be made to convey passive meaning by an internal vowel change. Only the passive formation processes in فصحى that you will encounter in the reading passages of the book will be discussed here. These are represented by the two verbs وُلِدَ "was born" and يُعتَقَد "it is believed." وُلِدَ is derived from the perfect verb وَلَدَ, which consists of the three root consonants and two short vowels, marked on the first and second consonants. (The vowel sometimes shown over the last consonant of a perfect verb in the third person singular masculine as in دَ of وَلَدَ is a person marker rather than part of the verb itself.) The change from active to passive involves changing the first two vowels of the verb (and all Form I sound verbs in the perfect). The first one is replaced by ضمّة (ُ) and the second by كسرة (ِ):

وَلَدَ (walada) ⇒ وُلِدَ (wulida).

In the imperfect Form VIII verb يُعتَقَد, the change is from يَفتَعِل (yaftaʕil) pattern to يُفتَعَل (yuftaʕal).

يَعتَقِد (yaʕtakid) ⇒ يُعتَقَد (yuʕtakad)

قد + Perfect

When the word قد precedes a verb in the perfect it simply affirms that the action has taken place.

وقد دخل الأكراد الإسلام في القرن السابع الميلادي.

"The Kurds embraced Islam in the seventh century A.D.

تمارين

١. اكتب

Fill in the blank spaces in the following.

وُلِد نَبيّ الإسلام ———— (صلّى الله عليه وسلّم) سنة ٥٧٠ م. في مدينة ———— التي هي الآن في ———— المملكة العربية ———— مات أبوه قبل ولادته وماتت ———— عندما كان عمره ٦ ———— اسم أبيه ———— واسم جده عبدالمطّلب، واسم عائلته "بني ————"، وهي من العائلات المعروفة في ———— قريش.

بعد موت أبيه ربّاه ———— عبدالمطلب، وبعد موت عبد المطلب ربّاه ———— أبو طالب. وعندما كان شابّاً ———— مع عمّه ابو طالب الى ———— (سوريا الآن) للتجارة، وكان يذهب الى ———— ويستمع الى ناس من أديان ———— يتناقشون في الدين.

٢. اقرأ واكتب

Rewrite the following words, grouping them into related families. For each family identify the root and give its general meaning in English.

موجود، يسلّمك، خارج، أخضر، مُسلم، واقف، إخراج، تكلّم، خارجيّة، وجد، كلام، موجودات، داخل، خُضار، استمرّ، دخول، مُستمرّ، رجع، موقف، سلام، مَرّ، استرجَع

٣١٠

الدرس رقم ٤٩

اسـمـع

أسئلة

1. What did Juha borrow from his neighbor?
_____
2. What did he put in the big pot?
_____
3. What was Juha's answer when the neighbor asked him about the small pot?
_____
4. Why was the neighbor happy when Juha borrowed the pot a second time?
_____
5. Why did the neighbor ask Juha for the pot?
_____
6. What did Juha tell his neighbor when he asked for the pot?
_____

كلمات جديدة

cooking pot	طنجَرة	to borrow	استعار
to give birth	ولَد	to put	حَطّ

٣١١

حوار

أسئلة

1. Where does Yousif live?
_____

2. What does he do?
_____

3. Is he married?
_____

4. What does Yousif think of the housing problem?
_____

كلمات جديدة

fruit	فَواكِه	businessman	رَجُل أعمال
other people	الناس الثانيين	gasoline	بنزين

٣١٢

اقرأ

فلسطين (١)

مدينة يافا الفلسطينية قبل قيام دولة إسرائيل سنة ١٩٤٨

دخل العرب المسلمون فلسطين سنة ٦٣٨ ميلاديّة وأصبحت جزءاً من الإمبراطوريّة الإسلاميّة. وفي نهاية القرن الحادي عشر دخلها الصليبيّون وأسّسوا مملكة مسيحيّة فيها عاصمتها القدس، ولكنها رجعت الى الحكم الإسلامي بعد معركة "حطّين" سنة ١١٨٧. وفي سنة ١٥١٧ صارت جزءاً من الامبراطورية العثمانية. استمرت تحت الحكم العثماني الى سنة ١٩١٨.

في سنة ١٨٨٢ ظهرت الحركة الصهيونية بقيادة "ثيودور هرتسل" نتيجة ظلم اليهود في روسيا وشرق اوروبا، وكان هدف الحركة تأسيس وطن قومي لليهود في فلسطين. وبدأ اليهود يهاجرون الى فلسطين في تلك السنة. وفي سنة ١٩١٨ كان عدد سكان فلسطين ٦٤٤ الف عربي (٩٢٪) و ٥٦ الف يهودي (٨٪). سكن الكثير من اليهود في مدن فلسطين ولكن بعضهم سكن في مستعمرات يهودية. وكان عدد تلك المستعمرات حوالي ٤٠ على ٢٪ من مساحة فلسطين.

وفي الحرب العالمية الأولى دخلت تركيا الحرب ضد بريطانيا، وفي سنة ١٩١٧ أصدرت بريطانيا وعد بلفور للمساعدة في تأسيس وطن قومي لليهود في فلسطين، واحتلّ الجيش البريطاني فلسطين بعد هزيمة تركيا في الحرب، وفتحت بريطانيا فلسطين لهجرة اليهود. ولكن سكان فلسطين العرب

لم يقبلوا أن تصبح فلسطين وطناً قومياً لليهود فقاوموا هجرة اليهود وطالبوا بدولة عربية مستقلة. وقويت مقاومة العرب عندما زاد عدد المهاجرين اليهود من اوروبا في الثلاثينات، فمثلاً في سنة ١٩٣٥ وصل عدد المهاجرين اليهود من المانيا وحدها ٦٦ الف مهاجر. وبسبب المقاومة العربية حاولت بريطانيا تحديد عدد المهاجرين اليهود الى فلسطين وتحديد بيع الأرض لليهود ولكن لم تنجح في ذلك.

أسئلة

1. When did Palestine become part of the Arab-Muslim empire?
_____

2. When did the Crusaders establish a kingdom in Palestine?
_____

3. When did the Zionist movement appear?
_____

4. When was the Balfour Declaration issued?
_____

5. What was the population of Palestine like in 1918?
_____

6. Why did the Palestinian Arabs resist Jewish immigration?
_____

7. Was England successful in limiting the flow of immigrants?
_____

كلمات جديدة

to appear	ظَهَر	eleventh	حادي عشر
Zionist	صهيوني	movement	حركة
persecution	ظُلم	as a result of	نتيجة
to immigrate	هاجَر	homeland	وطن قومي
to issue	أصدر	settlement	مستعمَرة
defeat	هزيمة	promise, declaration	وَعد
did not	لم	immigration	هِجرة
to resist	قاوَم	to accept	قَبِل (يقبَل)
independent	مُستقلّ	to demand	طالَب
by itself	وحدها	to become stronger	قَوِيَ
selling	بَيع	to try	حاوَل
		to succeed	نجَح

٣١٤

More on Using the Dictionary

The first step in looking up a word in the dictionary is to identify its root. To get to the root all affixes and modifications of the basic structure need to be removed. For example, suppose you do not know the meaning of the word يتعلّمون. First you take out the subject/person marker ي–ون, the ت, and the شدّة (ّ). The root علم is left, which is looked up alphabetically. All derivations of the root and their meanings are listed under the root, including تعلّم. تعلّم will not be shown, but its number (V) will instead: V *to learn*, *study*, etc.

Roots are not always easy to recognize, particulary in cases involving hollow and lame verbs. The more Arabic you know, however, the easier it will be to recognize relationships among families of words and the root of each family. The following hints may be helpful:

1. The consonants of a root generally stay stable from one form to another in the same family. If you look at the words طار، طيّارة، طيران, you will notice that the consonants ط and ر stay the same. This is an indication that they are part of the root.

2. ا and ى derive from و or ي. So, after taking out all suffixes and prefixes and arriving at the form طار, you do not look up the word under طار, but rather under طور or طير. Once you reached this stage, the work is mostly done, because if you cannot find the word under the first form, it will be under the second, which is listed next to the first in the dictionary. However, you can for the most part tell whether a verb derives from و or ي by looking at the other membrs of the family; if most of them tend to have a و in them, then it is a و-verb and if most of them tend to have a ي, then it is a ي-verb.

3. Certain consonants cannot be part of an affix and hence they are part of the root. These consonants include ث، ج، ح، خ، د، ذ، ر، ز، ص، ض، ط، ظ، ع، غ، ق. Some consonants like ب، ف، ل occur as prefixes but not as suffixes; the consonant ـه occurs as a suffix only.

Remembering the form numbers is necessary only when looking up verbs; all other parts of speech are listed without numbers.

تمارين

١.

استعمل القاموس

Look up the following words in the dictionary.

مختلِفون، تفكير، أخبر، اختيار، مخلوق، استعمار، قسّم، مهاجر

٢. اقرأ واكتب

Give the plural form of each of the following words.

هديّة

كنيسة

دكّان

ليلة

فلس

ضيف

٣. اقرأ واكتب

From which verbs (not roots) are the following verbal nouns derived?

مقاومة، استقلال، تصنيع، اقتصاد، محاولة، تحديد، استقبال، معاملة،
انقلاب، مساعدة، تصدير، انقسام، تحسين، ارتفاع، استمرار.

٤. اكتب

Fill in the blank spaces in the following.

دخل العرب المسلمون ـــــــــ سنة ٦٣٨ ميــلادية وأصبــحت
ـــــــــ من الإمبراطورية ـــــــــ وفي نهاية ـــــــــ الحادي عشر
دخلها الصليبيون وأسسوا ـــــــــ مسيحية فيها عاصمتها ـــــــــ
ولكنها رجعت الى ـــــــــ الإسلامي بعد معركة ـــــــــ سنة ١١٨٧. وفي
سنة ١٥١٧ صارت جزءاً من الامبراطورية ـــــــــ استمرت ـــــــــ
الحكم العثماني الى سنة ـــــــــ.

٥. اكتب

Write a short paragraph about the city of Jedda in Saudi Arabia. The following
words may be useful.

جدّة، المملكة العربية السعودية، غرب، البحر الأحمر، كبير، الطقس

ـ ممكن تنزّل راسك شويّة يا أخ، مش شايف شيء.

الدرس رقم ٥٠

والله اذا ما بتجيبوا كندرتي رايح اعمل مثل ما عمل ابوي لما انسرقت كندرته.

أسئلة

1. Where did Juha take off his shoes?
_____

2. Did Juha find his shoes when he left the mosque?
_____

3. What did the people say when Juha asked them about his shoes?
_____

4. What did Juha say when the people said that they did not see the shoes?
_____

5. Why were the people afraid?
_____

6. Did the people find the shoes in the end?
_____

7. What did Juha's father do when his shoes were stolen?
_____

to shout	صاح	to pray	صلّى (يصلّي)
to steal	سَرق	voice	صوت
		barefoot	حافي

الله يرحم ايام الشباب! كنت
من اول مرة اركبك وما أطّع.

وليش الكذب؟ لما كنت شاب كنت
اطّع كمان.

أسئلة

1. How long has Dan been in Jordan?

_____

2. Where does he live?

_____

3. Does he have a problem?

_____

4. How many bedrooms does his apartment have?

_____

5. How much does he pay with electricity and water?

_____

6. How much does a similar apartment in New York cost?

_____

كلمات جديدة

frankly	بِصَراحَة	citizen	مُواطِن
to cost	كلّف (يكلّف)	to believe	اعتقد (يعتقد)
		Mercy on us!	يا لطيف!

اقرأ

فلسطين (٢)

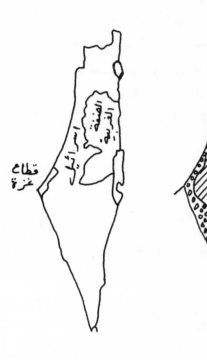

فلسطين بعد تأسيس إسرائيل سنة ١٩٤٨	فلسطين حسب قرار التقسيم (١٩٤٧)	العراق وبلاد الشام حسب معاهدة سايكس بيكو (١٩١٦)
	▨ دولة عربية	▨ تحت الانتداب البريطاني
	▨ دولة يهودية	☐ تحت الانتداب الفرنسي
	☐ إدارة دولية	

في سنة ١٩٤٧ أصدرت الأمم المتحدة قراراً بتقسيم فلسطين الى دولة عربية ودولة يهودية ولم يقبل العرب القرار لأنه أعطى اليهود ٥٦٪ من فلسطين بينما كانوا أقلية فيها. وعندما لم يتفق العرب واليهود على حل للمشكلة قررت بريطانيا الانسحاب وتحويل المشكلة للأمم المتحدة، وانسحب الجيش البريطاني من فلسطين في ١٤ مايو (ايار) ١٩٤٨ وأعلن اليهود تأسيس دولة اسرائيل في ١٥ مايو.

ثم قامت حرب بين الفلسطينيين واليهود ودخلت جيوش عربية من الأردن ومصر والعراق وسوريا ولبنان لمساعدة الفلسطينيين، ولكن الجيوش العربية خسرت الحرب واحتلت اسرائيل أجزاء أخرى من فلسطين. وفي نهاية تلك الحرب كانت اسرائيل تحتل ٧٧٪ من فلسطين بدلاً من ال ٥٦٪ التى

٣٢١

تقررت للدولة اليهودية في قرار تقسيم الأمم المتحدة.

ماذا حدث للفلسطينيين ولل ٢٣٪ التي بقيت من فلسطين؟ حوالي ٦٠٠ الف فلسطيني هربوا بسبب الحرب وصاروا لاجئين، وبقي حوالي ١٦٠ الف داخل الدولة اليهودية. وقد صدرت قرارات من الأمم المتحدة تُطالب اسرائيل بالسماح للفلسطينيين بالرجوع الى بيوتهم ولكن اسرائيل رفضت ذلك وفتحت أبوابها لهجرة اليهود من كل بلاد العالم.

بالنسبة لل٢٣٪ التي بقيت من فلسطين فهي ما يعرف الآن بالضفة الغربية وقطاع غزة. الضفة الغربية صارت جزءاً من الأردن وقطاع غزة جزءاً من مصر.

أسئلة

1. Why did the Palestinian Arabs not accept the U.N. partition plan?
_____

2. Why did Britain transfer the problem of Palestine to the United Nations?
_____

3. What happened in 1948?
_____

4. How much of Palestine did Israel occupy at the end of the 1948 war?
_____

5. How many Palestinians fled Palestine?
_____

6. What happened to the part of Palestine that was not taken over by Israel?
_____

كلمات جديدة

division, partition	تَقسيم	decision	قرار
solution	حَلّ	to agree	اتّفق (يتفق)
transfer	تحويل	withdrawal	انسحاب
instead of	بدلاً من	that, f.	تِلْكَ
what	ماذا=ايش	to be decided	تقرّر
allowing	سَماح	to happen	حدث
as for	بالنسبة لِ	to refuse	رفَض
		what is known	ما يُعرف

٣٢٢

Negation with لَمْ in فصحى

Perfect verbs are negated in فــصــحـى in one of two ways: (1) by using the negative particle ما before the verb in its perfect form:

كتب   "he wrote"   ما كتب   "he did not write"

and (2) by using لم followed by the imperfect form of the verb:

لم يكتُب   "he did not write"

Certain changes accompany the use of لم. Only those changes that you will encounter in the reading selections of this book will be discussed here. First, the ن of plural and dual verbs is dropped after لم:

يقبلون   "they, pl.m. accept"   لم يقبلوا   "they, pl.m. did not accept"

يقبلان   "they, dual, m. accept"   لم يقبلا   "they, dual m. did not accept"

(Notice plural ا at the end of يقبلوا.)

Second, the long vowel of a hollow verb in the imperfect is shortened in pronunciation and dropped in writing.

ينام	"he sleeps"	لم ينَم	"he did not sleep"
تنام	"she sleeps"	لم تنَم	"she did not sleep"
تنام	"you, m.s. sleep"	لم تنَم	"you, m.s. did not sleep"
أنام	"I sleep"	لم أنَم	"I did not sleep"
ننام	"we sleep"	لم ننَم	"we did not sleep"

تمارين

١. اقرأ واكتب

Give the plural form of each of the following words.

مملكة

جُزْء

بلَد

مسجد

درْس

سِعر

٢. اقرأ واكتب

Rewrite the following words, grouping them into related families. For each family identify the root and give its general meaning in English.

مماليك، حاول، زيادة، انولد، تقسيم، أقارب، قادم، وُلد، انقسم، توحيد، كلّف، استقبل، مملكة، واحد، قريب، تكاليف، قبل، وصل، قابل، زاد، قديم، توحّد، قدام، ولادة، مستقبل، مواصلات، يزيد، تحويل.

٣. استعمال القاموس

Look up the following words in the dictionary:

جامِع، محاسَبة، انتصر، مأكولات، اشتراكي، هاجَر، يستعملون، مُستشار

الدرس رقم ٥١

اسمع

شيء غريب، لما اركب الحمار باشوف اربع حمير، لكن لما انزل عنه
باشوف خمسة.

أسئلة

1. How many donkeys did Juha buy?

2. How did Juha return to his house?

3. Why did Juha think he had only four donkeys?

4. Why was Juha puzzled?

5. What did he decide to do in order to have five instead of four donkeys?

كلمات جديدة

to wonder	تعجّب	donkeys	حمير (حمار)
to be puzzled	تحيّر	to count	عدّ
		instead of	بدل ما

حوار

مشكلة الناس في هالأيام انهم ما بدهم يمشوا وما بدهم يستنوا.

أسئلة

1. What is today's segment of the program about?

2. What is the name of the person interviewed?

3. What does he do?

4. How many children does he have?

5. Where does he live?

6. How does he handle the transportation problem?

7. What is the problem that people these days have in Ibrahim's opinion?

كلمات جديدة

مُواصَلات — transportation

لعندهم — to them, to where they are

كم سُؤال — a few questions

٣٢٦

اقرأ

القدس

صورة قديمة للحرم الشريف (المسجد الأقصى ومسجد قبّة الصخرة) في القدس

تقع القدس على جبلين في وسط فلسطين، على بعد حوالي ٣٥ ميلاً شرق البحر الأبيض المتوسط وحوالي ١٣ ميلاً شمال غرب البحر الميت. وهي مدينة مقدسة عند اليهود والمسيحيين والمسلمين، ومن أهم الأماكن المقدّسة فيها حائط المبكى وكنيسة القيامة (القبر المقدّس) والمسجد الأقصى ومسجد قبّة الصخرة.

ذُكِرت مدينة القدس أوّل مرّة في رسائل "تل العمارنة" التي كُتبت حوالي سنة ١٣٧٠ ق.م. واحتل الملك داوود القدس حوالي سنة ١٠٠٠ ق.م. وصارت عاصمة مملكة اسرائيل، وبعد ذلك عاصمة مملكة يهودا. وفي سنة ٩٧٠ ق.م. بنى الملك سليمان سور المدينة والمعبد. وفي سنة ٥٨٦ ق.م. دمّرها نبوخذ نصّر البابلي، وفي سنة ٥٣٨ ق.م. أرجعها الملك سايروس ملك بلاد فارس لليهود، ثم حكمها الاسكندر الكبير وعائلة بطليموس والسلوقيون والرومان. وقد حكمها الرومان في زمن النبي عيسى المسيح. وفي سنة ٧٠

م. دمّرها تيتوس ثم دمّرها هادريان في سنة ١٣٥ م.، ولكنها بقيت تحت حكم الرومان. ثم احتلها الفرس من سنة ٦١٤ الى سنة ٦٢٩ م. ودخلها العرب المسلمون سنة ٦٣٨ م. وبنوا فيها قبّة الصخرة سنة ٦٩١-٦٩٢م. وفي سنة ١٠٩٩ احتلها الصليبيون وأقاموا فيها مملكة مسيحية، ولكن رجعت الى حكم المسلمين سنة ١١٨٧ بعد انتصار القائد المسلم المشهور صلاح الدين في معركة حطين. ثم حاول الصليبيون استرجاعها من المسلمين عدة مرات ولكنها ظلت تحت حكم المسلمين بشكل مستمر من سنة ١٢٤٤ الى سنة ١٩١٧. ودخلها الجيش البريطاني في ٩ كانون الأول (ديسمبر) سنة ١٩١٧ بعد هزيمة الأتراك العثمانيين في الحرب العالمية الاولى. وبعد حرب فلسطين بين العرب واليهود احتل الجيش الإسرائيلي الجزء الغربي من المدينة (المدينة الجديدة) واحتل الجيش الأردني الجزء الشرقي (المدينة القديمة). وفي سنة ١٩٥٠ عملت اسرائيل القدس الجديدة عاصمة الدولة. ثم احتل الجيش الإسرائيلي المدينة القديمة في حرب حزيران (يونيو) سنة ١٩٦٧ وضمّت اسرائيل المدينة القديمة الى المدينة الجديدة.

أسئلة

1. Where is Jerusalem located?

2. What Jewish, Christian, and Muslim religious sites are located in Jerusalem?

3. When was Jerusalem mentioned for the first time?

4. When was the Temple built?

5. When did Nebuchadnezzar destroy Jerusalem?

6. When did the Arabs enter Jerusalem?

7. What happened in 1187?

8. When did the British Army enter Jerusalem?

9. When did Israel declare Jerusalem its capital?

10. What happened in 1967?

the Wailing Wall	كلمات جديدة
Church of the Holy Sepulcher	حائط المبكى
al-Aqsa Mosque	كنيسة القيامة
Dome of the Rock	المسجد الأقصى
wall	قُبّة الصخرة
the Temple	سور
to return (something)	المعبد
Jesus Christ	أرجع=رجّع
victory	عيسى المسيح
getting back	انتصار
continuously	استرجاع
to annex	بشكل مستمر
	ضمّ

قواعد

بعض, كلّ, etc. with Pronominal Suffixes

The attached (possessive) pronouns can be suffixed to words like كُلّ "all," بعض "some," قدّام "in front of," and وراء "behind" in the same way that they are suffixed to nouns and prepositions. (بعض، كل، قدام، وراء are considered nouns in Arabic grammar.) This is shown in the following examples.

كلها	"all of it, f."
بعضهم	"some of them"
قُدّامنا	"in front of us"
وراءكم	"behind you, pl."

تمارين

١. اكتب

Fill in the blanks in the following:

ذُكِرت مدينة القدس أول مرّة في رسائل "تل العمارنة" التي كتبت
حوالي ـــــــ ١٣٧٠ ق. م. واحتل الملك داوود القدس ـــــــ سنة ١٠٠٠
ق.م. وصارت ـــــــ مملكة اسرائيل، وبعد ذلك عاصمة مملكة يهودا. وفي
سنة ٩٧٠ ق.م. بنى الملك سليمان ـــــــ المدينة والمعبد. وفي سنة ٥٨٦
ق.م. دمّرها نبوخذ نصّر ـــــــ، وفي سنة ٥٣٨ ق.م. أرجعها الملك سايروس
ملك ـــــــ فارس لليهود، ثم حكمها الاسكندر ـــــــ وعائلة بطليموس
والسلوقيون والرومان. وقد حكمها الرومان في زمن النبي ـــــــ المسيح.
وفي سنة ٧٠ م. دمّرها تيتوس ثم دمّرها هادريان في سنة ١٣٥ م.، ولكنها
بقيت تحت حكم ـــــــ ثم احتلها الفرس من سنة ٦١٤ الى سنة ٦٢٩ م.
ودخلها ـــــــ المسلمون سنة ٦٣٨ م. وبنوا فيها ـــــــ ـــــــ ـــــــ سنة
٦٩١-٦٩٢م.

٢. اكتب

Identify the root and the verb form in the following:

تقع، ذُكِرت، احتلّ، بنوا، دمّرها، حاول، يسترجع، ضمّت، انتهى، صار، اعتَبر،
يُركّز، استراح

٣. اكتب

Write a short paragraph about Kuwait. Use the following information as a basis.

الكويت

عدد السكان	٢ مليون
المساحة	١٧٨٢٠ كيلومتر مربع
العاصمة	الكويت
نوع الحكومة	إمارة
الحاكم	الأمير جابر الصباح

اسـمـع

أسئلة

1. Where did Juha and his son go one day?

_____

2. What did the people say when they saw Juha riding and his son walking behind him?

_____

3. What did the people say when Juha and his son were riding the donkey together?

_____

4. What did Juha decide to do at the end?

_____

كلمات جديدة

| strong | قَوِي | shame on you | عيب عليك |
| to carry | حَمَل (يحمِل) | old (person) | عَجوز |

حوار

أسئلة

1. What does Muhammad Salman do?

_____

2. Is he married?

_____

3. Does he have a car?

_____

4. What are some of the transportation problems that Muhammad faces?

_____

5. How long does it take Muhammad to get to the Teacher's Institute?

_____

كلمات جديدة

bachelor	أعزَب	Teacher's Institute	مَعهد معلّمـين
full	مَليان	barely, with difficulty	يالله يالله
to take	أخذ (ياخذ)	the whole time	طـول الوقت

٣٣٢

اقرأ ١

محمود درويش

وُلد الشاعر الفلسطيني المعروف محمود درويش في قرية "البروة" شرق مدينة عكّا في شمال فلسطين سنة ١٩٤٢. وفي ليلة من ليالي سنة ١٩٤٨ هجم الجيش الإسرائيلي على قرية البروة فهربت عائلة محمود درويش الى لبنان. وفي لبنان بقيت العائلة سنة تعيش على مساعدة الأمم المتحدة. وفي سنة ١٩٤٩ رجع محمود درويش وعمه الى قرية البروة ولكن لم تكن هناك لأن الجيش الإسرائيلي كان قد دمرها، فسكن في قرية "دير الأسد" في الجليل. قال محمود درويش إنه كان لاجئاً في لبنان وصار لاجئاً في بلده.

بدأ اهتمام محمود درويش بالشعر وهو صغير، وسبّب الشعر له مشاكل كثيرة مع الحكومة الإسرائيلية.

اشتغل محمود درويش صحفياً في حيفا وحرّر مجلة "الاتحاد". وفي سنة ١٩٧١ سافر الى بيروت وبقي فيها حتى سنة ١٩٨٢. ويعيش الآن في باريس ويحرر مجلة "الكرمل".

كتب محمود درويش أكثر من عشر مجموعات شعريّة وحصل على جائزة "لوتس" سنة ١٩٦٩ وجائزة لينين للسلام سنة ١٩٨٣. ويُعتَبَر أشهر شاعر فلسطيني. ومن أشهر كتبه "آخر الليل"، "عاشق من فلسطين"، و"أوراق زيتون".

كلمات جديدة

poet	شاعر
one night ("a night of the nights")	ليلة من الليالي
refugee	لاجئ
interest	اهتمام
poetry	شعر
journalist	صَحَفي
to edit	حرّر (يحرّر)
award, prize	جائزة

اقرأ ٢

سجّل، أنا عربي (محمود درويش)

سجّل! — Write down!

أنا عربي — I am an Arab,

ورقم بطاقتي خمسون ألف — My I.D. number is 50,000,

وأطفالي ثمانية — My children, eight

وتاسعهم ..سيأتي بعد صيف! — And the ninth is coming next summer.

فهل تغضب؟ — Are you angry?

سجّل! — Write down!

أنا عربي — I am an Arab.

وأعمل مع رفاق الكدح في محجر — I work with my struggling friends in a quarry,

وأطفالي ثمانية — And my children are eight.

أسلّ لهم رغيف الخبز — I pull out the loaf of bread for them,

والأثواب والدفتر — clothes and notebooks

من الصخر — from the rock.

ولا أتوسّل الصدقات من بابك — I do not beg for a handout at your door,

ولا أصغر — Nor do I humble myself

أمام بلاط أعتابك — at your threshold.

فهل تغضب؟ — Are you angry?

سجّل! — Write down!

أنا عربي — I am an Arab.

أنا اسم بلا لقب — A name without a title,

صبور في بلاد كل ما فيها — patient in a land, everything in it

يعيش بفورة الغضب — brimming with anger.

جذوري — My roots

قبل ميلاد الزمان رست — were entrenched before the birth of time

وقبل تفتّح الحقب — and before the opening of ages,

وقبل السرو والزيتون — before the pines, the olive tree,

وقبل ترعرع العشب — before the grass grew.

أبي من أسرة المحراث — My father came from the family of the plow

٣٣٤

لا من سادة نجب

not from grand gentlemen.

وجدي كان فلاحاً

My grandfather was a peasant

بلا حسب ولا نسب!

neither well-bred nor well-born.

وبيتي، كوخ ناطور

My house is a watchman's hut

من الأعواد والقصب

Made of sticks and reeds.

فهل ترضيك منزلتي؟

Do you like my status?

أنا اسم بلا لقب!

I am a name without a title.

سجّل!

Write down!

أنا عربي

I am an Arab.

ولون الشعر فحمي

Hair color: coal black,

ولون العينين بنّيّ

eye color: brown,

وميزاتي:

Special features

على رأسي عقال فوق كوفيّة

On my head: a *'iqal* on top of a *hatta*.

وكفي صلبة كالصخر

My hand is hard like a rock,

تخمش من يلامسها

It scratches those who touch it.

وأطيب ما أحب من الطعام

My favorite food is

الزيت والزعتر

zeit and *za'tar*.

وعنواني:

My address:

أنا من قرية عزلاء منسيّة

I am from a peaceful forgotten village,

شوارعها بلا أسماء

Its streets have no names.

وكل رجالها ... في الحقل والمحجر

All its men are . . . in the field and the quarry

فهل تغضب؟

Does that anger you?

سجّل!

Write down!

أنا عربي

I am an Arab.

سلبت كروم أجدادي

You stole the vineyards of my ancestors

وأرضاً كنت أفلحها

and the land I once plowed

أنا وجميع أولادي

Along with all my children.

ولم تترك لنا.. ولكل أحفادي

The only thing you left for us and for all the grandchildren

سوى هذي الصخور

is those rocks.

فهل ستأخذها

Will your government take those

As it has been said.	حكومتكم كما قيلَ
Write down then	إذن سجّل
On top of the first page	برأس الصفحة الأولى
I do not hate.	أنا لا أكره الناس
I do not steal.	ولا أسطو على أحد
But if I become hungry	ولكني..اذا ما جعت
I eat the flesh of my usurper.	آكل لحم مغتصبي
Beware, beware of my hunger	حذار.. حذار ..من جوعي
and of my anger.	ومن غضبي.

قواعد

The Resumptive Pronoun

The Arabic equivalent of the English phrase *the house which you live in* is rendered as البيت اللي انتَ ساكن فيه "the house which you live in it." Such a phrase derives from انت ساكن في البيت and البيت. When a relative clause is formed by replacing the second occurrence of البيت by the relative pronoun اللي (English *which*), the pronoun that replaces the object of the preposition (or the object of the verb) is retained in Arabic but not in English. Another example of the resumptive pronoun is found in phrases like:

البنت اللي شفتها.   "the girl who I saw" ("the girl who I saw her")

The Future in فصحى

Future tense is indicated in فصحى by attaching the prefix س to the imperfect form of the verb or placing the word سوف before such a verb. سيأتي and سوف يأتي mean the same thing: "will come."

تمارين

١. استعمل القاموس

Look up the meanings of the following words in the dictionary.

شاعِر، فهرَبت، مُساعدة، اهتمّ، مَجموعات، عاشِق

٢. اكتب

Identify the root and the verb form in the following:

يَتَوسّل، سجّل، (أنا) أفلح، تُعاني، يُبيّن، يَنزِل، ستَزيد، تَخاف

٣. اقرأ

Match each the words in the first column with their opposites in the second.

ميّت	بيع
متزوّج	نجح
ماضي	أعزب
كثير	انتصار
فشل	حيّ
شراء	قادِم
هزيمة	قليل

٤. اكتب

Write a short paragraph about Algeria. Use the following information as a basis.

الجزائر

٢٥ مليون	عدد السكان
٢،٣٨١،٧٥١ كيلومتر مربع	المساحة
الجزائر	العاصمة
جمهورية	نوع الحكومة
الإسلام	الدين
١٩٦٢	سنة الاستقلال

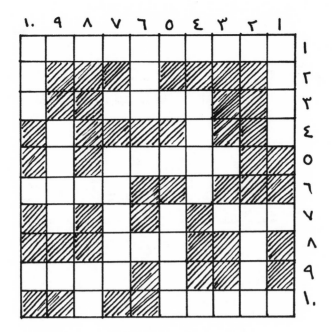

أفقي

١. شاعر فلسطيني معروف

٣. إسم سدّ في مصر (عكس مُنخَفَض)

٥. تفاح وموز وبرتقال

٦. جمع درس

٧. عكس تذكّر

٨. إبن أبي

٩. عكس أخذ

١٠. يصلّي فيها المسيحيون

عمودي

١. رسول الإسلام

٢. جمع ساكن

٤. يدرسها الطلاب في الجامعة والمدرسة

٥. مفرد موادّ

٦. بلاد

٧. تعطيها لأقاربك وأصحابك

٨. أخ الأب

٩. جمع فلس

١٠. إنسان

اسمع

أسئلة

1. What did Juha tell his wife one night?

_____

2. What did he say when his wife said: "Say 'God Willing'"?

_____

3. What happened to his money when he got to the *suq*?

_____

4. Did Juha buy a donkey that day?

_____

5. Who did he meet on the way back to his house?

_____

6. What did the soldiers want?

_____

7. Why did the soldiers get angry?

_____

8. What did the soldiers do when they got to the village?

_____

9. How was Juha when he got home at the end of the day?

_____

10. What did Juha say when his wife asked who was knocking at the door?

_____

كلمات جديدة

Note

The phrase إن شاء الله is used to express hope for something to happen in the future. It shows a certain degree of piety and the belief that things are not under our control but under God's. Juha refuses to say إن شاء الله before he goes to the market, but he learns a tough lesson and uses the phrase inappropriately when it is too late.

soldiers	جُنود	to forget	نِسِي
hunger	جوع	body	جِسم
to answer	رَدّ	thirst	عَطَش

أسئلة

1. What is the taxi fare to the airport?

_____

2. How long has Dan stayed in Jordan?

_____

3. Is he thinking of coming back to Jordan?

_____

4. How much was the meat in the old days?

_____

5. Was Jordan crowded in the past?

_____

6. What makes Jordan crowded in the summer?

_____

كلمات جديدة

what if, imagine if	كيف لو
Ah, the good old days! ("God bless the days of the past")	الله يرحم ايّام زَمـان
crowdedness	زَحمة
Bulgarian	بَلغاري
the (Arabian) Gulf	الخليج
Europe	أوروبا
Japan	اليابان

تكلّم

Create a dialogue with another student in which one asks questions and the other tells how good, bad, or hard things were at some point in the past.

اقرأ

الماء في الشرق الأوسط

مشكلة الماء مشكلة كبيرة في الشرق الأوسط، فماء المطر قليل وليس هناك أنهار وبحيرات كثيرة. تختلف حدّة مشكلة الماء من بلد الى بلد، فعلى سبيل المثال السعودية والأردن وليبيا تعاني أكثر من مصر والعراق وسوريا.

ويبيّن الجدول التالي كمية الماء في بعض البلاد العربية بالمقارنة بالولايات المتحدة:

	كمية الماء المتوفرة للشخص الواحد في السنة بالمتر المكعب (١٩٩٠)
الولايات المتحدة	١٠٠٠٠
العراق	٥٠٥٠٠
سوريا	٢٠٨٠٠
مصر	١٠٠٠٠
الأردن	٢٦٠

ينزل أكثر المطر في بلاد العالم العربي في فصل الشتاء فقط، وفي بعض المناطق قد لا ينزل المطر أبداً في بعض السنوات. ويبين الجدول التالي كمية ماء المطر في السنة في بعض المدن العربية:

	كمية ماء المطر بالمليمتر في السنة
الدار البيضاء	٣٨٤
الجزائر	٧٦٢
طرابلس-ليبيا	٣٨٤
القاهرة	٢٢
أسوان	١
الخرطوم	١٥٧
بيروت	٥١٧
دمشق	٢١٨
عمان	٢٨٠
بغداد	١٥١
الكويت	١١١
الرياض	٨٢
جدة	٢٥
مسقط	٩٩
الإسكندرية	١٧٥
صنعاء	٥٠٠

ومن الأمور التي تزيد في حدة مشكلة الماء في العالم العربي:
الزيادة السريعة في عدد السكان، تطور الزراعة والصناعة، والخلافات
السياسية بين دول المنطقة. ففي حرب١٩٦٧ قصف الجيش الإسرائيلي سداً
على نهر اليرموك على الحدود الأردنية السورية. وفي سنة ١٩٧٥ كادت أن
تقوم حرب بين العراق وسوريا بسبب بناء سدين على نهر الفرات في سوريا
وتركيا.

ويقول البعض إن أهمية الماء ستزيد في المستقبل. وقد قال
الدكتور بطرس بطرس غالي الأمين العام للأمم المتحدة في سنة ١٩٨٥: "إن
الحرب القادمة في الشرق الأوسط سيكون سببها الماء وليس السياسة." فالآن
تخاف سوريا والعراق أن تقل كمية الماء التي تصل لهما من دجلة والفرات
بسبب بناء سدود كبيرة لحجز الماء في تركيا. كذلك تخاف مصر والسودان أن
تبني اثيوبيا وأوغندا سدوداً لحجز ماء النيل. وفي الضفة الغربية تعتبر
مشكلة الماء من أهم المشاكل في العلاقات بين إسرائيل والفلسطينيين.

أسئلة
Indicate whether each of the following statements is true or false.
1. Libya suffers more than Syria from the shortage of water. _____
2. The amount of water available per person in Jordan is less than one-tenth of the
amount available per person in the U.S. _____
3. Most of the rainwater in the Arab world falls in the spring and summer. _____
4. More rain falls on Tripoli (Libya) than on Beirut. _____
5. More rain falls on Kuwait City than on Cairo. _____
6. One of the factors that contributes to the water shortage in the Arab world is the
development of agriculture. _____
7. Political differences do not contribute to the water problems of the Arab world.
_____
8. Syria and Iraq were about to go to war over water. _____
9. Some people think that the next war in the Middle East will be fought over water.
_____
10. Sudan is worried that the building of dams on the Nile in Egypt will affect its
water supply. _____

		seriousness, acuteness	حدّة
to suffer	عانى (يعاني)	as an example	على سبيل المثال
table	جدول	to show	بيّن (يبيّن)
amount	كمية	following	تالي
available	متوفر	comparison	مقارنة
cubic	مكعّب	person	شخص
increase	زيادة	things, factors	أمر (أمور)
disagreement	خلاف	development	تطوّر
future	مُستقبَل	was about to	كاد أن
coming, next	قادم	secretary general	أمين عام
to be afraid	خاف (يخاف)	cause	سبب
to block off	حَجَز	to decrease, to be less	قَلَّ (يقِلّ)

تمارين

١. اقرأ واكتب

Give the plural form of each of the following words.

دين
قريب
حمار
سُؤال
مكتبة
شخص
مكتب

٢. اقرأ واكتب

Identify the root and the verb form in the following:

انتظر، وافق، تَتَوقّف، تنام، يُفكّر، تستعمِل، ينفتح

٣. استعمل القاموس

Look up the meaning of the following words in the dictionary:

تكلّم، طلاقة، استأجر، يقولون، اتّفق، تحسّن

٤. اكتب

Fill in the blanks in the following.

ويقـول البـعض إن أهمّيّـة المـاء سـتـزيد فـي ـــــــ وقـد قـال
الدكتور بطرس بطرس غالي الأمين العام ـــــــ ـــــــ ـــــــ فـي سنة ١٩٨٥:
"إن الحـرب القـادمـة فـي ـــــــ ـــــــ ـــــــ سـيـكون سـبـبـها المـاء وليس
ـــــــ" فالآن تخاف سوريا والعراق أن تقل كمية الماء التي تصل لهما من
دجلة ـــــــ بسبب بناء سدود كبيرة لحجز ـــــــ فـي ـــــــ كذلك
تخاف مـصـر ـــــــ أن تبنـي اثيـوبيـا وأوغندا سـدوداً لحجـز ـــــــ
النيل. وفي الضفـة ـــــــ تعتبـر مشكلة الماء من أهم ـــــــ فـي
العلاقات بـين إسرائيل و ـــــــ

٥. اكتب

Write a short paragraph about Morocco. Use the following information as a basis.

المغرب

عدد السكان	٢٥ , ٤ مليون نسمة
المساحة	٤٤٦٥٥٠ كيلومتر مربع
العاصمة	الرباط
نوع الحكومة	مملكة
الحاكم	الملك الحسن الثاني
الدين	الإسلام
سنة الاستقلال	١٩٥٦
العملة	الدرهم

٦. اكتب

Imagine yourself in Dan's position. Write a letter to Abu Sharif thanking him for his help during your stay in Jordan. Use the form of the following letter as a guide.

فيرفاكس-فرجينيا
٧/٩/ ١٩٩٠

عزيزي أحمد
تحية طيّبة وبعد،

أكتب لك هذه الرسالة من مدينة فيرفاكس. فيرفاكس مدينة صغيرة في شمال ولاية فرجينيا، وهي قريبة من مدينة واشنطن العاصمة.

وصلت الى مطار كندي في نيويورك في صباح يوم الثلاثاء ٢٥/٨، ومن نيويورك ركبت الطائرة الى واشنطن. كان أبي وأمي في مطار واشنطن. ركبنا السيارة من المطار الى بيتنا في فيرفاكس.

بدأت الدراسة في جامعة جورجتاون قبل أسبوع، وأدرس الآن اللغة العربية والعلوم السياسية وتاريخ الشرق الأوسط. أسكن مع أبي وأمي في فيرفاكس وأذهب الى الجامعة "بالسبواي".

سلامي لك ولعائلتك وللأصدقاء، وأشكرك على كرمك وعلى مساعدتك لي وأنا في القاهرة.

والى اللقاء في رسالة أطول في المستقبل.

المخلص،

مارك

APPENDIX ملــحـق

Notes on Reading

1. ا+ل becomes لا.

2. م+ل is frequently written ـلـ.

3. Other symbols you will see are the following:

   a. ة ،ـة (taaʔ marbuuṭa). This is found only in the final position of a word. It is a feminine ending that appears on nouns and adjectives and is pronounced <u>a</u> or <u>i</u>, depending on the preceding consonant. However, if the word in which it occurs is the first part of a construct, then it is pronounced <u>at</u> or <u>it</u>. (See the sections on the Construct and Possession in lessons 7, 9, and 10.)

   b. The Arabic letter *hamza* is not considered a full member of the alphabet. It is sometimes written by itself, but it is mostly "tacked onto" a vowel. It always has the same pronunciation: a glottal stop or a glottal catch, the way you start a word like <u>apple</u> in English. The *hamza* may have any of the following shapes: أ، إ، ؤ، ئـ

ى، ئ، ء.

   c. ى (alif maqṣuura). This letter is found only at the end of words and is pronounced like the letter ا. When suffixes are attached it appears either as ا or ـي.

4. Short vowels are not generally indicated in Arabic writing. They are sometimes included to help certain groups of readers such as children or foreign learners. There are three reasons I have not included them fully in this book. The first is the belief that the sooner the learner is introduced to the Arabic that Arabs read the better. Second, the user of this book will not be decifering unfamiliar words for which he/she will need to know the exact pronunciaton, but rather will be reading familiar words that have been heard or read before. Third, I would like the course to focus on developing reading comprehension with the emphasis on the general meaning of a paragraph or a sentence rather than on the meaning and exact pronunciaton of individual words. However, in some contexts the short vowels are necessary; for example, in a vocabulary list where a distinction needs to be made between a pair of otherwise identical words.

The following list includes these vowels and the other most important diacritic symbols. I will use the letter ف (f) to illustrate shape, position, and pronunciation of these diacritics.

فَ fatḥa:	short ا following the consonant on which it appears (fa)	
فِ kasra:	short ي following the consonant on which it appears (fi)	
فُ ḍamma:	short و following the consonant on which it appears (fu)	
فّ shadda:	indicates doubling of the consonant on which it appears (ff)	
فاً	fan (Notice the ا with the diacritic.)	
فٍ	fin	
فٌ	fun	

The Numerals الأرقام

21	واحد وعشرين	٢١	1	واحد	١
22	اثنين وعشرين	٢٢	2	اثنين	٢
23	ثلاثة وعشرين	٢٣	3	ثلاثة	٣
24	أربعة وعشرين	٢٤	4	أربعة	٤
25	خمسة وعشرين	٢٥	5	خمسة	٥
26	ستة وعشرين	٢٦	6	ستة	٦
27	سبعة وعشرين	٢٧	7	سبعة	٧
28	ثمانية وعشرين	٢٨	8	ثمانية	٨
29	تسعة وعشرين	٢٩	9	تسعة	٩
30	ثلاثين	٣٠	10	عشرة	١٠
40	أربعين	٤٠	11	احداش	١١
50	خمسين	٥٠	12	اطناش	١٢
60	ستين	٦٠	13	ثلطّاش	١٣
70	سبعين	٧٠	14	أربعطاش	١٤
80	ثمانين	٨٠	15	خمسطاش	١٥
90	تسعين	٩٠	16	سطّاش	١٦
100	ميّة	١٠٠	17	سبعطاش	١٧
1,000	ألف	١٠٠٠	18	ثمنطاش	١٨
1,000,000	مليون	١٠٠٠٠٠٠	19	تسعطاش	١٩
			20	عشرين	٢٠

الأرقام الترتيبية Ordinal Numbers	
أوّل	first
ثاني	second
ثالث	third
رابع	fourth
خامس	fifth
سادس	sixth
سابع	seventh
ثامن	eighth
تاسع	ninth
عاشر	tenth

أيام الأسبوع Days of the Week

السبت	Saturday
الأحد	Sunday
الاثنين	Monday
الثلاثاء	Tuesday
الأربعاء	Wednesday
الخميس	Thursday
الجمعة	Friday

	Months of the Year	شهور السنة
	The Gregorian Calendar	التقويم الغربي
	(Syria, etc. سوريا، الخ.)	(Egypt, etc. مصر، الخ.)
January	كانون الثاني	يناير
February	شباط	فبراير
March	آذار	مارس
April	نيسان	أبريل
May	أيار	مايو
June	حزيران	يونيو
July	تموز	يوليو
August	أب	أغسطس
September	أيلول	سبتمبر
October	تشرين الأوّل	أكتوبر
November	تشرين الثاني	نوفمبر
December	كانون الأول	ديسمبر

The Islamic (Lunar) Calendar	التقويم الإسلامي
Muħarram	محرّم
ṣafar	صفر
Rabiiʕ al-Awwal	ربيع الأوّل
Rabiiʕ al-Thaani	ربيع الثاني
Jumaada al-Uula	جمادى الأولى
Jumaada al-Thaaniya	جمادى الثانية
Rajab	رجب
Shaʕbaan	شَعبان
Ramaḍaan	رمضان
Shawwaal	شوّال
Dhu al-ḳiʕda	ذو القعدة
Dhu al-ħijja	ذو الحجة

Seasons of the Year فصول السنة

summer	الصيف
fall	الخريف
winter	الشتاء
spring	الربيع

Arab Countries and Their Capitals الدول العربية وعواصمها

Capital	العاصمة	Country	الدولة
Cairo	القاهرة	Egypt	جمهورية مصر العربية
Algiers	الجزائر	Algeria	جمهورية الجزائر الشعبية الديمقراطية
Rabat	الرباط	Morocco	المملكة المغربية
Khartoum	الخرطوم	Sudan	الجمهورية السودانية
Baghdad	بغداد	Iraq	الجمهورية العراقية
Riyadh	الرياض	Saudi Arabia	المملكة العربية السعودية
Damascus	دمشق	Syria	الجمهورية العربية السورية
San'a	صنعاء	Yemen	جمهورية اليمن
Mogadishu	مغاديشو	Somalia	جمهورية الصومال الديمقراطية
Tunis	تونس	Tunisia	الجمهورية التونسية
Tripoli	طرابلس	Libya	الجماهيرية العربية الليبية الشعبية الاشتراكية
Amman	عمان	Jordan	المملكة الأردنية الهاشمية
Beirut	بيروت	Lebanon	الجمهورية اللبنانية
Kuwait	الكويت	Kuwait	دولة الكويت
Nouakshoute	نواكشوط	Mauritania	جمهورية موريتانيا الإسلامية
Abu Dhabi	أبو ظبي	United Arab Emirates	الإمارات العربية المتحدة
Muscat	مسقط	Oman	سلطنة عمان
Manama	المنامة	Bahrain	دولة البحرين
Doha	الدوحة	Qatar	دولة قطر
Djibouti	جيبوتي	Djibouti	جمهورية جيبوتي

Forms of the Arabic Verb
Summary
Table I

Example	Meaning	مصدر	Imperfect	Form/Perfect	
كتب	--	--	يفعُل	فعل	I
عرَف			يفعِل		
فتح			يفعَل		
علّم	causative/transitive	تَفعيل	يُفعّل	فَعّل	II
ساعَد	associative	مُفاعَلة	يُفاعل	فاعل	III
تعلّم	reflexive of II	---	يَتَفَعّل	تفعّل	V
تفاهَم	reflexive of III	--	يَتَفاعل	تفاعل	VI
انكسر	passive/reflexive of I	انفعال	يَنفَعِل	انفعل	VII
استمع	reflexive of I	افتعال	يَفتَعِل	افتَعَل	VIII
استقبل	causative/reflexive on I	استفعال	يَستفعِل	استفعل	X

Table II

Twice Derived		Once Derived		Basic
٥. تفعّل	reflexive	٢. فعّل	causative/transitive/intensive	فعل
٦. تفاعل	reflexive	٣. فاعَل	associative	"
		٧. انفَعَل	passive/reflexive	"
		٨. افتَعَل	reflexive	"
		١٠. استَفْعَل	reflexive/do for own advantage	"

قراءات إضافيّة Additional Readings

دان وليمز

١

دان وليمـز طالـب أمـريكي عمـره ٣٠ سنة. سافـر الى الأردن لدراسـة اللغـة العربيـة والأدب العـربي في الجامعـة الأردنيـة. كـان قـد درس اللغـة العربية في جامعة كورنيل وزار مصر لمدة أسبوعين قبل سفره للأردن. كان يفهم ويقرأ ويتكلّم العربية ولكنه كان يريد أن يتكلمها بطلاقة أكثر. في جامعـة كورنيل التقى دان بشريف سمارة وتكلّم معه باللغة العربية وصارا صديقين. وفي يوم من الأيام قال شريف لدان: "اذا بدك تحكي عربي وتكتب وتقرا مثل العرب لازم تروح لبلد عربي وتدرس وتسكن فيه." وقال شريف أيضا: "أهلي في الأردن، اذا رحت للأردن أبوي بيساعدك تستأجر شقّة وتسكن وتدرس في الجامعة هناك."

٢

 سافـر دان للأردن على شـركة طيـران عاليـة الأردنيـة، وكانت رحلتـه سـهلة. طـارت الطائـرة من نيـويورك السـاعة الثامنة في المساء ووصلت مطار علياء الدولي بعد ١٧ ساعة.

أخذ دان تكسي من المطار الى فندق الأندلس في عمان. وفي الفندق طلب الموظف جواز السفر من دان، وفتش دان على جواز سفره ولكن لم يجده، فترك شنطته في الفندق وأخذ تكسي الى المطار.

في التكسي كان دان غضباناً كثيراً لأنه ضيّع جواز سفره. وعندما وصل الي المطار ذهب الى شرطي المطار وأخبره عن مشكلته فطلب منه الشرطي أن ينتظر قليلاً حتى يفتش على الجواز في صندوق الموجودات. وفعلاً كان الجواز في صندوق الموجودات. أخذ دان جواز سفره وأخذ تكسي مرّة ثانية للفندق وأعطى الجواز للموظف وذهب الى غرفته.

كان دان جوعاناً، فسأل موظف الفندق عن مطعم قريب، فقال له الموظف إن هناك مطعم قريب ورخيص اسمه مطعم السلام. ذهب دان الى مطعم السلام وأكل فيه وأحب الأكل فيه كثيراً.

٣

رجع دان الى غرفتـه في الفندق وتكلم بـالتلفون مع أبيـه وأمـه في إثاكا، ونام في تلك الليلة، وفي صباح اليوم الثاني تكلم بالتلفون مع أبو

شريف في إربد. كان مع دان صور ورسالة من شريف لأهله في إربد.

أبو شريف دعا دان لزيارة العائلة وأكل الغداء في إربد. لم يذهب دان في نفس اليوم ولكنه ذهب في نهاية ذلك الأسبوع، أي يوم الجمعة.

وقبل أن يذهب تكلم بالتلفون مع أبو شريف، لأنه لم يعرف عنوان بيته في إربد. لكن بيت أبو شريف ليس له رقم، وكثير من الشوارع ليس لها أسماء. قال أبو شريف لدان: "إركب الباص وانا بستنّاك في محطة الباصات في إربد." وقال له إن هناك باصات اسمها باصات حجازي نظيفة وسريعة وكل ساعة هناك باص من عمان لإربد.

إنتظر أبو شريف دان في محطة الباصات، وعرف دان بسرعة لأنه لم يكن في الباص أمريكيون غير دان.

أخذ أبو شريف تكسي من محطة الباصات الى البيت. لم يكن البيت بعيداً عن المحطّة، حوالي عشر دقائق فقط.

التقى دان بأم شريف وأولاد أبو شريف: مريم وعبدالله وسعاد. قال دان إنه رأى شريف قبل سفره بأسبوع، وحكى لهم عن شقة شريف وعن دراسته في جامعة كورنيل.

بعد الغداء جلس دان مع عائلة أبو شريف وتحدّثوا وشربوا الشاي والقهوة. وحوالي الساعة الرابعة بعد الظهر قال دان إنه يريد أن يرجع الى عمان لأنه كان مشغولاً. لكن أبو شريف قال له: "لازم تنام هون الليلة حتى نحكي معك ونسألك عن شريف".

٤

بعد العشاء بقليل بدأ الجيران يجيئون الى بيت أبو شريف حتى يروا الضيف الذي جاء من أمريكا ويتكلموا معه ويسألوه عن أمريكا وعن شريف.

أولاً جاء أبو العبد وبعده بقليل جاء أبو محمود وبعد أبو محمود بحوالي ربع ساعة جاء أبو سامي. كلهم سألوا دان نفس السؤال: "مين في رأيك أحسن الأردن ولا أمريكا؟" طبعاً دان لم يعرف الأردن جيّداً لأنه وصل قبل أسبوع فقط.

بعدما رجع الجيران لبيوتهم سأل أبو شريف دان أين سيسكن، فقال له دان إنه يريد أن يسكن في عمان، في شقة قريبة من الجامعة الأردنية، واتفق دان وأبو شريف أن يفتّشا على شقة معاً، لأن أبو شريف يعرف عمان "من أولها لآخرها".

ذهب أبو شريف ودان الى سمسار بيوت في عمان، وأخذهم السمسار الى شقة مفروشة فيها غرفة نوم وغرفة جلوس ومطبخ وحمام غربي. كانت أجرة الشقة ٧٠ ديناراً في الشهر. ثم رجع أبو شريف الى إربد وذهب دان

للفندق وأخذ ملابسه وكتبه الى الشقة. وبعد ثلاثة أيام تكلم أبو شريف مع دان بالتلفون ودعاه ليأكل طعام الغداء مع العائلة في إربد يوم الجمعة القادم.

٥

ركب دان في باص من باصات حجازي الى إربد، وأخذ تكسي الى بيت أبو شريف، ووصل بعد الظهر بقليل. بعد الغداء جلس دان مع عائلة أبو شريف وشربوا قهوة وتكلموا عن أمريكا وعن شريف وعن الأردن، ثم طلب أبو شريف من دان أن يساعد بنته سعاد باللغة الإنجليزية حتى تنجح في امتحان التوجيهي.

ساعد دان سعاد في اللغة الإنجليزية ولكنه لم يقدر أن يساعدها في العلوم والرياضيّات لأنه لا يحب العلوم والرياضيات. واستمر في دراسة اللغة العربية والأدب العربي في الجامعة الأردنية وأحب دراسته كثيراً وتحسّنت لغته العربية وخصوصاً في الفهم والكلام. وأنهى دراسته في نهاية فصل الصيف ورجع الى أمريكا.

شريف سمارة

١

وُلد شريف سمارة في قرية صغيرة بالقرب من مدينة نابلس في الضفّة الغربية. كانت الضفّة الغربية جزءاً من الأردن في ذلك الوقت. وبعد حرب ال ١٩٦٧ بين العرب واسرائيل سافر شريف الى الأردن مع أبيه وأمه وأخته مريم وسكنوا في إربد.

درس شريف في مدارس إربد وحصل على علامات عالية في امتحان التوجيهي وحصل على مساعدة من وزارة التربية والتعليم الأردنية لدراسة الهندسة في الجامعة الأردنية.

بعد أن أنهى شريف دراسته في الجامعة الأردنية وحصل على شهادة البكالوريوس في الهندسة، عمل مهندساً. وبعد ثلاث سنوات حصل على مساعدة من جامعة اليرموك في إربد للسفر الى أمريكا والدراسة في جامعة كورنيل للحصول على شهادتي الماجستير والدكتوراة في الهندسة.

٢

سافر شريف بالطائرة من مطار عمان الدولي الى مطار كندي في نيويورك. إربد ليس فيها مطار، لذلك أخذ شريف وأبوه وأخوه عبدالله تكسي من إربد الى المطار. أخذ التكسي حوالي ساعة ونصف في الطريق. انتظر أبو شريف وهيثم وعبدالله في المطار أكثر من ثلاث ساعات، ثم ركب شريف الطائرة. كانت الطائرة كبيرة من نوع "بونج ٧٤٧" تابعة للخطوط الجويّة الملكيّة الأردنيّة-عالية.

طارت الطائرة الساعة الرابعة بعد الظهر. كانت الرحلة طويلة؛ أخذت أكثر من عشرين ساعة، منها ١٥ ساعة في الطائرة وخمس ساعات في مطار عمان وفي مطار أمستردام بهولندا.

وصل شريف الى مطار كندي في نيويورك الساعة السادسة والنصف صباحاً، كان تعبان وخائفاً لأن هذه كانت أول مرّة سافر فيها خارج الأردن. كان يتكلم اللغة الإنجليزية ولكن ليس بطلاقة، ولم يعرف أحداً في نيويورك أو إثاكا.

من نيويورك ركب شريف طائرة صغيرة الى إثاكا، وفي إثاكا نزل في فندق (موتيل) رخيص وقريب من الجامعة. كانت غرفة شريف نظيفة وكبيرة وفيها تلفون وتلفزيون ملوّن كبير، وكانت أجرتها ١٢٠ دولاراً في الأسبوع.

٣

نام شريف أول ليلة في أمريكا، وفي صباح اليوم الثاني قام من

النوم مبكّراً وسأل موظف الفندق عن مطعم قريب. ذهب شريف الى المطعم وأكل فيه وأحب الطعام فيه كثيراً، وصار يأكل فيه كل يوم.

وفي يوم من الأيام كان شريف يمشي في جامعة كورنيل فالتقى بطالب سوري اسمه محمد. وفي تلك الليلة أخبره محمد أن صاحبه وليد يفتش على شاب يسكن معه في شقّته، فوافق شريف أن يسكن مع وليد، لأنه كان قد تعب من السكن في الفندق ومن الأكل في المطعم.

أحبّ شريف الشقّة كثيراً لأنها نظيفة وكبيرة ورخيصة؛ أجرتها ٤٥٠ دولاراً في الشهر مع الماء والكهرباء. هي بعيدة عن الجامعة لكن موقف الباص قريب جداً منها. يأخذ الباص حوالي ربع ساعة من شقة شريف ووليد الى الجامعة. شريف يحب الباص كثيراً لأنه لا يريد أن يشتري سيّارة، كذلك يحب السكن مع وليد لأن وليد طالب جيّد، وصار شريف ووليد صديقين عزيزين.

وليد يدرس علم الإجتماع في جامعة كورنيل ويريد الحصول على شهادة الدكتوراة.

٤

في يوم من الأيام تكلمت بنت اسمها "كاثي" بالتلفون مع شريف، وقالت له إنها ستسافر الى مصر وتريد أن تتعلم اللغة العربية بسرعة. فاتفق شريف معها أن يلتقيا في مكتبة الجامعة خمس مرات في الأسبوع ويعلمها اللغة العربية وتدفع له ١٥ دولاراً لكل ساعة.

تعلّمت كاثي كلمات عربية كثيرة، وتعلّمت القراءة، ولكنها قررت أن تتوقف عن دراسة العربية، وعندما سألها شريف عن السبب قالت إنه يعلّمها عربية "غلط"، فقد قالت لها صديقتها المصريّة إن المصريين لا يقولون "سيّارة" ولكن "عربية" ولا يقولون "كيف حالك" ولكن "إزّيّك".

سمعت أم شريف أن ابنها يمشي مع بنت أمريكية ويجلس معها في المكتبة، فخافت أنه يريد أن يتزوّجها. لذلك طلبت من أبو شريف أن يكتب لشريف رسالة يقول فيها إن أمه لا تنام الليل لأنها تفكر فيه دائماً وتخاف أن يتزوّج بنتاً أمريكية.

ردّ شريف على رسالة أمه وأبيه وقال إنه لا يفكّر بالزواج من أمريكية ولا من أي بنت أخرى في هذا الوقت، وإنه كان يجلس مع بنت أمريكية في المكتبة لأنه كان يعلّمها اللغة العربية.

الفلاح وبيته الصغير

كان يا ما كان، في قديم الزمان، كان فيه فلاّح، وكان الفلاّح فقير، وكان هو ومرته واولاده ساكنين في بيت صغير، بيت صغير كثير، فيه غرفة واحدة بسّ، يطبخوا فيها وياكلوا فيها وينامو فيها.

كل يوم كانت مرة الفلاّح تقول له: "شوف ما أصغر هالبيت! غرفة واحدة بسّ، بنطبخ فيها وبناكل فيها وبننام فيها، ابني لنا بيت أكبر." وكان الفلاّح يقول: "لكن كيف أبني بيت أكبر؟ من وين المصاري؟"

في يوم من الأيام قالت مرة الفلاح: "روح إحكي مع الشيخ، ممكن يساعدنا."

راح الفلاّح للشيخ وقال له: "يا سيدي الشيخ، بيتنا صغير، فيه غرفة واحدة بسّ، بنطبخ فيها وبناكل فيها وبننام فيها، وأولادي دايماً يصيّحوا ومرتي تقول بدها بيت أكبر وأنا فقير وما معي مصاري." ايش أعمل يا سيدي الشيخ؟"

قال الشيخ: "روح لبيتك وحطّ الديك فيه."

قال الفلاّح: "وليش أحطّ الديك في البيت؟"

لكن الشيخ ظل ساكت وما قال شيء.

رجع الفلاّح لبيته وحطّ الديك فيه.

ثاني يوم راح الفلاّح للشيخ وقال له: "يا سيدي الشيخ، مبارح طول الليل والديك يصيّح والأولاد يصيّحوا، ومرتي تقول بدها بيت أكبر. ايش أعمل يا سيدي الشيخ؟"

قال الشيخ: "حطّ العنزة في البيت." وسكت.

رجع الفلاّح لبيته وحطّ العنزة فيه.

ثالث يوم راح الفلاّح للشيخ وقال له: "يا سيدي الشيخ، مبارح طول الليل والديك يصيّح والأولاد يصيّحوا والعنزة تذغّي ومرتي تقول بدها بيت أكبر. ايش أعمل يا سيدي الشيخ؟"

قال الشيخ: "حطّ الخروف في البيت."

رجع الفلاّح لبيته وحطّ الخروف فيه.

رابع يوم راح الفلاّح للشيخ وقال له: "يا سيدي الشيخ، مبارح طول الليل والديك يصيّح والأولاد يصيّحوا والعنزة تذغّي والخروف يذغّي ومرتي

تقول بدها بيت أكبر. ايش أعمل يا سيدي الشيخ؟"

قال الشيخ: "حطّ الحمار في البيت."

رجع الفلّاح لبيته وحطّ الحمار فيه.

خامس يوم راح الفلّاح للشيخ وقال له: "يا سيدي الشيخ، مبارح طول الليل ما نمنا، الديك يصيّح والأولاد يصيّحوا والعنزة تذغّي والخروف يذغّي والحمار ينهّق ومرتي تقول بدها بيت أكبر. ايش أعمل يا سيدي الشيخ؟"

قال الشيخ: "حطّ البقرة في البيت."

رجع الفلّاح لبيته وحطّ البقرة فيه.

سادس يوم راح الفلّاح للشيخ وقال له: "يا سيدي الشيخ، ليلة مبارح ما نمنا أبداً؛ الديك يصيّح والأولاد يصيّحوا والعنزة تذغّي والخروف يذغّي والحمار ينهّق ومرتي تقول بدها بيت أكبر. ايش أعمل يا سيدي الشيخ؟"

قال الشيخ: "طلّع الديك والعنزة والخروف والحمار والبقرة من البيت."

قال الفلّاح: "وليش أطلّعهم من البيت؟"

لكن الشيخ ظل ساكت وما قال شيء.

رجع الفلّاح لبيته وطلّع الجاجات والعنزة والخروف والحمار والبقرة.

بعد ما طلعت الحيوانات من البيت قال الفلّاح لمرته: "شوفي ما أهدا البيت!"

وقالت مرته: "وشوف ما أكبره!"

قاموس عربي-انجليزي
ARABIC-ENGLISH GLOSSARY

Abbreviations

ج.	جمع (plural)	
pl.	plural	
f.	feminine	
m.	masculine	
s.	singular	
#	generally used in Modern Standard Arabic (MSA) but not in Levantine	
*	generally used in Levantine but not in MSA	

father	أب
with possessive pronouns and as first term of أبو :إضافة	
at all, never	أبداً
son	ابن
relics, antiquities	آثار
	أجر
rent, fare	أجرة
tenant	مُستأجر
	أجل
for the sake of	من أجل#
	أحد
eleven	حادي عشر#
we	احنا*
brother	أخ
sister	أخت
to take	أخذ–ياخذ
	أخر
to be late	V
last	آخِر
other, another	آخَر #
last time	آخِر مرّة
(other, another, f.)	أخرى
finally	أخيراً#
literature	أدب
if	اذا
therefore	إذن

	أرخ
history, date	تاريخ
historian	مؤرّخ
rabbit	أرنب
	أسّ
to establish, found	II (أسّس-يؤسس)
to be founded	V
founding	تأسيس
founder	مؤسّس
professor	أستاذ
strategic	استراتيجي
sorry	آسف
name	اسم (ج. أسامي)
your name (polite/formal)	الاسم الكريم
	أشر
entry visa	تأشيرة دخول
the Assyrians	الآشوريين
origin	أصل
the Royal Academy	الأكاديميّة الملكيّة
	أكد
certainly	أكيد
to eat	أكل-ياكُل
dining room	غرفة أكل
foods	مأكولات
except, to (time)	الاّ
which, who (f.s.)	#التي
which, who (m.s.)	#الذي
which, who (m.p.)	#الذين
thousand	ألف (ج. آلاف)
God	الله
God be with you!	الله معك!
may God keep them (safe)!	الله يخلّيهم*
God bless the good old days!	الله يرحم أيام زمان
may God keep you safe and sound (answer to الحمدلله على السلامة)	الله يسلّمك
God willing	إن شاء الله
let's	يالله*
barely, with difficulty	يالله يالله*

that, which	اللي*
(a) god	إله
mother	أمّ
to nationalize	VIII (أمّم-يؤمم)
the United Nations	الأمم المتحدة
empire	امبراطوريّة
when?	امتى؟*
matter, affair	أمْر (ج. أمور)
to hope for	أمل-يأمُل
	أمن
to believe	IV
secretary general	أمين عام
the Umayyads	الأمويّين
I	أنا
you, m.s.	انتَ
it depends ("you and your luck")	انتَ ونصيبك
you, f.s.	انتِ
female	أنثى
	أني
to wait	X (استنّى-يستنّى)*
people, family	أهل
welcome, hello (response to مرحبا)	أهلاً وسهلاً
Europe	اوروبا
	أول
first	أوّل
first thing	أوّل شيء
the day before yesterday	أوّل مبارح*
all of it (from its beginning to its end)	من أوّلها لآخرها
	أون
now	الآن#
which	أيّ
what	ايش*
also	أيضاً#
yes	أيوا*
in, by, with	ب
well (oil, water)	بئر
bus	باص
to discuss	بحث

sea	بحـر
the Mediterranean Sea	البحر الأبيض المتوسط
the Red Sea	البحر الأحمر
the Black Sea	البحر الأسود
the Dead Sea	البحر الميّت
lake	بُحيرة
(with pronominal suffixes) to want	بدّ*
to start	بدأ-يبدأ
starting with	ابتداءً بـ
	بدل
instead of (before a verb)	بدل ما
instead of (before a noun)	بدلاً من#
land as opposed to بحـر sea	برّ
oranges	برتقال
	برد
cold (adj.)	بارد
	برد
post office	بريد
parliament	برلمان
program	برنامج
only	بسّ*
	بسط
to be happy	VII
simple	بسيط
happy	مبسوط*
onions	بصل
potatoes	بطاطا
	بطخ
watermelon	بطّيخ
nonsense	بلا ... بلاد بطّيخ*
hero	بطل
bad	بطّال *
not bad	مش بطّال*
belly, stomach	بَطن
after	بَعد
after that	بعدين*
distance	بُعد
at a distance of	على بُعد

٣٦٦

far	بعيد
some	بَعض
together	مع بعض
cows	بقر
beef	لحم بقر
	بقل
grocery store	بقّالة
to remain	بقي-يبقى
remaining	باقي
bachelor's (degree)	بكالوريوس
	بكر
tomorrow	بُكرة*
the day after tomorrow	بعد بكرة*
	بكي
to cry	بكى-يبكي
country	بلد
downtown	البلد
Greater Syria	بلاد الشام
local, domestic	بلدي
Bulgarian	بلغاري
girl, daughter	بنت
daughter of good people	بنت حلال
girl from a good family	بنت ناس
tomatoes	بندورة
gasoline	بنزين
pants	بنطلون
bank	بنك (ج. بنوك)
brown	بُنّي
	بني
to build	بنى-يبني
(act of) building	بناء
building	بناية
	بوب
door	باب
house	بيت
dormitory	بيت الطلاب

	بيض
eggs	بيض
white	أبيض
	بيع
seller	بيّاع
selling	بيع
	بين
to show	II
between	بين
meanwhile, at that time	بينما#
	تبل
spices	توابل
	تجر
commerce, trade	تجارة
under	تحت
to translate	ترجَم-يترجم
to leave	ترك-يترُك
to get tired	تعِب-يتعَب
fatigue	تَعَب
tired	تعبان
	تفح
apples	تُفّاح
that, f.	تلك#
	تلو
following	تالي
	ثقف
cultural	ثقافي
(one) third	ثُلث
snow	ثَلج
then	ثُمّ#
	ثَمّ
then, after that	مِن ثَمّ #
	ثني
secondary	ثانوي
	ثور
revolution	ثورة
Gabriel	جبريل
mountain	جبل (ج. جبال)

mountainous	جبلي
grandfather	جَدّ
grandmother	جدّة
new	جديد
	جِدّ
very	جدّاً#
schedule	جدول
part	جُزْء (ج أجزاء)
carrots	جزر
body	جِسم
	جلّ
magazine	مجلّة
	جلس
council	مجلس
sitting	جلوس
to collect	جمع-يجمَع
gathering, collecting	جَمع
total	مجموع
mosque	جامع
university	جامعة
the Arab League	الجامعة العربية
	جمل
beautiful	جميل
republic	جمهورية
	جنّ
insane, crazy	مجنون
next to	جَنب
foreign, foreigner	أجنَبي (ج. أجانِب)
south	جنوب
	جند
soldiers	جنود
sex	جِنس
nationality	جنسيّة
	جهز
ready	جاهز
	جود
good	جيّد#

	جور
neighbors	جيران
	جوز
passport	جواز سفر
prize	جائزة
hunger	جوع
hungry	جوعان
famine	مجاعة
	جيء
to come	جاء-يجيء،# أجا-ييجي*
coming, next	جاي*
	جيب
to bring	جاب *
	جير
neighbor	جار
army	جيش
	حبّ
to like	حَبّ-يحبّ*، أحبّ-يُحبّ#
in order to, until, even	حتّى
pilgrim, pilgrimage	حَجّ
to reserve	حجَز
reserved	محجوز
to border	حَدّ-يحُدّ
to limit	حدّد-يحدّد II
border	حدّ (ج. حدود)
sharpness, acuteness	حِدّة
limiting	تحديد
until	لحدّ
until now	لحدّ هلّأ*
to happen	حدث-يحدُث
to speak	V
accident	حادِث
modern	حديث
events	أحداث
talks, negotiations	محادثات
	حدق
yard	حديقة

heat	حَرّ
hot	حارّ
free	حُرّ (ج. أحرار)
freedom	حُرّيّة
	حَرّ
to edit	II (حرّر-يحرّر)
editor	مُحرّر
war	حرب
to fight	III
civil war	حرب أهليّة
World War I	الحرب العالمية الأولى
	حرك
movement	حركة
	حرم
don't be unfair	حرام عليك
(political) party	حِزب
according to	حَسَب
accountant	مُحاسِب
	حسن
better	أحسن
improving	تحسين
to obtain	حصل-يحصُل
	حضر
you (polite/formal)	حضرتَك، حضرتِك
civilization	حضارة
to put	حَطّ-يحُطّ*
station	محطّة
	حفظ
to keep, retain	VIII
	حفي
barefoot	حافي
	حقّ
rights	حقوق
true, actual	حقيقي
	حكر
to monpolize	VIII
to rule	حكم-يحكُم
ruler	حاكم
governmental	حكومي

self-rule	حُكم ذاتي
	حكي
to speak, tell	حكى-يحكي
solution	حلّ
to occupy	VIII
	حلب
milk	حليب
	حلق
episode (of a program)	حلقة
sweet	حِلو
sweets	حلويات
	حمّ
bathroom	حمّام
	حمد
thank God	الحمد لله
thank God for your safety, welcome	الحمد لله على السلامة
	حمر
red	أحمر
donkey	حمار (ج. حمير)
to carry	حمل-يحمِل
carrier, holder	حامِل
	حمي
hot	حامي×
	حور
neighborhood, quarter of city	حارة
	حوط
reserve	احتياطي
the Wailing Wall	حائط المبكى
ocean	محيط
	حول
to try	III
condition	حال
in any case	على كل حال
transforming, changing	تحويل
approximately	حوالي
attempt	مُحاولة
	حوي
to contain	VIII (احتوى-يحتوي)

alive	حيّ
life	حياة
quarter of a city	حيّ
	حير
to be puzzled	V
time	حين (ج. أحيان)#
sometimes	أحياناً
	خبر
to inform	IV
	خبز
bakery	مخبز
	خدم
service	خدمة
	خرج
expelling	إخراج
	خرط
map	خريطة
	خرف
lamb	خَروف
to lose	خسِر-يخسَر
	خصّ
special, private	خاصّ
especially	خاصّةً
especially	خصوصاً
specialization	تخصّص
fertile	خَصب
	خضر
green	أخضر
vegetables	خُضار
	خطّ
airlines	خطوط جوّية
	خفض
low	منخفِض#
	خلج
gulf	خليج
	خلص
to finish	II
	خلف
to vary, be different	VIII

disagreement, dispute	خِلاف
different	مُختلف
	خلق
creator	خالق
	خلو
to let, leave	II (خلّى-يخلّي)
	خنزر
pig	خنزير
	خوف
to be afraid, worried	خاف-يخاف
afraid, worried	خايف
	خول
maternal uncle	خال
good	خير
to choose	VIII (اختار-يختار)
cucumbers	خيار
well, fine	بخير
	دجّ
chicken	دجاج
the Tigris River	دِجلة
	دخل
to intervene	V
inside	داخل
annual income	دخل سنوي
	درج
temperature	درجة الحرارة
the Roman amphitheater	المدرّج الروماني
lesson	درْس (ج. دروس)
study	دراسة
teaching	تدريس
school	مدرسة
secondary school	مدرسة ثانوية
	دعو
to invite	دعا-يدعو
invitation	دعوة
straight	دُغري*
to pay	دفع-يدفَع
defense	دفاع

to bury	دفن-يدفِن
to knock	دقّ-يدُقّ
minute	دقيقة (ج. دقايق)
	دكّ
shop	دكان (ج. دكاكين)
doctor, physician	دُكتور
	دلّ
proof, evidence	دليل
	دمر
to destroy	II
	دول
country	دَولة (ج. دُول)
international	دَولي
	دوم
always	دائماً
see ما دام	دام
	دون
without	بدون
	دوي
cure, medicine (check)	دواء
	دير
beware, watch out	دير بالك*
religion	دين (ج. أديان)
religious, spiritual	ديني
city	مدينة (ج. مُدن)
dinar (currency)	دينار
to mention; remember	ذكر-يذكُر
to remind	II
ticket	تذكرة
that	ذلك#
after that	بعد ذلك #
also	كذلك #
to go	ذهب-يذهَب#
	ذيع
broadcasting station	إذاعة
head	رأس
president	رئيس
prime minister	رئيس وزراء
main	رئيسي

	دأي
to see	رأى-يرى#
opinion	رأي
God	ربّ
housewife	ربّة بيت
quarter, one-fourth	رُبع
the Empty Quarter	الربع الخالي
	دبي
to raise	II (ربّى-يربّي)
to return	رجع-يرجَع
to return (something)	II, IV
recovering, getting back	استرجاع
	رجل
man	رجُل#، راجل*
businessman	رجُل أعمال
leg, foot	رِجل
	رحب
hi, hello	مرحبا
	رحل
trip	رحلة
	رخص
cheap	رخيص
to answer, respond	ردّ-يرُدّ
rice	دزّ
	رسل
to correspond with	VI
letter, message	رسالة (ج. رسائل)
	رسم
official	رسمي
	رغم
in spite of	على الرغم من
to refuse	رفض-يرفُض
	رفع
rise	ارتفاع
number	رقم (ج. أرقام)
to ride	ركب-يركَب
	ركز
to focus, concentrate	II
center	مركَز

	رمل
widow	أرملة
	دوح
to go	داح-يروح*
going (active participle)	رايح*
Russia	روسيا
	دوض
physical education	رياضة
mathematics	رياضيات
	ريح
to rest	X (استراح-يستريح)
	ريد
to want	VIII (أراد-يريد)#
feathers	ريش
	زبط
exactly	بالزبط*
correct	مزبوط*
	زحم
congestion, crowdedness	زحمة
	ذرع
agriculture	زراعة
farm	مزرعة
farmer	مُزارِع
thyme	زعتر
to be upset, angry	زعل-يزعَل
upset, angry	زعلان
time, era	زمَن
for a long time	من زمان
	زهر
flowers	زهور
husband	زوج
to get married	V
husband	زوج
married	متزوِّج
	زور
to visit	زار-يزور
visit	زيارة
as, like	زيّ*

oil	زيت
olive oil	زيت زيتون
	زيد
to increase, to exceed	زاد-يزيد
plus, in addition to	زائد
increase	زيادة
to ask	سأل-يسأل
question	سؤال
cause	سَبَب
to swim	سبح-يسبَح
	سبع
week	أسبوع (ج. أسابيع)
	سبل
as an example	على سبيل المثال
lady, woman	سِتّ*
	سجد
mosque	مسجِد (ج. مساجد)
al-Aqsa Mosque	المسجد الأقصى
	سجل
to record, write down	II
registered (letter)	مسجّل
to imprison	سجَن-يسجن
	سحب
to withdraw	VII
withdrawal	انسحاب
	سحل
coast	ساحِل
dam	سدّ (ج. سدود)
the High Dam	السدّ العالي
	سرّ
secret	سِرّي
	سرع
fast, quick	سريع
speed	سُرعة
quickly	بسُرعة
to steal	سرق-يسرق
roof, (sea) level	سَطح
	سعد
to help	III

help	مساعدة
price	سِعر (ج. أسعار)
pricing, price regulation	تسعيرة
	سفر
to travel	III
traveling (noun)	سفر
embassy	سفارة
passport	جواز سفر
	سكر
sugar	سُكَّر
	سكر
to close	II
secretary	سكرتير
to live, reside	سكن-يسكُن
living, residing, inhabitant	ساكِن (ج. سُكَّان)
residential	سكني
poor, unlucky	مسكين
knife	سِكّين
	سلط
authority	سُلطة
sultanate	سَلطنة
salad	سَلَطة
to be safe	سلم-يسلَم
to greet	II
peace	سلام
peace be upon you (and God's mercy and blessings)	السلام عليكم (ورحمة الله وبركاته)
upon you peace (answer to السلام عليكم)	عليكم السلام
I hope you are well (to someone sick or hurt)	سلامتك
bless the hands of . . .	يسلموا ايدين...
good-bye	مع السلامة
Muslim	مُسلِم
to allow	سمح-يسمَح
allowing, forgiving (noun)	سماح
to hear	سمع-يسمَع
do not pay attention (pointing to the ears, "hear from here and let go from here")	اسمع من هون وطيّر من هون*
listener	مُستمع
fish	سمك

٣٧٩

	سمي
to name	II (سمّى-يسمّي)
	سن
year	سنة (ج. سنوات)
centimeter	سنتمتر (سم)
easy; plain	سَهل
	سود
Mr.	سيّد
excellency	سيادة
my (dear) sir	سيدي
ladies and gentlemen	سيداتي وسادتي
black	أسود
fence, wall	سور
	سوع
watch, clock, hour	ساعة
abbreviated to س will (future)	سوف#
Soviet	سوفييتي
market	سوق (ج. أسواق)
	سيح
tourist	سايح
tourism	سياحة
	سير
car	سيّارة
ambulance	سيّارة إسعاف
	شأن
for the sake of	على شان*
tea	شاي
	شبّ
young man	شابّ (ج. شباب)
to be full, satisfied	شبِع-يشبَع
	شبه
peninsula	شبه جزيرة
	شجر
tree	شجرة (ج. شجر)
palm trees	شجر النخيل
person	شخص
personal	شخصي
to drink	شرب-يشرَب

	شرط
police	شُرطة
policemen	شرطي
	شرع
street	شارع
	شرف
to be honored	V
east	شَرق
the Middle East	الشرق الأوسط
	شرك
company	شَرِكة
airline company	شركة طيران
socialist	اشتراكي
Circassians	شركس
	شري
to buy	VIII (اشترى-يشتري)
	شطء
coast	شاطئ
	شعب
popular	شعبي
hair	شعَر
poetry	شعِر
poet	شاعِر
	شغل
to work	VIII
busy	مشغول
	شفي
hospital	مستشفى
	شقّ
apartment	شقّة (ج. شقق)
	شكر
thank you	شُكراً
thank you very much	شكراً جزيلاً
don't mention it, you are welcome	لا شكراً على واجب
	شكل
in particular	بشكل خاص
in general	بشكل عام
continuously	بشكل مستمرّ
problem	مشكلة

to take off (clothes)	شلح-يشلَح*
	شمل
north	شمال
	شنط
suitcase, briefcase	شنطة
handbag	شنطة يَد
	شهد
certificate, degree	شهادة
month	شَهر (ج. شهور)
famous	مشهور
	شور
advisor, consultant	مستشار
	شوف
to see	شاف-يشوف*
	شوي
baked, roasted	مشوي
thing	شيء
little	شويّة *
living room	صالون معيشة
	صبح
to become	IV
morning	صُبح
good morning	صباح الخير
good morning (response to صباح الخير)	صباح النور
in the morning	صباحاً#
good night	تصبح على خير
	صحّ
true, correct	صحيح
health	صحّة
bon appetit	صحّة وهنا،
	صحب
friend; owner	صاحب
	صحر
desert	صحراء
	صحف
journalist	صَحفي
	صحي
to wake up	صحي-يصحى

	صخر
rocky	صخري
	صدر
to issue	IV
exporting	تصدير
issuing	صدور
exporter	مصدّر
	صدق
to believe	II
	صرح
frankly	بصراحة
difficult	صَعب
	صعد
elevator	مَصعَد
	صغر
small	صغير
class, grade (in school)	صَفّ
	صفح
page	صفحة
zero	صِفر
	صلب
the Crusaders	الصليبيين
	صلو
to pray	II (صلّى-يصلّي)
peace be upon him	صلّى الله عليه وسلّم
	صندق
lost and found box	صندوق الموجودات
	صنع
industry	صناعة
industrialization	تصنيع
artificial	اصطناعي
idol	صنم (ج. أصنام)
Zionist	صهيوني
voice, sound	صوت
	صور
picture	صورة (ج. صور)
	صيح
to shout	صاح-يصيح

	صير
to become	صار-يصير
Chinese	صيني
	ضبط
officer	ضابِط (ج. ضُبّاط)
against	ضِدّ
to hit	ضرب-يضرُب
double, twice as much	ضِعف
weak	ضعيف
to pressure	ضغط-يضغَط
	ضفّ
the West Bank	الضِفّة الغربية
to annex	ضمّ-يضُمّ
	ضيع
to be lost	ضاع-يضيع
to lose	II (ضيّع-يضيّع)
guest	ضيف (ج. ضيوف)
steward	مُضيف
fresh	طازة
	طبّ
physician	طبيب (ج. أطبّاء)
to cook	طبخ-يطبُخ
kitchen	مطبخ
	طبع
of course	طبعاً
(postage) stamp	طابِع (ج. طوابِع)
to expell	طرد-يطرُد
package	طرْد
	طرق
way, road	طريق (ج. طُرُق)
soft	طري
	طعم
restaurant	مطعم
weather	طَقس
to request, ask for	طلب-يطلُب
to demand	III
student	طالِب
request, application	طلب

to go out	طلع-يطلَع
to look	V
	طلق
divorce	طلاق
	طور
development	تطوّر
	طوف
sects	طوائف
the length of	طول
straightaway	على طول*
the whole time	طول الوقت
long	طويل
	طيب
OK, good, delicious	طيّب
	طير
airplane	طائرة، طيّارة
pilot	طيّار
Gulf Air	طيَران الخليج
airport	مطار
to remain	ظلّ-يظَلّ
persecution	ظُلم
to appear	ظهر-يظهَر
noon	ظُهر
	عبد
slaves	عبيد
worship	عبادة
nature worship	عبادة الطبيعة
temple	مَعبد
	عبر
to be considered (VIII passive)	يُعتبَر
the Hebrews	العبرانيين
to please	عجب IV
to wonder about	V
miracle, great achievement	أعجوبة
	عجز
old (person)	عجوز
to count	عدّ-يعدّ
a few, a number of	عدّة
number	عدد

population	عدد سُكّان
ready, willing	مستعدّ
	عدل
moderate	معتدل
	عرب
Arab, Arabic	عربي (ج. عرب)
width	عَرْض
to know	عرف-يعرف
to recognize, acknowledge	VIII
known	معروف
	عرك
battle	معركة
	عزب
bachelor	أعزب
honey	عسَل
	عصر
juice	عصير
	عصف
Desert Storm	عاصفة الصحراء
	عصم
capital	عاصمة
thirst	عطَش
	عطل
vacation	عُطلة
	عطي
to give	IV (أعطى-يعطي)
bones	عَظم
	عفو
you're welcome (answer to شكراً)	عفواً
	عقد
to believe	VIII
mind	عَقل
sensible, reasonable	معقول
opposite	عكس
	علب
box of chocolate	علبة شوكولاتة
	علق
relationship	علاقة

	علم
to learn	V
science, branch of knowledge	علِم (ج. علوم)
sociology	علم الاجتماع
political science	علوم سياسية
grade, mark	علامة
world	عالَم
teacher	معلّم
educated	متعلّم
	علن
to announce	IV
	علو
high	عالي
paternal uncle	عمّ
	عمد
to depend	VIII
age	عُمر
settlement	مستعمرة
to work	عمِل-يعمَل
work	عمَل
currency	عُملة
treatment	مَعاملة
use, using	استعمال
grapes	عنَب
at, close to (with a pronominal suffix it indicates possession)	عند
	عنون
address	عنوان
	عني
to suffer	III (عانى-يعاني)
in other words, it means	يعني
	عهد
institute	معهد
	عود
to return	عاد-يعود
habit, custom	عادة
shame	عيب
	عير
to borrow	X (استعار-يستعير)
Jesus Christ	عيسى المسيح

	عيش
to live (survive)	عاش - يعيش
	عيل
family	عائلة
the royal family	العائلة المالكة
eye	عين (ج. عيون)
	غدو
to have lunch	V (تغدّى - يتغدّى)
lunch	غداء
west	غَرب
strange, foreign	غريب
	غرف
room	غرفة
dining room	غرفة أكل
living (sitting) room	غرفة جلوس
bedroom	غرفة نوم
	غزو
the Three-Way Invasion (of Egypt in 1956)	الغزو الثلاثي
	غضب
to anger	IV
	غلب
most of	غالب#
wrong	غَلَط
	غلق
closing	إغلاق
	غلو
expensive	غالي
high prices	غلاء
rich	غَني
	غور
cave	مغارة
un-, not, other than	غير
unfit, unsuitable	غير صالح#
to open	فتح - يفتَح
key	مفتاح
	فتر
period, era	فَترة
	فتش
to look for	II

the Euphrates River	الفُرات
individual	فَرْد
the Persians	الفُرس
	فرش
furnished	مفروش
branch	فَرع (ج. فروع)
to fail	فشِل-يفشَل
season	فصل (ج. فصول)
	فضل
please, go ahead	تفضّل
if you please	من فضلك
	فطر
breakfast	فُطور
	فعل
indeed	فعلاً
to lose	فقد-يفقِد
	فقر
poor	فقير
only	فقط#
	فكر
to think	II
thinking	تفكير
idea	فِكرة
by the way	على فكرة
intellectual	فِكري
	فكه
fruit	فواكه
	فلح
peasant, farmer	فلاح
fils (monetary unit, one-thousandth of a dinar)	فِلس
money	فلوس
art	فَنّ
hotel	فُندق (ج. فنادق)
to understand	فهم-يفهَم
fava beans	فول
	فيد
benefit	فائدة
the Phoenicians	الفينيقيين

English	Arabic
in	في
in it, there is,* there are*	فيه
	قبّ
the Dome of the Rock	قُبّة الصخرة
grave	قَبر
before	قبل
B.C.	قبل الميلاد
to accept	قبل-يقبَل
to meet	III
to receive, meet	X
future	مستقبَل
tribe	قبيلة (ج. قبائل)
to kill	قتل-يقتُل
before perfect verb indicates termination of an action; before imperfect verb: may, might	قَد
to be able to	قدر-يقدر
	قدس
holy	مقدّس
	قدم
next, coming	قادم
ancient	قديم
in front of	قُدّام
how much	قدّيش*
	قرّ
to decide	II
to be decided	V
decision	قرار
to read	قرأ-يقرأ
	قرب
close	قريب
relatives	أقارب
approximately	تقريباً
close to, in the vicinity of	قُرب
piastre	قِرش
century	قَرن
comparison	مقارنة
	قري
village	قرية (ج. قرى)

قسم	
VII	to be divided
تقسيم	division, partition
قصد	
اقتصاد	economy, economics
قصر	
قصير	short
قصف-يقصِف	to bomb
قضي	
قضى-يقضي	to spend time
قطّ	
قِطّة	cat
قطع	
VII	to be cut, to stop
قطاع غزّة	the Gaza Strip
قُطن	cotton
قعد-يقعُد	to sit
قواعد	grammar
قلّ-يقلّ	to decrease, diminish
X	to become independent
استقلال	independence
مُستقلّ	independent
أقلّ	less, fewer than
أقلّيّة	minority
قلب	
انقلاب عسكري	military coup
قَمح	wheat
قمص	
قميص	shirt
قنّ	
قانون (ج. قوانين)	law
قنو	
قناة السويس	the Suez Canal
قهوة	coffee
قوت	
قات	qat
قود	
قاد-يقود	to lead
قائد	commander

	قول
to say	قال-يقول
	قوم
to erupt, take place	قام-يقوم
to undertake	قام-يقوم بـ
to resist	III
residence	إقامة
resistance	مقاومة
to become strong	قَوِي-يقوى
strong	قَوِي
	كبر
big	كبير
to write	كتب-يكتُب
book	كتاب
writing	كتابة
office	مكتب
library	مكتبة
written	مكتوب
	كثر
many, a lot, very	كثير
also	كذلك#
to break	كسَر-يكسِر
	كشف
to discover	VIII
	كعب
cubic	مكعّب
	كفي
sufficient	كافي
every, each, all	كُلّ
everything	كل شيء
college	كلّية
college of commerce, business	كلية التجارة
college of medicine	كلية الطبّ
the Chaldeans	الكلدانيين
	كلف
to cost	II
costs	تكاليف
	كلم
to speak	V

word	كلمة
speech, what is said	كلام
how many, a number of	كَم
quantity	كمّيّة
also	كمان*
	كمل
complete, full	كامِل
completing	مكمّل
shoes	كندرة
	كنس
church	كنيسة (ج. كنائس)
Church of the Holy Sepulcher	كنيسة القيامة
	كهرب
electricity	كهرباء
	كود
to be about to	كاد أن#
	كوس
good	كويّس*
	كون
to be	كان-يكون
to consist of	V (تكوّن-يتكوّن)
place	مكان
how	كيف
how are you	كيف حالك
what if	كيف لو
as you wish	على كيفك
kilogram	كيلوغرام
kilometer	كيلومتر
to, for	ل
no	لا
because	لأنّ
to put on, wear	لبس-يلبس
clothes	ملابس
yogurt	لَبن
	لجأ
refugee	لاجئ
grave	لَحد

	لحم
meat	لحم، لحمة
butcher	لحّام
butcher shop	ملحمة
	لزم
must, it is necessary that	لازم*
	لسن
tongue	لسان
still, until now	لِسَّه*
	لطف
kind	لطيف
Oh, my God, God have mercy!	يا لطيف!
	لغو
language	لُغة
to find	لقي-يلقى
to meet	VIII (التقى-يلتقي)
but	لكن
did not	لم#
when	لمّا
if	لو
if you please	لو سمحت
color	لون (ج. ألوان)
not	ليس#
why	ليش*
night	ليل
tonight	الليلة
one night	ليلة من الليالي
not; what	ما
as long as	ما دام
	مئة
of a hundred, centigrade	مئوي
master's (degree)	ماجستير
what	ماذا#
Maronite	ماروني
yesterday	مبارح*
like	مِثل
for example	مثلاً

	محن
examination	امتحان
	مدّ
period, duration	مُدّة
subject	مادّة (ج. مواد)
to pass	مرّ-يمُرّ
to continue	X
time	مرّة
another time	مرّة ثانية
	مرأ
wife, woman	مرأة#، مرة*
to be sick	مرِض-يمرَض
sickness	مرَض
sick	مريض
	مرق
sauce	مرقة
	مسح
area	مساحة
Christian	مسيحي
	مسو
evening	مساء
good evening	مساء الخير
good evening (answer to مشاء الخير)	مساء النور
not	مِش*
	مشي
to walking	مشى-يمشي
walking (active participle)	ماشي
walking (noun, gerund)	مشي
	مضي
past	ماضي
rain	مطر
with	مع
Mongols	مغول
	مكن
possible	مُمكن
	ملك
king	ملك
kingdom	مملكة (ج. ممالك)

monarchy	ملَكية
ownership	ملِكيّة
angel	ملاك
the Mamlukes	المماليك
millimeter	ملمتر
	ملي
full	مليان*
from	مِن
who	مَن#
cradle	مَهد
profession	مِهنة
	موت
to die	مات-يموت
death	موت
bananas	موز
music	موسيقى
	موه
water	ماء#
	ميز
excellent	ممتاز
who?	مين؟*
	مين
port	ميناء (ج. موانئ)
water	ميّة*
to result	نتج-ينتُج
production	إنتاج
producer	مُنتِج
result	نتيجة
	نثي
female	أنثى
to succeed	نجح-ينجَح
success	نجاح
to go down, land, stay (in a hotel)	نزل-ينزِل
	نسب
ratio	نسبة
as for	بالنسبة لِ
to forget	نسي-ينسى
to publish	نشر-ينشُر

half	نُصّ*
the middle of the night	نُصّ الليل*
	نصب
to appoint	II
luck, lot	نصيب
	نصر
to be victorious	VIII
victory	انتصار
victorious	منتصِر
half	نصف#
middle	منتصف#
	نطق
area, region	منطقة (ج. مناطق)
	نظر
in the eyes of	في نظر
	نظف
clean	نظيف
	نظم
to arrange	II
organization	منظّمة
yes, what can I do for you?	نعم
same, self	نفس
	نقب
association	نقابة
	نقش
to discuss	VI
river	نهر
	نهي
to end	VIII (انتهى-ينتهي)
end	نهاية
	نوس
people	ناس
type, kind	نوع
	نوم
to sleep	نام-ينام
	هتف
telephone	هاتِف
	هجر
to immigrate, emigrate	III

immigration, emigration	هِجرة
to attack	هجم-يهجِم
goal	هدَف
	هدي
gift	هديّة (ج. هدايا)
this	هذا
that	هذاك*
to flee, run away	هرب-يهرُب
	هزم
defeat	هزيمة
now	هلّأ*
	همّ
interest	اهتمام
important	مهمّ
more important	أهمّ
there, there is,# there are#	هُناك
India	الهند
Indian	هندي (ج. هنود)
	هندس
engineering	هندسة
engineering (adj.), architectural	هندسي
engineer	مهندس
here	هون*
and, while (circumstantial clauses)	و
to find	وجد-يجِد#، يوجَد*
there is, there are	يوجَد#
present, available, found, exisiting	موجود
	وجع
to hurt	IV
pain	وجع
	وجه
the Tawjihi exam	توجيهي
	وحد
to be united	V
to be united	VIII (اتّحد-يتّحد)
alone	وحد... ,لوحد...
the Soviet Union	الاتّحاد السوفييتي
united	متّحد

	ورث
inheritance	ميراث
	ودي
behind	وراء
	وذر
ministry	وزارة
ministry of education	وزارة التربية والتعليم
ministry of the interior	وزارة الداخلية
minister	وزير
minister of foreign affairs	وزير خارجية
to weigh	وزن-يزِن#، يوزَن*
weight	وزن
scale	ميزان
middle, medium	وسط
average, middle	متوسّط
to arrive, reach	وصل-يصِل#، يوصَل*
transportation	مواصلات
situation	وضع
	وطن
national	وطني
homeland	وطن قومي
	وظف
employee	موظّف
job	وظيفة
promise	وعْد
	وفر
available	مُتوفّر
	وفق
to agree	III, VIII
agreement	اتّفاقيّة
time	وقت
to be located	وقع-يقع
to sign	II
signature	توقيع
in reality	في الواقع
location	موقع
	وقف
to stop	II
stop	موقِف

Photograph Credits